Women Ageing

Women Ageing

Social Work Intervention

Vineeta Srivastava

RAWAT PUBLICATIONS

Jaipur • New Delhi • Bangalore • Mumbai • Hyderabad • Guwahati

ISBN 81-316-0207-9

The publication of this book was financially supported by ICSSR and the responsibility for the facts stated, opinions expressed, or conclusions reached, is entirely that of the author and that ICSSR accepts no responsibility for them.

ICSSR Consultant: Prof. D. Jamuna

Published by
Prem Rawat for **Rawat Publications**
Satyam Apts, Sector 3, Jawahar Nagar, Jaipur 302 004 (India)
Phone: 0141 265 1748 / 7006 Fax: 0141 265 1748
E-mail: info@rawatbooks.com
Website: www.rawatbooks.com

New Delhi Office
4858/24, Ansari Road, Daryaganj, New Delhi 110 002
Phone: 011 2326 3290

Also at Bangalore, Mumbai, Hyderabad and Guwahati

Typeset by Rawat Computers, Jaipur
Printed at Nice Printing Press, New Delhi

To my parents,
Smt. Bimla Srivastava and *Late Sh. N.K. Srivastava*

and my siblings
Geeta and *Tarun*

Contents

Acknowledgement

Successful completion of any study, more so challenging as the present one has been, requires continuous encouragement, guidance, co-operation and support from a number of persons. I shall be failing in my duty, if I do not acknowledge my gratitude to all those who have contributed in one way or another in presenting this work.

It gives me great pleasure in acknowledging my immense debt of gratitude to my research guide and mentor, Professor Rajeshwar Prasad, for his generous advice and inspiring guidance in all academic matters. It has claimed his time and constant care till the completion of the thesis. His judicious direction and discussions enabled me to have a thorough insight into the subject of the study. Without his unstinted patience, help and keen insight, this study would not have been possible.

I am immensely thankful to Mr. Dalbir Singh Ji, Seva Mandir, as his extensive writing expertise helped me in objectively visualizing and revising my study. His critical analysis and useful advice have proved instrumental in shaping the present form of this book.

I am also thankful to the Research and Consultancy Cell, ICSSR, New Delhi, in the matter of regulating and shaping my research. My special thanks are due to Mr. Anil Kumar, Asstt. Director (Systems), ICSSR and Mr. Shankar Bose, the Director (Systems), ICSSR. I drew extensively on their vast experience in data processing in the field of social research.

I owe a lot to the learned authors whose works I have studied and referred to in the completion of this research. My special thanks go to Kalyan Bagchi, Amrita Bagga, Arun P. Bali, H.S. Bhatia, A.B. Bose, N.K. Chadha, T.M. Dak, K.D. Gangrade, D. Jamuna, Malini Karkar, M.Z. Khan, Vijaya S. Kumar, Vinod Kumar, U.S. Mishra, Indira Jai Prakash, Irudaya S. Rajan, C.R. Ramachandran, P.V. Ramamurti, Rajeshwar Prasad, P.N. Sati, P.S. Sharma, Bela Shah, R.R. Singh, S.K. Verma and all those who have enlightened me in the field of gerontology by their in-depth knowledge and valuable views, articulated in different books and journals.

No doubt, it was the co-operation and support of the staff of different libraries, which made referral work possible. I am thankful to the library staff, particularly of the Helpage India, New Delhi; Economic Growth, New Delhi; Ratan Tata Library, University of Delhi; ICSSR, Mandi House, New Delhi; Department of Social Work, University of Delhi; Tata Institute of Social Sciences, Mumbai; SNDT, Mumbai; Tribal Research Centre, Udaipur, and Udaipur School of Social Work, Udaipur.

I owe a great deal to all the respondents for their kind co-operation. I am also thankful to Ms. Richa Sharma, Ms. Asha Suyal and Ms. Deepika Nagada who have assisted me in the processing of the data.

I am grateful to Mr. Cyriac who patiently went through the draft of the study at different points of time and made useful corrections, comments and suggestions.

This work has become possible because of the ever-willing help, assistance and encouragement of my friends and colleagues. I am grateful particularly to Chandra Bhandari, Ginny Srivastava, Kavita Srivastava, Mamta Jaitly, Renuka Ji and Tara Ahluwalia.

I will be failing in my duty if I do not thank the members of my family. Words fail to express my deep sense of gratitude to my mother Smt. Bimla Srivastava, my sister Geeta and my brother Tarun, who have sacrificed a lot of their interests for the smooth accomplishment of this work. I am profoundly grateful to all the members of my joint family, particularly my cousins, Arun and Kuldeep, and the inmates of my aunt Karuna's house who have shown great interest in my research.

My *didi* the Late Mrs. Sunita Srivastava, had been a benign inspirer in pursuing my task. Sadly, the absence of her inspiration and encouragement in the later years had resulted in the delay completion of the work. At this moment, I miss her more.

The work is dedicated solely to my beloved *Papa* the Late Shri N.K. Srivastava, Retired Director of Enquiries, MCD, New Delhi, whose dreams have come true posthumously in the form of this book. Perhaps, his wishes and dreams sustained my interest and endeavour from the beginning to the last. The work is a loving homage towards his aspirations about me.

Finally, I am deeply indebted to God for having given me the intellect, fortitude and endurance to fulfil my personal and professional commitments.

Vineeta Srivastava

1

Gender and Ageing

The World and Indian Scenarios

Old age is not a problem of 'age' but the intermingling of socio-cultural and other demographic variables. There is a continuous interplay between adult development and social forces; and gender is a potent social factor in determining ageing experience. 'Gender' and 'ageing' have become the core of any genuine development concern at national and international levels. In terms of sheer acknowledgement of this fact, there are no two views, no matter what the arguments are. The study, in hand, is an attempt to analyse ageing from gender perspective with the ultimate focus on the lifestyle, needs and problems of the aged women.

This chapter attempts to elaborate the problem under study as well as the design of research. Some basic questions are also being raised about general conditions of the aged women across the globe. The discussion also covers the impact of prevalent social norms and practices with regard to the aged women. The aim is to highlight the global scenario of how the gender-based disparities have influenced their conditions. The socio-economic and demographic changes that are taking place in the contemporary Indian society add to the existing situation of vulnerability of the aged women. Hence, the demography of the aged women in the Indian context has been described with the aim of highlighting their marginalized position in the Indian society and the gloomy part of the problems faced by them.

The concluding part of the present chapter deals with the design of research. Besides highlighting the significance of the study, it describes various steps of the research. It also gives a small introduction to the study area and ends with the chapter plan of the work.

The Aged Women: The World Scenario

The aged are not homogenous even within a well-defined group. The heterogeneity gets accentuated when gender-based comparisons are made. The experiences of men and women across the life span differ considerably depending upon the equality in and similarity of opportunities, status and access to resources. And women, irrespective of their age, are worse off than men with regard to so many dimensions of human existence.

Lower Socio-Political Status

"Let the woman get the status of a human being on this earth in the next millennium", was touchingly the expressed life dream of a famous Indian writer. "Is woman not being treated as a human being?", is the obvious question variously asked by social scientists and activists. The answer can be derived from the following statistics:

> Norway was the first country, which granted women the right to vote (in 1913). In Bangladesh, it was in the year 1972, and the Central African Republic granted the right only too late, i.e., 1986. Arabian countries present the worst situation in this regard. Women's right to vote and to stand for election has still not been recognized by Brunei, Darussalum, Kuwait, Quatar, Saudi Arabia and Oman. Although Djibouti and United Arab Emirates have recognized the right of vote, they have not yet elected or nominated a woman to the National Parliament (HDR, 1999).

This political situation is just a reflection of the social status of women in general. Let us consider the following statement made by Mickey Lewis in a conference in this regard:

> When I was young, I heard my father say to my mother, 'what do you know about it? You are only a woman'. And I remembered

> that I vowed that no one was going to say that about me. At that time, girls were expected to get married. Education and careers were not important. We were expected to be carers, loving wives and mothers—always putting others first. We were brought up to feel devalued, not worth much (United Nations, 1991).

Resultant Ageing Experience

It indicates that the special problems confronting the aged women have their origins, in part, in their very early life. The problems of an ageing woman are not so much a product of the 'ageing' as they are a product of widespread perceptions of the inferior status of a woman throughout her life.

One does not come up by autonomy, sense of personal control, feelings of self-esteem, competence, self-worth, self-confidence and the like qualities in old age by accident. To be able to grow into an active, skilled, confident and mature woman who can realize her potential, a girl must be nurtured in an environment of dignity and equal opportunity. A supportive society, a gerophilic culture and a facilitating environment will permit smooth transition from the earlier stages of life to old age. Otherwise, with age, women may only get more and more marginalized in societies where the general status of women is low, and in cultures, which devalue feminity.

Overall Challenges

A global analysis reveals that almost all societies devalue females. The Human Development Reports of UNDP (from 1990 onwards) give a live proof to illustrate the point. The Human Development Index (HDI), Gender Development Index (GDI) and Gender Empowerment Measure (GEM)—all unfold the current grim story. Women, all over the world, have a comparatively low status than men. The degrees of disparities, of course, vary from country to country. But, as a matter of fact, the 'second sex' of the world has been facing the multiple challenges of physical and mental health hazards, economic vulnerability, burden of care-giving responsibilities, social isolation, family rejection, humiliation, social insecurity and neglect.

Still, Higher Life Expectancy

The remarkable thing is that women still survive against all odds. They tend to live longer, and outnumber men in old age. Therefore, unless something radical is done to improve the status of women in general and the aged women in particular, the number of sick, dependent, disheartened, isolated, neglected and insecure aged women will go on increasing. The worldwide demographic pattern, discussed below, further validates the point.

The Demographic Changes

Growing Number of Aged People

In 1950, there were about 200 million persons aged 60 and above, evenly distributed between developed and developing countries; and constituting about eight per cent of the total global population (Figure I-III). By 1975, there were 350 million elderly people, with a similar distribution. Projections indicated a definite change in the pattern by the year 2000. The total elderly population in 2000 was estimated to be 614 million (Figure II) and the proportion of elderly population in developing countries was supposed to be over 62 per cent (Figure III). By 2025, there will be a six-fold increase in the number of elderly population: of 200 million in 1950, the elderly population is projected to be 1.2 billion people in 2025 (Figure II), about 14 per cent of the total population (Figure I). Seventy-two per cent of this 1.2 billion, about 858 million people are projected to be living in developing countries (Figure III) (UN, 1991). The population explosions in the developing countries along with the improving health facilities and increasing life expectancy are some of the reasons behind this disequilibrium.

Thus, the developed countries will have a smaller share of the world's elderly; there will be decline in elderly population in Europe, North America and USSR. The developing countries, by contrast, will have a larger share of the world's elderly population; there will be an increase in Asia, Latin America and Africa. The median age of the world population will jump from 23.4 years in 1950 to 31.1 years in 2025 (Figure IV) (UN, 1991).

Figure I
Share of World Population Aged 60 and Over, 1950–2025

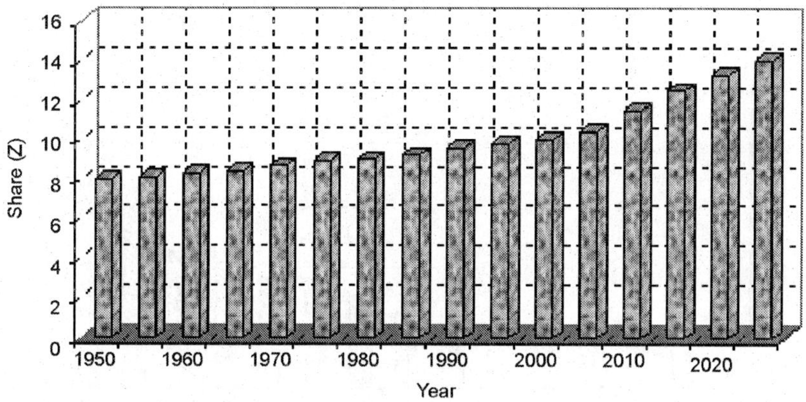

Source: U.N. (1991): *The World Ageing Situation.*

Figure II
World Population Aged 60 and Over, 1950–2025

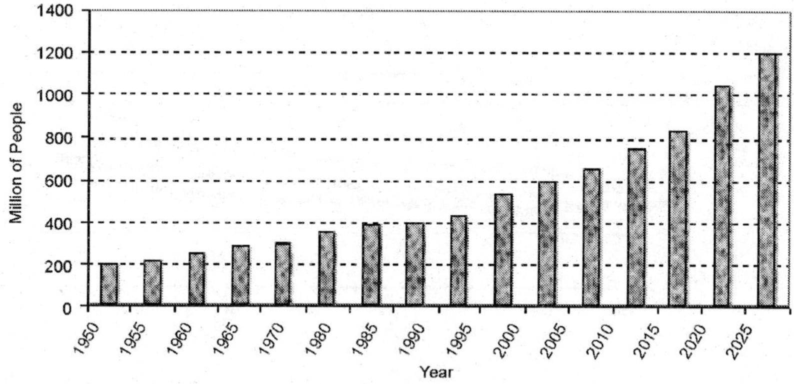

Source: U.N. (1991): *The World Ageing Situation.*

Figure III

Population Aged 60 and Over: More Developed and Less Developed Regions, 1950–2025

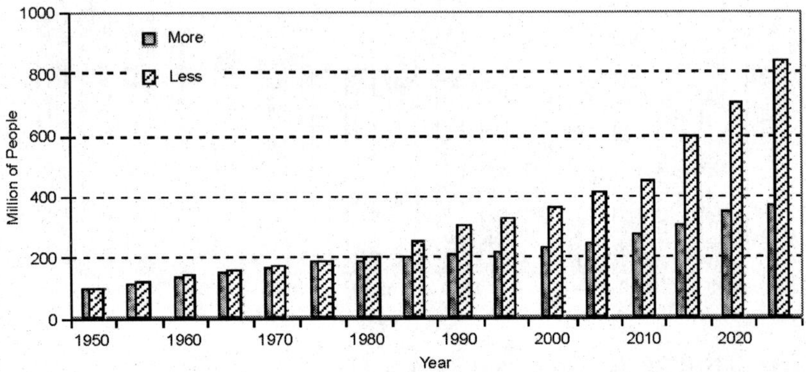

Source: U.N. (1991): *The World Ageing Situation.*

Figure IV

Share of World Population Aged 60 and Over, 1950–2025

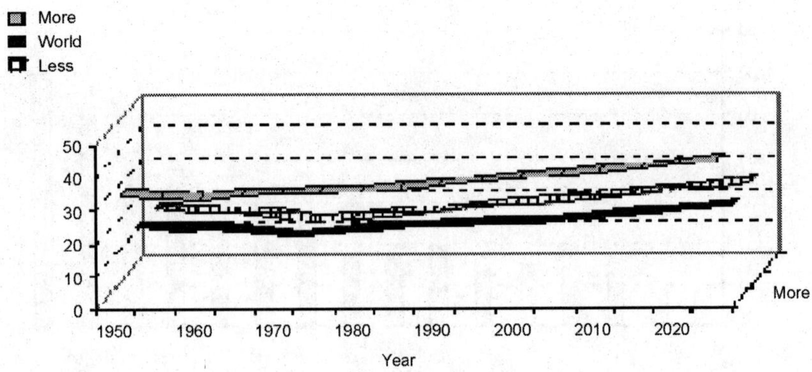

Source: U.N. (1991): *The World Ageing Situation.*

Differences by Sex

In developed countries, women on an average live longer than men. Women live five to seven years longer in most of them. This gap has been widening over the past several decades.

"In developing countries, differences in life expectancy by sex are usually smaller than in developed countries. The typical worldwide pattern is even reversed in a few developing societies of South Asia and the Middle East, where the interplay of various cultural factors (for example, lower social status of females and preference for male over female offspring) contributes to higher male than female life expectancy at birth" (UN, 1991).

Given the age patterns, growth of the elderly population implies an increase in the sex ratio with regard to the total aged population; and a greater increase in the number of older (80+ years) women than of older men. Between 1985 and 2025, projected increase for persons aged 70 years and above is 32 million (5% of the total increase in the population of the world) for males and 38 million (6%) for females in developed regions; and 284 million (42%) for males and 317 million (47%) for females in the developing regions. Sex differences in absolute increments are more apparent in elder ages. Thus, over the same period, projected increases in the aged 80+ population are 8 million (10%) for males and 14 million (17%) for females in the developed regions; and 24 million (30%) for males and 35 million (43%) for females in the developing regions (UN, 1991). Obviously, the developing regions will have a larger share of world's aged population, and particularly the aged female population.

Health Status

Women are More Prone to Health Problems than Men

With increasing longevity and higher women to men ratio in old age, one would expect a larger number of women outliving men in the coming years. It only adds disability and dependency to her last years (Jamuna, 1995). In epidemiological terms, women experience greater morbidity but lesser mortality (Maclean, 1984).

Health of the elderly is determined by several factors such as gender, economic status, marital status, living standards, availability of social support, etc. Normal ageing and diseased ageing interact with each other. Hence, there are differences in men's and women's health and ways of living, and they become more pronounced in later life (Kalche and Kickbusch, 1998). The irony is that most adult women, to fulfil the family responsibilities, put their own physical and mental health at jeopardy at some point of their lives.

Malnutrition is an index of poor health in developing countries. Malnutrition is disproportionately higher among women. This is traced in certain social customs and inimical cultural practices. In most of the Asian countries, food taboos are imposed on women, for example, serving first to males; the better food, quantity and quality-wise; and eating themselves in the last, the left-out food. There is little awareness of the type of diet suitable for an ageing person that is right in terms of bodily needs, debilitating conditions and systematic disorders.

Main Diseases

In general, the last two or three decades of life of the elderly females are dominated by two broad categories of health disorders: gynecological disorders accumulated during their reproductive years and compounded by post-menopausal morbidities; and the clinical disorders commonly associated with ageing diseases like diabetes, hypertension, osteoporosis and cardio-vascular disorders. The other important health problems faced by the elderly women, as also reported by others (for example Rao, 1990; UN, 1991; Ramamurti et al., 1992; Jamuna, 1995 and Mansharamani et al., 1998), are arthritis, anaemia, digestive disorders, Alzeimer disease, breast and vaginal cancers and respiratory complaints.

Depression is the most common psychiatric disorders among people over 65 (*IJG*, 1998). Though there is a lack of consistent evidence of greater psychological impairment among older females than older males, yet, it is reasonable to assume that older females would be particularly vulnerable to mental disorders because "the mental health among elderly females is frequently related to low income, widowhood and social isolation (see Jamuna, 1995)".

Utilization of Health Care Services

Needless to say that the aged women need health and support services of all types, which regrettably are not available to most of them. In developed countries, women are greater users of health services in all ages. There is also a big difference between men and women in the utilization of nursing homes. In the United States, for example, three quarters of nursing home residents are women (UN, 1991). But this, however, is not the case in the developing countries. Here, because of poverty, older women are unable to buy sufficient goods and services. Even those who have some resources, tend to outlive them due to prolonged health expenses.

According to the available estimates, there are 208 million aged women in the world, and about half of them live in rural areas of developing countries. Obviously, majority of the world's aged women has limited access to the health care services.

Widowhood

Prevalence Rate

In spite of their poor health and limited access to health services, women tend to outlive men, and hence, are more likely to face widowhood. Around the world, widowhood is a reality for the increasing number of elderly women. The percentage of women aged 65 and above are widows, for example, is 75 per cent in the Republic of Korea, 70 per cent in India, 61 per cent in Japan, 44 per cent in Switzerland, 41 per cent in Mexico and 35 per cent in Cuba (UN, 1991).

When an elderly woman is a widow, the widowhood stigma gets added to the travails of ageing and compounds her miseries. Women experience decline in status due to the loss of spouse.

Economic Repercussions

When a woman becomes widow, her economic condition deteriorates drastically. One reason for this is that most of the deceased husbands had been working before death and the women were only housewives; as a result, an important source of income shared by the couple suddenly stops. Since, this is the trend in most countries; the majority of widows remain poor.

Social Repercussions

According to Bengtson, Rosenthal and Burton (as quoted in UN, 1991), "widowhood is a profound life-course transition bringing a number of losses and changes in objective and subjective levels. Widowhood has negative effects on health, exhibited in the higher rates of depression, mortality and mental illness". Widowhood is also likely to cause changes in social and friendly relationships and, in a way, blocks social participation; a widow starts interaction with different and often with fewer people. In her study of two villages of Bangladesh, Ellickson (1988) writes that she did never see elderly widows being mistreated in their son's homes, but she saw a definite change in interactions upon the death of the elderly husband. The elderly widow changed from an "official, vocal, wifely head of the domestic realm", into an "old widow, much quieter in voice and demeanour".

Superstitions towards Widowhood

In some Asian countries, widowhood is considered a sign of bad omen. A widow is held responsible for the death of her husband. As a result, she is blamed and cursed throughout her life. Considering her presence as a bad sign *(apshagun)*, her presence is avoided at sacred ceremonies and social functions. In rural communities, the widows are given inhuman treatment. In some parts of India, her head is shaved, she is made to wear white dress, follow a code of restricted interaction, *purdah* (covering the face with clothes), denied the basic comforts, and a strict time-schedule in daily routine. These are some of the examples of the inhuman treatment, which a widow has to face on account of her widowhood.

In a nutshell, widowhood brings degrading changes in the life of the aged women in most societies of the world, particularly the traditional societies.

Care-giving Responsibilities

Care-giving: Mainly Women's Job

Giving of care is viewed in almost all cultures as women's work. Women provide more health care than all the health services put together (UN, 1991). In almost all the countries, care-giving remains largely a responsibility of the family. The primary responsibility falls upon the wife/woman. After her, the female members like daughters and daughters-in-law are considered responsible for the same.

Aged Women: Overburdened with Care-giving Responsibilities

When any 'old' person becomes seriously sick or disabled, the women of the family continue to look after that senior member. These women themselves may be middle-aged or elderly. They have to sacrifice much of their comfort to serve the sick senior member. When women grow older, they often need special care; still they continue to work hard till functional disability cripples them (Prakash, 1996).

Still they also face demands from their own children and husband. They are expected to continue performing routine domestic chores in addition to serving the sick. For the working women, parental care is just another addition to their already existing long list of responsibilities. Most dual career families in urban areas depend on elder women of the family for child care. In rural areas, domestic farm work is still being managed by women. Even frail old women continue to do the household work, child care or caring her older spouse. In fact, there is no retirement for an elderly woman. She has to toil till death or earlier when dementia or disability overtakes her.

Repercussions

There is increasing evidence of the stress that arises from the care-giving responsibilities. Depression, psychological stress, less satisfaction with life, decline in health and adverse effects on leisure and family activities have all been reported in recent researches (Sharan and Sandhwar, 1990; UN, 1991).

State Response towards Care-giving Responsibilities

In developing countries, the state has not yet accepted its responsibility towards the elderly care. The state has been slow to recognize that successful care-giving, even from non-governmental sources, such as the family also, requires special support services to the care-givers. Yet, it is heartening that recently in India, the State has offered a few incentives to the families, which take care of their elderly. However "a modern telling example of general failure to understand this role is the current struggle of every developed nation to provide health care to the elderly that was formerly given by female family members" (Lewis, 1987). Research clearly shows that without such support, informal care mechanisms break down more quickly, often forcing the government to assume the whole responsibility, usually at a higher cost. One kind of support, in this context, is 'respite care', which provides caregivers access to non-family service providers (e.g., social workers) on a temporary basis, giving them time off and a change for relieving their stress.

The Economic Perils of Long Life

Invisibility of Domestic Work

Women do almost all the world's domestic work. Their domestic role, which is vital to the well-being of the society, consumes more than half of their time and energy. It is estimated that unpaid housework done by women in industrialized society contributes about 25 to 40 per cent of Gross National Product (UN, 1991). But, it is generally underestimated since 'existing methods of measuring labour impose a statistical *purdah*' on women's work, which render much of their work invisible (Bandyopadhyay, 2000). Prakash (1996) has rightly asked, "if men who were once active in the labour force and had made substantial tangible contribution to national economics are considered as 'burden' in old age, then how women, who always had been invisible contributors, will be treated when they are old and no longer useful?". Older women throughout the world are more likely to be living in poverty than older men. To understand the reason for this, the economic realities facing women before they are old must be looked at.

Determinants of Economic Conditions

A married elderly woman's economic condition usually depends directly on the earning sources, which both the spouses had before they became old. Alternatively, when a woman remains unmarried, is divorced or becomes a widow, her economic situation in old age generally depends very much on her own sources of income which she had before she became old. In both the cases, income in old age depends on savings out of earlier income or on pensions.

Present Working Status regarding Paid Work

Women often do not work in the formal labour force due to either family responsibilities or the cultural barriers. If they work at all, their careers are often interrupted and limited by these and other family responsibilities (Lebra et al., 1984; Tripathi and Das, 1991; UN, 1991).Women form just one-third of the world's official labour force. Actually, they generally face severe labour force discrimination, and are often forced or steered into the lowest paying jobs, i.e., there is widespread occupational segregation all over the world (UN, 1991; Varghese, 1993; Thakur, 1999). They are much more vulnerable to unemployment.

In case of pensions, the retirement benefits are usually depend upon the type of employment, the amount of pre-retirement earnings and the years of creditable service. Women are less likely to be covered by pensions, they tend to have fewer years of creditable service and earning histories that put them at a disadvantage in the pension benefit calculation process (UN, 1991; Duraisamy and Duraisamy, 1999).

Thus, women fall into poverty as they age, mainly because they have very little to start with, and have no way of compensating what has been lost in terms of health, support, etc. Obviously, the poverty among women in old age is not the result of a random or accidental process. It is largely due to the fact that most societies push women to inferior economic positions throughout their lives. It is not just in the Third World societies that women are poor. Even Canada, with one of the best social security programmes for the elderly, confesses that its aged women are living in 'genteel poverty' compared to more 'abject poverty' of many aged women in the United States of America (Prakash, 1996). If that is so, then how are we to describe the poverty of elderly women in countries like India?

In a nutshell, a woman all over the world gets the secondary status. On becoming old, her earlier life experience combined with other socio-economic factors lead her to a miserable existence. Poor health, widowhood, poverty, isolation and neglect prove to be the hard facts of her life.

The home for 500 million women, a country steeped in its plurality of traditions, customs and institutions and proud of its heritage of eclecticism—India is no exception. Indian women are far poorer than men not only in health but also in education and income levels. Adult literacy in India was 54 per cent for females as compared to 76 per cent for males (Census of India, 2001). The share of National Income earned by Indian women amounted in 1992 to a mere 19 per cent (Mehta, 1996). India performs poorly in terms of both GDI and GEM, occupying, during 2000, 112th rank out of 174 countries and 95th in field of 174 nations respectively. The GDI ranking of India during 2003 became 103 out of 144 countries. Only 9 per cent of parliamentarians (2003), 2 per cent of managers and administrators and 21 per cent of technical workers (Lalitha, 1996) and 30 per cent of main and marginal workers (Census of India, 2001) are women.

Obviously, India has miles to go in the struggle of gender equality.

The Aged Women: The Indian Scenario

The present section is an attempt to analyse the situation of the aged women in India. In Indian society, old age has been associated with virtues, knowledge and wisdom. The Indian joint family itself provides an element of social security as well as status to the aged and mitigates the loneliness to some extent.

Demographic trends have made 'population ageing' inevitable in almost every country today. The longevity of population has increased from 1920s, first in the developed countries followed by the developing ones, thanks to health and medical services. Mere rhetoric that our tradition or culture will take care of problems of the elderly is a pathological denial of reality.

General Picture of the Aged in Society

In the present context, aged people have been assigned a negative role by all the societies. They are portrayed as dependent individuals, characterized by lack of social autonomy, isolation and neglect. They are considered as if posing a threat to the living standards of younger age groups by being a burden, who only consume without producing. However, the nature of the problems that the aged face varies in different societies and cultures. While bringing aged persons into the mainstream of socio-political life is a common problem faced in developed countries, the problems and aspects of ageing in a developing country would portray mainly the picture of intense poverty, hard work, dependency and bed-ridden sick aged persons. In other words, the aged in the developed countries face the disheartening experiences of marginalization, while in a developing country they are subject to physical ageing mainly due to malnutrition, ill health and poor economic conditions. But at the same time, the aged in traditional societies enjoy a relatively high level of warmth and affection among their kith and kin.

Indian Scenario of the Aged

Indian social fabric is closely knit and its unique nature and value system has attached a sustained respect for the elders. Both the age and experiences are respected here. Interdependency among family members and between generations is encouraged from childhood. A westerner would probably be puzzled to see the typical Indian joint family system where the younger generation traditionally gathers around older persons for advice and sanction; where voluntary dependency on younger generation causes no loss of self-esteem; where without earning, the aged enjoy social security, respect and high status in decision-making in family matters. Those who have no family are looked after by the community or caste organizations through institutions like temple, *dharamshala*, *math*, the village council or the panchayat (Nag, 1987). The aged have been considered as an 'asset' rather than a burden in the Indian society. It must be the reason why India has only recently started taking note of 'population ageing'[1] and the accompanying problems.

Diminishing Status of the Aged in the Changing Society

But now, it can be safely surmised that changes in kinship and family organization in conjunction with urbanization and industrialization have been more to the disadvantage of the aged. It may be seen that industrialization and urbanization have impinged upon the 'inbuilt' mechanism of the Indian joint family system to provide social security to its members. Weakening of several beneficial value systems, namely, respect, love and affection and familial affinity has become apparent. The generation gap is widening. It is experienced that attitude of youngsters is now becoming more individualistic and has come to disregard the authority of and disrespecting their elders.

Economy of the individualized and urbanized society is in many ways incompatible with stable family structures. A division in joint families and landed property, migration of children to far off urban areas in search of new jobs and change in marital pattern, i.e., from arranged to love marriage has adversely affected the social security of the aged and their authority in the family (Nag, 1987; Bose, 1988; Sati, 1988). The paucity of space in urban areas, the reduction in living space per family unit and the escalating costs of living in the urban pattern have pushed the aged parents into an isolated and lonely life. The lower income groups have no savings for the old age. Due to economic pressures and self-centred tendencies, the individuals may not be in positions to fulfil the basic needs of their parents. The parents often expect that in their old age they will be taken care of by their children (Bose, 1988; Nagesh, 1992). And, the failure on the children's part easily upsets the aged parents causing them great emotional strain as well as economic trauma.

The Indian Aged Women

For Indian women, ageing is not a trauma. Indian culture has enough buffers to promote natural acceptance of the process of ageing. Religious and cultural ideas such as "life is endless"; "death is not the end of all" and "the cycle of birth and death are ever recurring" help one to remove the fear of death and the apprehension of personal annihilation. The Indian aged women suffer more socially, economically as well as emotionally. Understanding their psycho-social condition needs an evaluation of the Indian view of feminity.

Perception of Society Towards a Woman

Woman in India, throughout her life, is considered a liability on others, no matter whether she is educated or an earning individual. Indian society has been a hierarchical, rigid and patriarchal system. Passages are often quoted from the *Manusmriti* to illustrate the subservient role of women. The Hindu *Dharma Shastras* (religious books) give a subordinate status to women. When they discussed *Vanaprasthashram*[2] and *Sanyasashram*,[3] they referred to only men. In fact, woman's role had been described just as a facilitator in the performance of men's social duties. That is why; the psycho-social realities of a woman's life are generally described to be encapsulated into three—as a daughter to her parents, wife to her husband and mother to her children. Female socialization practices are described as oppressive and not allowing female identity to develop. How Indian women perceive their own roles and their identity is deeply rooted in the myths, legends and the religious traditions of India.

On the birth of a girl child, even the educated parents become sad, and to overcome the shock they have to console themselves by thinking that "girls are equal to boys".

The discrimination begins even before birth. For most couples, a girl child is unwanted, and in almost every facet of her life, she gets a raw deal. If her life is not snuffed out by foeticide or infanticide, and if she is given a chance of life at all, it is a hard journey for her all through.

Adverse Sex Ratio

Biologically, females are the superior sex. During pregnancy, more male foetuses are spontaneously aborted. Male babies have higher rates of still births and in most societies, more males than females die in the early years of infancy and childhood.

To compensate this, it is believed, nature ensures that the preponderance of conceptions are male and that the sex ratio at birth is approximately around 1,050 males per 1,000 females. In

India, official statistics put the sex ratio at birth closer to 1,120 males per 1,000 females. However, the sex ratio for general population as per the 2001 census was 933. Thus, in India, the number of missing women comes out to be 40 to 50 million (Bandyopadhyay, 2000). But, where do these missing girls go? In all probability, they are made victims of female foeticide or infanticide. In India, about 20 lakh cases of female infanticide are reported every year, whereas Indian Medical Association considers this number to be about one crore. Owing to the availability of ultrasound facilities, more of foeticide cases are reported in the urban areas than in the rural areas where infantiside is more practised a phenomenon.

This discrimination against a girl child is often directed by family members other than the mother. Among some communities of Rajasthan and Tamil Nadu, a woman who dares not to destroy her daughter may be abandoned by her husband. A woman going against the wishes of her in-laws is bound to face mental tensions and social pressures.

There are certain related evidences highlighted by the media. For example, recently, a woman in Rajasthan killed her female child only after a few hours of the birth. The traumatic statement of the lady reads: "It was my third child. The sex determination test indicated a male child. Even then my in-laws who, anyhow accepted my two girl children, had warned me before I was hospitalized that their doors would be closed in case I returned with a female child. I have no regrets of my act since I had no other alternative". Obviously, this is only one among the many such cases which go unreported.

Here, it is worthwhile to mention a special case. In a village called Devra in Rajasthan, a girl child not only survived through a series of accidental circumstances but also brought a groom's marriage party *(barat)* to the village for the first time after 110 years. Girl children were routinely killed in such villages (Bandyopadhyay, 2000). The early Indian censuses also reported villages with no girls in some parts of the north-west. Presumably, such villages still do exist.

Education

Literacy, the first step towards formal education, also reveals a grim scenario. The population of women who are literate has increased just by 15 per cent over the last decade from 39 per cent in 1991 to 54 per cent in 2001. And, even today, 193 million women lack the basic capability to read and write.

The enrolment of girls in schools even at the primary level is lower when compared to boys. In 1999–2000, the enrolment ratio for girls was 85 per cent in class I-V (6–11 years) (GoI, 2001). The emphasis laid upon their household responsibilities such as cooking and child/elderly care, training them for marriage, inadequate facilities for girls in schools, absence of adequate female teachers, fear for their safety and so on are among the reasons for low enrolment of girls in schools. This is further compounded by higher levels of dropouts among girls. In 1999–2000, 42 per cent of girls in primary schools had dropped out. Given low keeping up, very few girls reach primary (13%), middle (9%), secondary school (5%) or higher levels (4%) of education (while 61% receive no schooling) (GoI, 2001).

This implies low human capital development, poor levels of skill/training to meet market demands, lowering the probability of women joining the labour market except in jobs that are in the informal sector, which are lowly paid, and virtually with no protection and security. Lower literacy also impacts upon women's awareness levels regarding their own health needs, thereby foreclosing the possibility of improving their access to the available services for their well-being. And this severely continues curtailing their chances of participating in the social, economic and political spheres.

Health

The indicators selected to reflect the health status of women are: mean age at marriage, total fertility rates, anaemia levels in women and couple protection rate.

Despite the legally stipulated age of 18 years at marriage, girls still get married before attaining this age in India. Here, the mean age at marriage for females stands out at 17 years (Rustogi, 2004). And the NFHS-II (1998–99) states that nearly 60 to 80 per cent of married women surveyed between the ages of 25 to 49 years were married before they were 18 years old. Early marriage often accompanies early pregnancy, with young unprepared mothers being burdened with responsibilities beyond their capacities. Pregnancies at young age are more likely to result in underweight babies, stillbirth and abortions, especially where mothers suffer from poor health and dietary deficiencies.

The fertility rate as per the NFHS-II is an average of three babies per women for the country as a whole. Frequent child bearing, often an offshoot of the predominant preference for a son in our society, takes a heavy toll on women. During childbirth, several serious complications are commonly reported, such as haemorrhage, excessive bleeding, anaemia, toxicity, premature babies and other associated problems.

Among these, anaemia is a prominent cause leading to maternal deaths, apart from resulting in physically weak children. Every second women in India suffer from some degree of anaemia, according to NFHS-II. Severe anaemia is reported by 2 per cent women while 35 per cent and 15 per cent are affected by mild and moderate anaemia levels respectively.

In spite of all this, the additional responsibility of contraception also falls overwhelmingly on women. The latest data available from the Department of Family Welfare (Ministry of Health and Family Welfare) reveals that female sterilizations account for 95 per cent of all sterilizations (Rustogi, 2004). Since women are viewed mainly as the means of reproduction, it is supposed to be their sole responsibility to control or protect themselves against further pregnancies.

Health Care

In India, medical needs of women are often ignored. They are not brought to hospitals till their illness reaches an advanced stage. Even in serious conditions, the withdrawal rate from the hospitals is also quite high for females.

Avoidance of Health Care Needs of Women

A girl of about five years, who had lost a lot of blood in an accident, was brought to a hospital in Jammu. The doctor approached her father to get a unit of blood donated. The father was reluctant: "*Yeh to paraya dhan hai. Iske liye main apni sehat kyon kharaab karoon*?" (She is to go away after her marriage, why should I harm my health for her?) he said. All persuasive efforts resulted in vain. He did not relent and finally walked away. The girl died a few days after (Srivastava, 2000).

This was way back in early 70s. But three decades later, the condition has not changed much. It is not at all feasible to obtain the actual statistics about the health care services available for and utilized by females in India. Yet an humble effort is, hereby, being made in this context by providing some statistics from the All India Institute of Medical Sciences (AIIMS).[4]

More Health Care Services to Males

At AIIMS, of all the surgeries, which are conducted on infants and children, only 30 per cent are on girls. To illustrate, from 1986 to 1999, the number of neonatal surgeries carried out in intensive care were 2089. Of these, only 648 (30.02%) were on girls. Remaining 1,441 were on boys. In 1998, while 117 boys were operated in the intensive care unit, the number of girls operated was only 57. In 1999, out of the total 152 surgeries in this category, only 52 were on girls. In the general ward category of surgeries, around 1,800 to 2,000 operations are conducted each year. Of these too, around 70 per cent are on boys (Srivastava, 2000).

Health Care Needs: Males versus Females

It is not that more boys fall sick and need medical care as compared to girls. Women/girls are severely malnourished, especially in lower and middle castes and classes of India. Just to quote, around 80 per cent of the pregnant women brought to the Guru Teg Bahadur Hospital in Delhi are reportedly anaemic. The situation is worse in Rajasthan. Obviously, the chances of females getting sick are the higher. But their health care needs are rarely given due consideration. The following statistics validate the point: over a period of almost two years (1998–99), ten girls were referred to a liver transplant in AIIMS. Most of the families were economically well off. Still, families of eight of them dropped out. Not all the dropouts were worse off.

Gender Biased Attitude of Parents about Health Care Needs

The overall attitude of the parents of boys, according to doctors, is different from those of girls. While the former are alert and receptive to the treatment, the latter are not willing to take much trouble and tend to give in more easily. The lurking feeling is, perhaps, that the scarce resources of time and money should not be spent on girls; that they must learn early to tolerate and endure punishments and pains that will come naturally in their way throughout their lives (Srivastava, 2000).

There are several factors, which lead to discrimination against girls in a family. First is the financial constraint. Most families when forced to make a choice, prefer to spend money on boys as they are considered as the future of the family. These biases are pronounced in both the rich as well as the poor families. In private hospitals expenses are high and even the fairly wealthy families hesitate to bring their daughters in for surgery/treatment. Parents, many a time, back out on the information that their girls require complicated surgeries, lengthy treatment or treatment in some other city (out of station) even if it is free of cost. The family is generally unwilling to bear the cost of living in another city (Srivastava, 2000). It appears that the expenses on a girl's medical care are not considered worthwhile as they add to the expenditure the family will have to bear on her marriage. Scars, which may emerge after surgeries, are considered as barriers in her marriage. And if there are more than four or five children in the family, it is most likely that the girls suffer the worst neglect.

If the state of health care services available to women in their childhood, young age or reproductive age (when they are in the family way) is so poor, one can very well imagine the kind of services which will be available to them in the twilight phase of their life.

Widowhood

Apart from the trends discussed earlier, the Indian widows are particularly prone to risks of social isolation and cultural castigation.

Religious Discourse

According to the Hindu *Dharama Shastras*, the man needs a wife, mainly for the fulfilment of religious duties, especially procreation; on the death of the wife, man was, therefore, obliged to immediately remarry. However, on the death of the husband, the women if she survives, lives a life devoid of any status in the society. She is supposed to be bound to her husband even after his death. Sexuality outside of marriage is out of question for her. She also has to renounce all the other joys of life. And, that may be the reason why "the widow's reaction to the death of the spouse was mostly in terms of a sense of loss or feeling of deterioration in their livelihood and status, neglect by the family, loneliness, loss of respect, added responsibilities and burden" (Muthayya, 1995).

Social Realities

Widows amongst the Hindus are, in fact, socially marginalized, ritually inauspicious and cruelly segmented, as also found by the Horward Institute of International Development. They, in fact, are an exploited lot. Widowhood weakens the kinship network from the husband's side. Loss of wife's role restricts certain social interactions (Prakash, 1994). A further loss of status is expected by older widows who have to give up their own home and find a shelter with their children. It is thought that the widow must realign her relationship with other family members in the absence of her spouse (Bali, 1997). Widows in certain regions of India have been 'dispatched' to Varanasi, Mathura and Brindavan to spend the rest of their lives in so called 'religious pursuits', but in reality to live in homes for widows on alms and charity. Even during the year 2000, about twenty thousand aged widows were left behind by their families in the famous *Kumbh Mela* of Allahabad (Uttar Pradesh), India. (Kumbh Mela refers to a huge religious gathering, which takes place once in every twelve years, on the occasion of

Mauni Amavasya, at the *Triveni (Sangam)* area of Allahabad city of Uttar Pradesh. The last gathering had about three crore people. The poor widows are still spending their lives in the hope that one day the members of their families would turn up to take them back to their homes.

Widowhood is called social death as a woman has no existence without a husband (Prakash, 1997). Bali (1997) is of the same view that widowed elderly females, who are poverty-stricken and emotionally wrecked, are left without a meaningful life pattern or social function. Prevalence of restrictions of widow remarriage, particularly among higher status groups, makes the life of ageing females even more problematic.

Economic Hardships

Economic dependency is the other major problem faced by the Indian aged women, especially the Hindu widows. Money handling is considered as a male prerogative. Woman is habituated to depend on male members of the family for handling the economic resources. She, even though educated, does not directly handle money matters of the family, and hence, is largely ignorant of them. When an elderly woman becomes widow, she also loses control over the economic resources left by her husband or the household due to lack of skills to deal with them. She has to lean heavily on her adult children and/or relatives; and even depend on them for economic help. At times, she is deceived of her property by the relatives and/or children. This is true mainly of middle and upper classes. The situation is worse in the case of lower class women and it is not unusual to find her socially deserted.

Social Response to the Problem

Problems of the widows have yet not given due recognition in the society. That's why the condition of widows is considered as one of India's most neglected social issues in Social Sciences,[5] in the agenda of the women's movements, and in the media which reacts only to the dramatic incidents of *sati* or *witch hunting*.

The above description makes it clear that the life of a woman in India is, indeed, a tough journey. The harsh experiences of the journey ultimately affect her status and position in old age.

Throughout, she is exposed to numerous hazards. Given on the next page is an attempt to explain the situation through a diagram.

Demography of the Aged Women in India

Demography of the aged women in India will further highlight their marginalized position and the gravity of the problems they face.

International Demography of the Aged

According to worldwide estimates, 9.5 per cent of the world population is aged 60 years or older. However, the proportion of the aged in the more developed countries was quite high (that is 18%) than that in the less developed ones (7%). At the same time, the aged comprised just 7 per cent of the total population of South Asia. Amongst the countries, Japan had the highest proportion of the aged with 20 per cent while the lowest proportion was in Africa (i.e., 5%). To be noticed, China (9%) has more aged population than America (6.5%) and India.

Demography of Aged in India

The physical context of ageing is changing in India leading to a growing number and a new profile of older persons. In 1995, India belonged to the category of 'mature nations'[6] with the aged proportion being 6.6 of the total population. And during 2001, India entered in the 'old population'[7] category with the aged comprising 7.5 per cent of the total population (see Table 1.3).

Proportion and Growth Rate of the Aged

In India, the population in the age group of 60+ is increasing due to reduction in the death rate; increase in the expectancy of life at birth; and decrease in the birth rate.

The older population is growing at a rate faster than the rest of the population. In 1901, India had 12 million aged persons. It increased to 77 million during 2001 indicating a rise of 542 per cent just in 100 years (Figure V, Table 1.2 and Census of India, 2001). Obviously, the decadal rate of increase, except for the decades 1921–31 and 1941–51, had been higher for the aged than for the total population. (These exceptions may be attributed to: the

Diagram 1

Life of a Woman in India

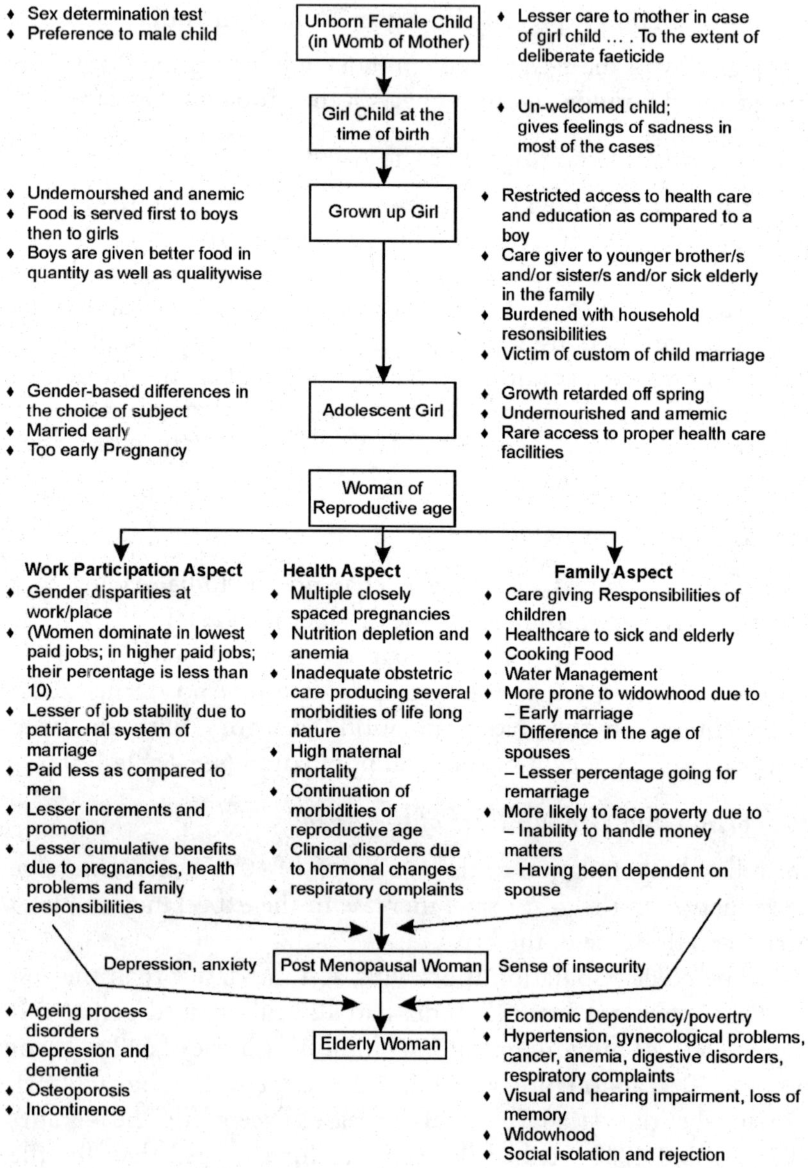

Figure V
Population and Proportion of the Aged in India

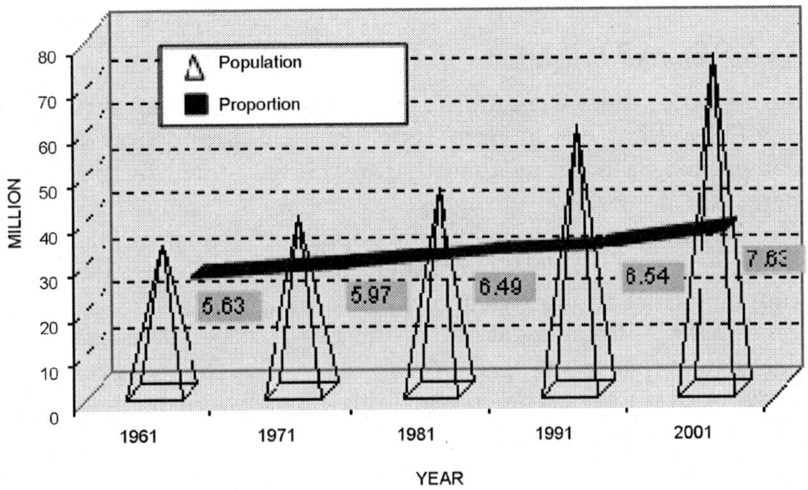

Figure VI
Sex Ratio of General Population and Aged Population of India (1901–2001)

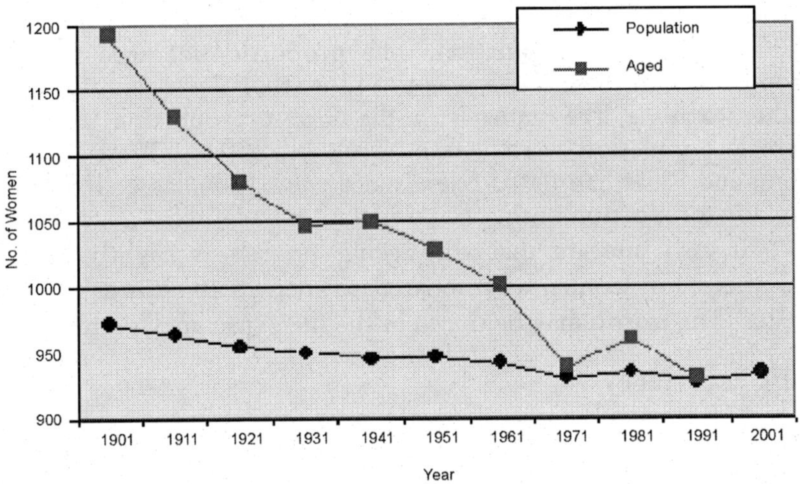

epidemic of 1931 that took a heavier toll of the aged; and the migration of the young due to partition of the country in 1947) (see Table 1.2).

Proportion and Progression of Aged Females

During 2001, there were more aged women (39 million) than aged men (38 million). Even from 1901–1951, the proportion of aged women had been higher than that of the aged men. But in 1961, there was a marginal advantage to the men. Thereafter, there remained fewer aged women in the population than aged men. The trend continued till 1991, when there were 27 million aged women compared to 28 million aged men.

Till 1971, the decadal rate of increase for aged men had been higher than that of the aged women. After that the trend reversed in favour of the aged women (see Table 1.2). Obviously, the Indian population is ageing with greater increase in the number of aged women as against the aged men.

The Female Dimension: Inter-State Differences

In 1991, among the major states of India, the proportion of aged female population (out of total female population) was highest in Kerala (9%) and the lowest in Assam (5%). Kerala along with Punjab, Haryana and Tamil Nadu belonged to the category of 'mature populations' with the aged comprising more than 7 per cent of the total population. The proportion of aged female population, in these states, was also more than 7 per cent. On the other extreme, the states with the lowest proportion of aged female population were: Assam (5%), Bihar (6%), West Bengal (6%) and Rajasthan (6%). These states were also characterized by the low proportion of the aged population (see Table 1.3).

It also appears that the ageing process is slightly more advanced for women as compared to men in two-thirds of the states. The reason may be traced in the life expectancy pattern.

Life Expectancy

At Birth

Even as recently as 1951, life expectancy at birth of Indian women was only 32.5 years. Virtually one-third of the women were likely

Table 1.1

Proportion of the Aged, 1995

Major Regions	*Proportion of Aged 60+*
World	9.49
More developed regions	18.28
Less developed regions	7.24
Africa	4.97
South Asia	6.65
Europe	18.82
Asia	8.13
Countries	
China	9.35
India	6.58
Japan	20.13
America	6.45

Source: *Global Estimates and Projections by Sex and Age: The 1994 Assessment*, New York: Department of International Economic and Social Affairs, United Nations, 1996.

Table 1.2

Elderly (60+) Population, Women and Men, India, 1901–2001

Year	*Aged as per cent of Total Population*	*Number (in millions)*			*Decadal per cent Change*			
					Aged Population			*Total Population*
		Persons	*Women*	*Men*	*Persons*	*Women*	*Men*	
(1)	*(2)*	*(3)*	*(4)*	*(5)*	*(6)*	*(7)*	*(8)*	*(9)*
1901	5.06	12.06	6.56	5.50				
1911	5.22	13.17	6.99	6.18	9.20	6.55	12.35	5.75
1921	5.37	13.48	7.00	6.48	2.40	0.21	4.87	0.31
1931	5.09	14.21	7.27	6.94	5.37	3.74	7.12	11.00
1941	5.66	18.04	9.15	8.89	26.97	25.95	28.03	14.22
1951	5.43	19.61	9.94	9.67	8.72	8.66	8.78	13.31
1961	5.63	24.71	12.35	12.36	26.00	24.28	27.77	21.51
1971	5.97	32.70	15.83	16.87	32.32	28.04	36.56	24.80
1981	6.42	43.98	21.49	22.49	34.50	35.80	33.28	24.66
1991	6.55	55.30	27.07	28.23	25.73	25.96	25.51	23.16
2001	7.45	76.62	38.85	37.77	38.55	43.52	33.79	21.80

Source: Registrar General of India, Censuses of respective years.
For 1981 and 1991, Registrar General Census Data.
For 2001 India.www.censusindia.net

Table 1.3
Proportion of Aged Population by Gender: India (1991, 2001) and Major States, 1991

State/Country	*Total*	*Female*	*Male*
Andhra Pradesh	6.47	6.64	6.32
Assam	5.29	4.94	5.62
Bihar	6.05	5.83	6.25
Gujarat	6.15	6.58	5.74
Haryana	7.47	7.74	7.24
Karnataka	6.76	6.95	6.58
Kerala	8.77	9.23	8.29
Madhya Pradesh	6.43	6.61	6.27
Maharashtra	6.91	7.20	6.64
Orissa	6.98	7.05	6.92
Punjab	7.56	7.31	7.77
Rajasthan	6.06	6.31	5.83
Tamil Nadu	7.29	7.10	7.48
Uttar Pradesh	6.65	6.34	6.92
West Bengal	6.00	6.13	5.89
India 1991	6.58	6.61	6.55
India 2001*	7.45	7.83	7.10

Source: Census of India, 1991 Population Projections for India and Major States; cited from Ganguli and Rajan, 1999:P.WS–46.

Source: Census of India, 2001 cited from India.www.censusindia.net.

Table 1.3 highlights the inter-state differences of the aged population by sex in 1991. Before analysing Table 1.3, it should be noted that the percentage given refers to 100 of total persons and hundred of each sex. This percentage cannot be compared horizontally, viz. '6.61 per cent of females and 6.55 per cent of males in India are aged' does not indicate that there are more aged women. It was already seen that in 1991, there were fewer women than men even among the aged.

to have lost their own mothers prior to the birth of their first child, and nearly half of the women would have lost at least one of their parents. With the expectation of life at birth going up to nearly 60 years, 90 per cent of women will survive to become grandmother (Ganguli and Rajan, 1999).

During 1973, male life expectancy at birth was 50.5, which was 1.5 years higher than the female life (49). But during 1991, the situation was reversed. The female life expectancy at birth (59.7) became greater than the male life expectancy (59). This trend continues till today when the female life expectancy at birth is 64.7 compared to 64.1 that of the male (see Table 1.4).

At Age 60

At higher ages, women's life expectancy in India has further caught up with men's. It may be due to an addiction-free life, lower exposure to road accidents and lower suicide rate besides the earlier described factors (Desai, 1999). As per the famous social worker, Ginnie Srivastava, "Men are more prone to heart attack while women are more likely to suffer from arthritis. And a person can die of heart attack but not of arthritis". And this may also be an important factor.

Presently, at national level, at the age 60, both men and women are expected to live for an additional 15 years on an average. However, male-female gap in the extension of life is of one year, which is expected to further increase in favour of women in the near future (see Table 1.5).

One of the implications of higher longevity among women is reflected in the sex ratio.

Sex Ratio

The sex ratio of Indian population has always been unfavourable to women. But, in the aged population (60+), a reverse trend had been persisted till 1961, i.e., the sex ratio had been favourable to women. Thereafter, following the trend of the general population, it also became unfavourable to women. However, the sex ratio of the aged population has throughout been more favourable for women than that of the general population (see Table 1.6).

Table 1.4
Changes in Expectancy of Life at Birth

Urban/Rural	*Year*	*Male*	*Female*	*Persons*
All	1973	50.5	49.0	49.7
	1991	59.0	59.7	59.4
	2001	64.1	64.7	64.4
Rural	1973	48.9	47.1	48.0
	1991	57.9	58.1	58.0
	2001	—	—	—
Urban	1973	58.8	59.2	58.9
	1991	63.5	66.3	64.9

Source: SRS based Life Tables, 1989–93 cited in *India*, Ministry of Human Resource Development, 1997: 33.
For the data of 2001, J.K. Banthia: *Census of India 2001 Series 1 Provisional Population Totals*, Registrar General and Census Commissioner, India, 151.

Table 1.5
Added Years at 60 by Sex, India

Years	*Males*	*Females*	*Gap*
1981–85	14.6	15.8	1.2
1986–90	14.9	16.2	1.3
1991–95	15.3	16.6	1.3
1996–2000	15.7	16.7	1.0
2001–2005	15.8	17.2	1.4

Source: Computed by N.B. Suresh Kumar, Department of Demography, University of Kerala, on the basis of Coole and Demeny Life Table, cited from Ganguli and Rajan, 1999: WS–48.

Table 1.6

Sex Ratio (F/M × 1,000) for Population and for Aged

Year	*Population*	*Aged*
1901	972	1,192
1911	964	1,130
1921	955	1,080
1931	950	1,046
1941	945	1,049
1951	946	1,028
1961	941	1,000
1971	930	938
1981	934	960
1991	927	930
2001	933	1,029

Table 1.7

Sex Ratio for the Elderly in India 1961–2021

Year	*60+*	*60–64*	*65–69*	*70+*
1961	1,000	770	960	1,060
1971	938	920	920	970
1981	960	940	960	980
1991	930	940	940	930
2001	1,029	1,025	1,090	1,006
2011 P	970	920	950	1,030
2021 P	990	990	960	1,030

Note: P = Projected.

Source: Census of India and S.I. Rajan, U.S. Mishra and P.S. Sharma (1999).

The sex ratio in the aged population had been continuously declining till 1991. From 1,192 in 1901, it reduced to 930 in 1991. And then it showed a remarkable improvement to 1,029 during 2001 (Table 1.6). The 65–69 group showed a remarkable increase to 1,090 (during 2001) in the sex ratio (Table 1.7). This sex ratio seems further to improve among the older aged. Obviously, in the near future, the sex ratio is projected to improve in favour of women, especially in the higher age groups.

Literacy

Women are more illiterate than men, especially in old age. Almost three-fourths of the total 60+ population (73%) was illiterate in 1991. The literacy rate among the older females was worse (13%) than that of the older males (41%) (Census of India, 1991). However, the literacy rate among the aged (women included) will improve in the coming years, as today's young literates grow old.

Marital Status

In 2001, while a large majority of elderly male (82%) lived with a married status, only 47 per cent of the elderly females carried this status. While a majority of the elderly women (51%) was widowed, for the aged men, this incidence of widowhood was only 15 per cent (Table 1.8 II). The incidence of widowhood increases rather sharply for women with advancing age (Tables 1.8 I and II).

Three main reasons for a greater incidence of widowhood among women than widower men are: (a) substantial age difference between marriage partners, because of differences in the ages at which men and women marry; (b) the differential life expectancy between males and females; and (c) the differing proportion of aged men and women who remarry. Rate of remarriage among males is much higher than among the females.

Has this overlap between age and widowhood undergone any major change over recent years, is obviously the next question. Actually, the incidence of widowhood in total population as well as in 60+ category continues to be substantially higher among women as compared to that among men becoming widower in India. The proportion of widows (women) in the general population has shown an increase from 6.5 per cent in 1991 to 6.9

Table 1.8 (I)
Marital Status for 60+, 1991

Marital Status	*Male*	*Female*	*Total*
Never married (million)	1.0 (3.4)[1]	0.4 (1.4)[2]	1.4 (2.5)
Married (million)	23.7 (80.7)[1]	12.1 (44.2)[2]	35.8 (63.1)
Widowed (million)	4.5 (15.5)[1]	14.8 (54.0)[2]	19.3 (34.0)
Divorced/separated (number)	93,190 (0.3)[1]	1,09,420 (0.4)[2]	2,02,610 (0.4)
Total 60+ population (million)	29.4 (6.7% of all males)	27.3 (6.8% of all females)	56.7 (6.8% of population)

Notes: 1. Per cent of all 60+ males; 2. Per cent of 60+ females; 3. Per cent of all 60+ population.
Source: Census of India, 1991 cited from *India*: Ministry of HRD, 1997: 12.

Table 1.8 (II)
Marital Status for 60+, 2001

Marital Status	*Male*	*Female*	*Total*
Never married (million)	0.96(2.54)[1]	0.58(1.49)[2]	1.55(2.02)[3]
Married (million)	31.02(82.15)[1]	18.39(47.34)[2]	49.42(64.5)[3]
Widowed ()	56,58,187(14.99)[1]	1,96,83,873 (50.65)[2]	2,53,42,060 (33.07)[3]
Divorced/separated (number)	1,25,377(0.34)[1]	1,91,269(0.49)[2]	3,16,646(0.42)[3]
Total 60+ population (million)	37.76 (7.1% of all males)	38.85 (7.83% of all females)	76.62(7.45% of population

Notes: 1. Per cent of all 60+ males; 2. Per cent of 60+ females; 3. Per cent of all 60+ population.
Source: Census of India, 1991 cited from *India*: Ministry of HRD, 1997: 12.

Table 1.9
Incidence of Widowhood by Sex and Age

Incidence of Widowhood	*INDIA*				
	1961	*1971*	*1981*	*1991*	*2001*
All men	3.7	2.9	2.4	1.9	1.8
All women	10.8	8.9	8.1	6.5	6.9
Men (60+)	27.5	22.4	19.4	15.5	15.0
Women (60+)	75.4	69.2	64.3	54.0	50.7
Widows (60+) as a proportion of all widows	40.4	46.8	52.8	56.3	57.4
Widowers (60+) as a proportion of all widowers	40.7	45.3	51.1	53.9	58.2

Sources: Computed from Census of India reports for 1961, 1971, 1981, 1991 reports for social and cultural tables, age and marital status.
From: Ganguli and Rajan, 1999: WS–48–49.

per cent in 2001. However, the incidence of widowhood shows a decline from 1961–2001 in all the other categories: of aged men, aged women and all men. Also, the incidence of widowhood is increasingly becoming an aged phenomenon with increasing number of widows and widowers belonging to the aged 60+ category (see Table 1.9).

Obviously, the overlap between incidence of widowhood and ageing is rather striking among women with serious economic and social implications.

Health Status

Greater Morbidity but Lesser Mortality

Although women live longer than men, elderly women always suffer from poorer health compared to men (Dandekar, 1996). There is a paucity of data about the health status of the aged of our country. Whatever data is available, it generally do not give sexwise details. Almost all the information on elderly female morbidity in our country has come from hospital in-patient and out-patient records. Very little information is available from population surveys.

Main Diseases

However, some of the important health problems among elderly women were reported to be arthritis, hypertension, diabetes, gynecological problems, cancer, anaemia, respiratory complaints, and digestive disorders. The two or three decades of reproductive years of the lives of millions of women produce adverse effects of diverse types. The chronological ageing interacts with the disease ageing. "For one case of pregnancy related death, due mostly to major obstetric causes like haemorrhage, obstructed labour, sepsis, eclambsia and abortion, there will be ten women having life worse when they get old" (Bagchi, 1997). The post-menopausal phase brings about a series of morbidities, which quite often accentuate those damages acquired during the reproductive years. Uterine prolapse and urinary incontinence are two glaring examples. Far more sinister are personality changes like depression and dementia. Loss of memory is also reported in the cases of aged women. They, in fact, have to face multiple diseases.

Impairment

As per the National Sample Survey, 1991, weak eyesight, difficulties in walking and hearing were the three major infirmities reported in descending frequencies by the aged. It is clear that the aged women suffer more from these infirmities as compared to the aged men. Just to specify, as per 1991 National Sample Survey, there were 68 physically infirm females compared to 46 males on per 1,000 aged population.

With advancing age, one is unable to perform common tasks of daily activities like going to toilet, dressing, getting up from bed, etc. Incapacity was more common in elderly females as compared to elderly males. And one-fifth of the elderly women were unable to perform common tasks of daily routine (Mansharamani and Chakravarty, 1998).

Morbidity and Socio-economic Status

Rates of morbidity are high among the poor and marginalized older women. However, they are not inherently vulnerable. Their poor health is a result of lifetime's inadequate nutrition, hard physical work, repeated pregnancies, systematic gender discrimination and lack of access to primary health care. "There is a definite relation of health to richness, education, social status and family status. Rich aged with higher education, married and with living spouse have low rates of chronic illness compared to the poor, widows and single people" (Mansharamani and Chakravarty, 1998).

This, in brief, is the present scenario in India as far as social condition of the aged women is concerned. Here, like in most developing countries, ageing brings with it dependency, ill health, insecurity and loss of control over one's own life, that put a woman in miserable position. But, the aged women themselves do not know how disadvantaged they really are. And perhaps, that is why they do still survive.

Design of Research

The demographic ageing of population has implications at the macro as well as household levels. It has been accompanied by changes in society and economy. The aged, particularly, women and those belonging to the lower income group, are the worst victims of these changes. The National Policy on Older Persons, 1999, concludes that a growing number of persons aged 60+ in the coming decades will belong to the middle and upper income groups (GoI, 1999). Obviously, the lower income group will find it hard to survive till 60 years or more. But a just society must have gender justice as well as economic equilibrium. For this, we need to plan our economy and institutions, keeping in view the probable demographic transitions and the prevailing gender and economic disparities. The present study is a humble effort in this direction. It aims at comparing the lifestyle, needs and problems of urban aged woman of the lower, middle and higher income groups. The aim is to suggest, keeping in view our meagre resources, a plan of action, which can easily be operationalized.

Significance of the Study

The present study promises to be useful in addressing the problems and issues of the aged women and in analysing gender perspectives towards ageing. The gravity of the 'problem' is being further highlighted below:

The Aged: Increasing Number and Diminishing Status

In fact, ageing is a subject that should be treated as priority number one. By 2025 A.D., one in every four persons is likely to be an aged person. It means that we are entering a world, where the aged would outnumber children. And that is something we are not well prepared for. This fact becomes clear when we look around for special doctors and find a lot of pediatricians and not a single geriatrician. Nevertheless, any visit to a general ward of a hospital or nursing home shows the preponderance of old people requiring health care and medical attention. Michael Lake, the Director General of the Help the Aged, in Britain rightly says that "if a long term strategy for tackling the problems associated with ageing and providing adequate financial, economic and emotional support to the growing elderly population of the world is not formulated now, it will cause havoc in the next 25 years" (*ToI*, 2000).

The aged are the people hit hardest by the socio-economic changes occurring in the society. Due to the erosion of several beneficial value systems and institutions, the aged are forced to live a life of loneliness, boredom, frustration and dissatisfaction. In old age, they need more money due to the increasing health problems and rising costs of medical care, but with no support they find it increasingly hard to sustain themselves. Social apathy towards them is also increasing day by day.

The Aged Women: More Vulnerable Section

Women amongst the aged are the worst victims of apathy and neglect. There are localized investigations adequate enough to give a fairly good idea of their situation in the country. Today, more of the aged men (82%) as compared to the aged women (47%) are living with their spouses. And while men are likely to be cared for by their spouses, the same may not be true for women. There are several reports of elderly abuse and especially so of the 'single' and more so for women. That 91 per cent of elderly men and only 14 per cent of elderly women are independent also speak of women's dependence. Women are known to contribute to family work in many ways but usual invisibility of women in work seems to have affected these data too (Karkar, 1999). Being silent sufferers, a large number of the elderly women is likely to face social, economic and psychological problems.

In a society like the one in India, women have been neglected all along. The system of patriarchy subordinates a woman right from her birth by controlling her sexuality, reproduction and labour through institutions such as marriage, religion, market and the state. Discrimination and devaluation that women are exposed to throughout their lives has a major impact on their health and well-being as they go through the process of ageing.

As a result, older women face special problems related to employment, income, health, social and emotional security and their care-giving responsibilities. They are rarely cared for by the family members. "The United Nations Commission on the Status of Women in 1992 reported that older women are seldom part of the development agenda. Their contributions are slighted, discussions on their situations are usually 'after thoughts', and remedial actions are seldom taken. Their work is not considered economically productive, and their contributions throughout their life spans are not quantified or valued" (as cited by Karkar, 1999). In fact, the aged women have been the worst victims of economic development, particularly in the developing countries where they previously used to hold the positions of command and respect both in the family and community. Work participation by women (daughters and daughters-in-law) has entrusted them not only with the domestic burden but also the responsibility to look after their grandchildren. When they grow old, and can no longer carry on with their tasks, they are looked upon as 'burden'. The quick increase in the number of such 'dependent' aged women will, in turn, hamper the economic growth, decrease the per capita income, and decline the quality of life of not only the aged women but the society as a whole.

The Aged: International versus National Concern

Developed countries like America, Britain, Canada and Japan have shown considerable interest in this regard. Frequent efforts, including intense research and better health care facilities, have been undertaken there to deal with the old age problems. Due to their awakening on the subject, these countries have observed not only higher life expectancy but also healthier longevity.

Just to illustrate, as per many of the recent researches, life is not only getting longer in the U.S. but it appears to be getting better also, particularly for the women. The overall quality of life in their last years improved among all women but was most prominent in those 85 years and older (*ToI*, January 28, 2000). People above 85 years in 1993 were found to be more independent and healthier than those of the same age in 1986, according to the report (January 26th issue, *Journal of American Medical Association*). The researchers also found that compared to 1986, in 1993, women of the age group 65–84 spent 18 fewer nights on an average in a nursing home, and women over age 85 spent 42 fewer nights in a nursing home. The proportion of women over the age of 85 who had difficulty in the activities of daily living such as walking, dressing, bathing, using the toilet or eating, dropped from 62 per cent in 1986 to 52 per cent in 1993. The findings indicate that the developed countries have realized their responsibilities towards their aged, which resulted in the improved quality of their lives.

But, in India, the government has been slow to recognize the state's responsibilities towards the aged. To our politicians, ageing seems to be an issue, which may easily be shifted to the last priority. In such a situation, the National Policy on Older Persons, 1999 is definitely a landmark. Keeping in view our scarce resources and the apathetic attitude of the society, it is yet doubtful whether there will be a drastic change in the status of the aged, particularly the aged women, because the policies and programmes we have, are not free from the gender bias, and do not give due consideration to the special needs of the aged women. In the present context, it is not sufficient to promote the equal treatment of men and women and to develop so-called sex neutral laws. Recognizing the special problems of the aged women, each country should carefully review the options for dealing with their special needs.

State of Research in the Field of Gerontology

Research plays a vital role in guiding the policies and programmes. But the research on gerontology has also not been free from gender bias. The early researches focussed explicitly or implicitly only on issues relating to elderly males. Gerontology did not give importance to women's issues until 1970s. Afterwards, the women's movements, launched primarily by younger professional women, could successfully define ageing as a feminist issue so as to seek the attention of a few of the researchers (Desai, 1999). Then onwards, the researches were undertaken on this aspect. But the efforts have been sporadic and scanty.

Relevance of the Present Study

The present study is an attempt to fulfil the gap. The study is hoped to be of a good deal of significance for those interested in the field of gerontology, gender justice and human rights of the aged women. The aged women do not form a homogenous group. There exist among them socio-economic and cultural diversities. The economic status of the aged women definitely influences their lifestyles, likes and dislikes, needs and aspirations and problems and difficulties. Hence, no serious study, which aims at developing some workable strategies to improve their status, can afford to avoid the economic diversities they live in and with. As of today, a few studies have tried to analyse and describe the economic status of the aged women; and to highlight the economic problems they encounter. Yet, rarely any attempt has been made to compare the lifestyles and problems of the aged women belonging to different income groups. This study is singular in the sense that it considers the economic diversities while analysing the needs and problems of the urban aged women and ultimately attempts to suggest some course of action to improve their status. A uniform pattern of strategies will not only lead to wastage of resources but will also prove to be ineffective. Every specific group needs a different treatment. And, this study may well provide a basis for planning such treatment.

Objectives of the Study

The specific objectives of the study are:

1. To examine the personal profile and (economic and non-economic) resource endowment of the urban aged women.
2. To analyse the health status, physical mobility and leisure time activities of the urban aged women.
3. To examine the emerging challenges faced by the urban aged women.
4. To compare the urban aged women of lower, middle and higher income groups with respect to the various variables included in the objectives 1–3 above.
5. To analyse perceptions and policy implications in encountering challenges and to suggest, in line with the prevailing provisions and efforts, a plan of action so as to deal with the problems of the urban aged women of the three income groups.

Hypotheses

1. Housing condition, household composition and family pattern of the urban aged women depend on the income group they belong to.

2. Generally, physical mobility declines as age increases.
3. Utilization of free time differs according to age, educational level, health status and income group.
4. Those who had been engaged in some occupation face lesser economic problems as compared to those who had never been in any occupation.
5. The aged women who are educated do not have so much financial difficulties as the aged women who are uneducated or less educated.
6. The aged women face problems—physical, social, economic and psychological—irrespective of the income group they belong to.
7. The kind of services required by the aged women depends on their physical mobility and health status; their relationship with their family and kin; and the income group they belong to.

The study is focused on the 60+ aged women residing in the municipal territories of Girwa tehsil of the Udaipur district.

Research Design

The study employs exploratory-cum-descriptive research design with primary emphasis on the descriptive one. It aims at gaining new insights into the comparative lifestyle, needs and problems of the aged women of the three income groups: lower, middle and higher. Though scattered evidences are available, yet no systematic study has so far been available the findings of which could become the basis of the present study. So, it resembles with exploratory studies. The study also aims at portraying as faithfully as possible the characteristics of the aged women of the three income groups. At various points, the study plans to determine the association of one variable with the other, for example, age and income group, educational status and income group, satisfaction and income group, etc. The study also makes use of various hypotheses. The efforts have also been made to minimize bias and maximize the reliability of the data collected. And the author asserts that the similar findings will be obtained if the collection of evidence is repeated. All this reflects the characteristics of any descriptive study.

Area of Study

Rajasthan, geographically the largest state in India after the separation of Chattisgarh from Madhya Pradesh, has an aerial extent of 3,42,239 sq. km. It covers about one-tenth geographical area of the country.

The state is situated between north latitudes 23E03' and 30E12' and east longitudes 69E30' and 78E17'. Its western border is part of the international boundary with Pakistan. It is surrounded by Gujarat on the south-west, Madhya Pradesh on the south-east, Punjab towards the north, and Haryana and Uttar Pradesh towards the north-east (Chouhan, 1996; Gupta, 1998).

Population-wise, the state of Rajasthan ranks ninth in the descending order. As per 1991 census, its population was approximately 4.40 crores, which contributes around 5.2 per cent of total population of the country (Chouhan, 1996). The population,

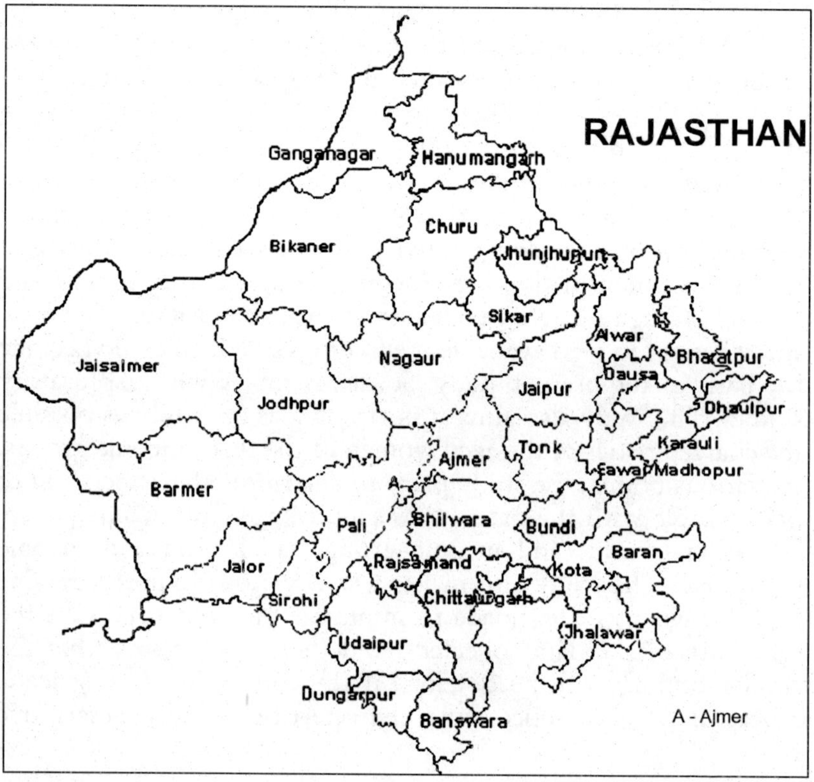

according to 2001 census, increased to 5.65 crores so as to contribute 5.5 per cent of the country's total population (GoI, 2002).

Divided into 32 districts, Rajasthan exhibits a varied range with regard to the density of population. Being sparsely populated, the state had a density of 129 persons per square kilometre in 1991 which, in 2001, increased to 165 persons a square kilometre (GoI, 2002). The density within the state ranges from 9 persons a square kilometre in the desert district of Jaisalmer to 336 in Jaipur district (Gupta, 1998).

Rajasthan has a low degree of urbanization and the extent of urban influence extended by the urban centres upto their surrounding areas is also, generally, low. Around 22.38 per cent of the population in Rajasthan resides in the urban areas [*District Census Handbook* (DCHB) and Gupta, 1998]. Seven major towns, viz., Jaipur, Jodhpur, Ajmer, Kota, Bikaner, Udaipur and Alwar, form the nuclei of urban concentration.

The climate of Rajasthan varies from arid to sub-humid and the annual rainfall in the state also varies significantly. The distinct physiographic features of Rajasthan limit the possibilities of economic development. Consequently, the level of per capita state domestic product is one of the lowest in the country. The state is not industrially developed.

Rajasthan is distinct from the rest of the country in two different aspects: regular droughts and a history of feudalism.

By all commonly accepted indicators of the status of women, Rajasthan ranks as one of the lowest in the country. Figures of female literacy and enrolment of girls in schools are among the lowest in India; and those of female mortality and infant and child mortality are among the highest. In 2001, the sex ratio in Rajasthan was 922; the national figure being 933. The literacy rate among women, as per 1991 census, was 20 per cent; and was increased to 44 per cent in 2001, still one of the lowest in the country (GoI, 2002). The female rural literacy rate was only 12 per cent. The literacy rate among SC and ST women was just 8 and 4 per cent respectively (*Village Prakriya Census Abstracts*, Rajasthan State, 1991). There were 27 districts in the country with a female rural literacy of less than 10 per cent; of which 15 districts were in

Rajasthan alone. There were 5,000 villages in Rajasthan where there was not a single literate woman. Barmer and Jalor districts of Rajasthan had female literacy rates (rural + urban both) of 7.7 and 7.8 per cent respectively (Nanda, 1992).

The people of Rajasthan represent a mosaic of many social patterns. While for a millennium, the region had been dominated by Rajputs, the Bhils and Gujars are the oldest known inhabitants. Brahmins, Jats, Gurassias, Gujars (who practice livestock rearing for livelihood), Lohars, Ahirs, Raigers (leather workers), Berwas (SCs), Rebari (nomads keeping goats, sheep and camels) and Khati (carpenters) are among the other important groups. The common characteristic of all the castes, however, is the marginal position of women.

Women, in Rajasthan, do not have authority in sociological sense. By law, women have the right to inheritance of land. But, in practice they inherit land only in the absence of a male heir. In joint families, woman's, particularly the widow's rights of inheritance, occupancy and disposal are at times violated by their own children and relatives. Women are expected to work throughout the day. Leisure for women is frowned upon and women sitting in groups invite severe criticism from the male members and aged women of their families. Drawing, fetching and management of water is considered exclusively a woman's job.

People of Rajasthan, generally, have typically orthodox mindset, which worsens the plight of women. Cases of foeticide, sexual abuse (including child rape, rape and gang rape), domestic or otherwise violence against women to the extent of killing on the suspicion of her being a 'witch', etc., are often reported by the media, provide ample evidence of the miserable condition of the women in Rajasthan. Women are supposed to cover their faces in front of men other than the husband. In fact, there is rarely any other state in India where women are so much suppressed, tortured and humiliated.

Udaipur District

Situated in the southern part of Rajasthan, the district of Udaipur lies between 23°46' and 26°2' north latitudes and 73°0' and 74°35' east longitudes. Its geographical area covers 13,618 sq. km. From the sea level, its height is measured to be 577 metres.

It is bounded on the west by Chittorgarh, on the north by newly formed Rajsamand district, on the northwest by Pali district, on the west by Sirohi, on the south by Dungurpur and on the southwest by Banswara district. On the west-south, the district touches the border of Gujarat (Gupta, 1998).

Administrative Structure

From administrative point of view, the district is divided into four sub-divisions, 10 tehsils (see map below), six sub-tehsils, 11 Panchayat Samitis, 361 Gram Panchayats and 2,271 villages.

At the same time, the district has one municipal council and four municipalities (one *Nagar Parishad* and four *Nagar Palika*). From the democratic point of view, the district has been divided into two Lok Sabha and 10 Vidhan Sabha electoral areas (Gupta, 1998).

Population

As per 1991 census, the district has a population of 29 lakhs and contributes around 6.6 per cent to the population of the state

Map
Udaipur District

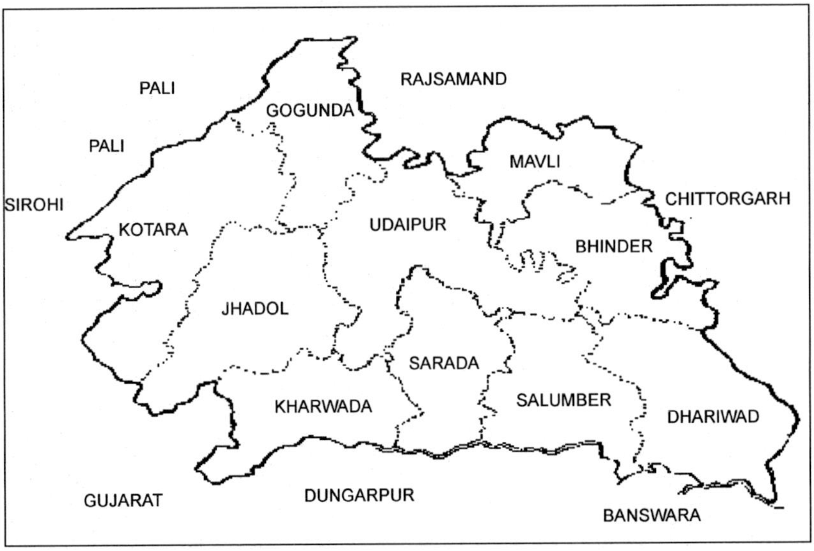

(DCHB, 1991). It has a density of 151 to 200 (average 167) persons per square kilometre and is one among the seven major towns of Rajasthan forming the nuclei of urban concentration (Gupta, 1998). The sex ratio, as per 1991 census, is 965, which is much higher than that of the whole Rajasthan (910) and India (927).

Literacy

The district has a literacy rate of only 34 per cent. The female literacy rate is just 19 per cent (DCHB, Udaipur, 1991). The female literacy rate is found to be the higher in urban areas (i.e., 62% with a maximum of 68% in the Udaipur city and the lowest of 41% in the Deogarh town) than in rural areas (i.e., 10% ranging from a maximum of 15% in the Bargaon Panchayat Samiti to a meagre minimum of 3% in the Kotra Panchayat Samiti) (DCHB, Udaipur, 1991).

Girwa Udaipur: The Urban Area

Lying almost at the centre of the district, Girwa Udaipur covers a total geographical area of 1,751 sq. km. The urban area of the tehsil amounts for only 64 sq. km. and is under the charge of the Udaipur Municipal Council (UMC) (DCHB, 1991).

As per 1991 survey, the population of the tehsil was 5.58 lakhs with 53 per cent living in the urban areas. The urban population accounted for 3.09 lakh (1.65 lakh males + 1.44 lakh females) and was divided into 19 wards. The UMC had sex ratio of 876 (DCHB, 1991).

The slums cover about 5 sq. km. of the urban area. The area is divided into 34 slums and approximately 15 per cent of the tehsil's population resides here (DCHB, 1991).

The majority of the UMC population (69%) consists of 'non-workers'. The remaining population includes 30 per cent main workers and 1 per cent marginal workers. As far as females are concerned, only 9 per cent belong to the working population. It includes 7.8 per cent main workers and 1.1 per cent marginal workers. It may be noted that contrary to the general trend, women outnumber men in the 'marginal worker' category (DCHB, 1991).

As per 1991 survey, the population of the tehsil was 5.58 lakhs with 53 per cent living in the urban areas. The urban population accounted for 3.09 lakhs (1.65 lakh males + 1.44 lakh females) and was divided into 19 wards. The UMC had sex ratio of 876 (DCHB, 1991).

The slums cover about 5 sq. km. of the urban area. The area is divided into 34 slums and approximately 15 per cent of the tehsil's population resides here (DCHB, 1991).

The majority of the UMC population (69%) consists of 'non-workers'. The remaining population includes 30 per cent main workers and 1 per cent marginal workers. As far as females are concerned, only 9 per cent belong to the working population. It includes 7.8 per cent main workers and 1.1 per cent marginal workers. It may be noted that contrary to the general trend, women outnumber men in the 'marginal worker' category (DCHB, 1991).

The overall literacy rate of the area is 78 per cent, while the female literacy rate is 68 per cent. The UMC has the highest literacy rate in the various urban towns of the district (DCHB, 1991).

As far as educational facilities in the UMC are concerned, there are various schools. The area has two main libraries and 15 reading rooms. The UMC has three universities: the JRN Rajasthan Vidyapeeth (Deemed University), the Sukhadia University and the Agriculture University. These universities have made UMC into an important educational centre. A number of professional and non-professional colleges are run under these universities or otherwise. Coming to medical facilities, UMC has a government hospital and nine government dispensaries. Yet, the number of beds per 1,000 population is just four (DCHB, 1991).

Universe of Discourse

The aged women residing in the urban areas of Girwa tehsil of Udaipur district constitute the universe of this study.

The female population of the tehsil is 1,44,055 (DCHB, 1991). The census does not provide statistics by 60+ age. So, it is not at all possible to give the exact number of the 60+ aged women who comprise the universe of this study. As per the 1991 census, in

Rajasthan, the aged female population comprised 6.31 per cent of the total female population (Census of India, 1991; see Table 1.3) That way, 6.31 per cent of the female population (1,44,055), i.e., the aged female population, comes out to be 9,090. Since, the 15 per cent of the population of UMC lives in slums (DCHB, 1991), thus 15 per cent of 9,090 comes out to be about 1363. Since the study excludes slum areas from its purview, the universe of the study is supposed to be comprised of about 7,727 (9,090–1,363) aged women of the Girwa tehsil, Udaipur.

Sampling

Identification was made of the higher, middle and lower economic status localities (clusters) of UMC. Out of the identified localities, three localities (approximately equal in size) were selected from each of the three strata, using purposive sampling. From each of the nine selected localities, 25 aged women were contacted on the basis of the quota sampling.

The random sampling has its own limitations and difficulties. It was first intended to adopt random sampling. But, due to incorrect and back dated electoral list; the delay in obtaining the up-to-date/corrected list; difficulty in approaching the specific respondents (due to their migration, sickness, death or busy schedule); and the limited time span available for collecting data, the scholar was, in a way, compelled to shift to a mix of purposive and quota sampling because of its practical feasibility. In spite of the fact that this sampling might yield probable results, it was thought satisfactory for the purpose at hand.

To sum up, taking 75 aged women from each of the categories: the lower, the middle and the higher income group, in all 225 respondents were included in the sample. This sample forms approximately 3 per cent of the estimated size of the universe (7727). Table 1.10 specifies the sampling plan.

Data Collection

Both primary and secondary sources of data were used for the present study.

Table 1.10
Sampling Plan

Income Groups	*Udaipur City*		*Total*
	Localities Selected by Purposive Sampling	*Respondents Chosen by Quota Sampling*	
Lower*	1. Sindhi Colony	25	
	2. Sundarwas	25	75
	3. Kishan Pole	25	
Middle	1. Glass Factory (Arvind Nagar)	25	
	2. Bohra Ganesh Ji (Ganesh Nagar)	25	75
	3. Hiran Magri (Sector 13)	25	
Higher	1. Polo Ground	25	
	2. Moti Magri	25	75
	3. Saheli Marg	25	
	All	215	215

* The lower income group area excludes slums (Jhuggi-Jhopri), unapproved and temporary settlements (e.g., that of Gadaria Lohars). The study takes into account only permanent, regular and approved localities of the Udaipur city.

Primary Sources of Data

Keeping in view the low literacy rate among the aged women; the problems associated with ageing like weak eye-sight, sickness, etc.; low turnout rate of 'questionnaire'; and the limited time span available for data collection, interview schedule was considered as the best suitable tool for the data collection, and was, therefore, opted for the study.

The present researcher, herself, had collected the primary data with the help of a structured interview schedule. The schedule, divided into various sections, covered different aspects of life of an aged woman, in addition to her views and expectations regarding old age (the schedule is provided in the Appendix 'B' of the study).

Secondary Sources of Data

The secondary sources of data included books, journals, periodicals, newspapers, published and unpublished government records, etc. These sources helped the researcher in visualizing the universe of the study, understanding the approaches to the old age and the demographic changes which have proliferated the problems of the aged.

To trace foreign studies on the subject and the latest demographic data, Internet was used. For this, the researcher obtained the expert assistance of National Social Science Documentation Centre (NASSDOC) of ICSSR, New Delhi.

Data Processing

The data were processed into bivariate or multivariate tables, and were analysed employing appropriate statistical measures like percentage, mean and chi-square test. The researcher availed herself of the opportunity to get the expert advice of the Guidance and Consultancy Cell of ICSSR, New Delhi in the data processing.

Scaling

To measure the level of physical mobility, the level of competence in the house hold work, and the level of social interaction; scaling technique, as described in the Appendix, was used.

Limitations

The study was confined just to the Girwa tehsil of the district Udaipur. For the analysis, impact of only a few of the variables, like economic status, income group, age and education, have been analysed with relation to the lifestyle, needs and problems of the aged women while ignoring the others that were thought not so important. And to define various income groups, the study developed its own criterion that was deemed suitable to serve the purpose of the study. These factors, however, may be considered as the limitations of this study.

In a nutshell, all over the world, a woman gets the secondary status. On becoming old, her earlier life experiences combined with other socio-economic factors lead her to a miserable state of existence. Poor health, widowhood, poverty, isolation and neglect prove to be the hard facts of her life. Either due to lack of education or due to lack of exposure to modern ideas, they perpetuate stereotypes about womanhood. An attitude of helplessness, that is culturally conditioned, may prevent women from avoiding dependency and vulnerability in old age. Designed to develop some workable strategies to deal with the challenges of the aged women, this study aims at comparing their lifestyles, needs and problems in relation to their income groups. The study is specific in the sense that it considers gender and economic disparities for planning the treatment. However, the government, NGOs, social workers and social scientists all must join hands towards this treatment. This support is also, in a way, the fundamental requisite for social justice, gender justice and protection of human rights of the aged women.

Notes

1. 'Population ageing' refers to the changes of structure of a population. It is defined in terms of the proportion of persons aged 60 and over in the total population.
2. *Vanaprasthashram* and *Sanyasashram* are two of the four *Ashrams* according to Aryan division of life cycle. The Hindu view of life has divided a man's life in four stages, viz., *Brahmacharya, Grihastha, Vanprastha and Sannyas* for the pursuit of *Dharma, Artha, Kaama* and *Moksha*. In *Vanaprastha*, the individual makes a conscious effort to withdraw himself from active participation in social life so as to enter the final stage of *Sannyas*.
3. Ibid.
4. All India Institute of Medical Sciences, Delhi is considered as one of the best government hospitals of India. It attracts patients from all over India.
5. There are only a few studies on the status and problems of elderly widows (Jamuna, 1992; Jamuna, Reddy and Ramamurti, 1991; Ramamurti, 1989; Ramamurti and Jamuna, 1993; Reddy, Jamuna and Ramamurti 1992; Muthayya, 1995).
6. United Nations defines populations with 4 to 7 per cent persons in ages 60+ as 'mature' and those with the percentage as 7+ as 'old' or 'aged'.
7. Ibid.

2

Gender Ageing

Conceptual and Theoretical Framework

On an average, women live longer than men, and some researchers have categorized 'very old' as primarily a *female experience*. This chapter attempts to analyse the concepts of ageing with special reference to women. We propose to proceed with a concise review of related studies on the subject and incorporate an analysis of National Policy on Older Persons from gender perspectives. The concluding but utmost important part of this chapter is going to be an attempt to develop the theoretical framework of the study. The various theories of gerontology are to be analysed critically. And, we shall select two theories—Activity Theory and Disengagement Theory—for testing and appraisal.

Conceptual Perspectives

Ageing: A Process of Deterioration

Ageing is a continued process and 'the aged' is a category. The word 'ageing' has been defined by researchers in different contexts. Tyagi (1996) says, "Ageing means the effect of age, i.e., the deterioration in physiological capabilities". Becker defines ageing in the broadest sense "as those changes occurring in an individual, as a result of passage of time" (see Khan, 1997). According to Stieglitz (1954), "Ageing is a part of living. It begins with conception and terminates with death". Obviously, ageing is a biological process, experienced by mankind at all times. But, at what age people become old in their life cycle is not clear. There is no single point at which people automatically cross a magic line and become old.

Approaches to Ageing

A man ages biologically as a continuing process, socially as perceived by the members of the society, economically when retired from the workforce; and throughout some chronological criterion is attached to this ageing process. Besides, some scholars have also mentioned psychological (Hooman and Kiyan, 1988; Prakash, 1998), socio-cultural (Khan, 1997; Tyagi, 1996) and functional dimensions of ageing (Kumar, 1997). By and large, the overall approaches to ageing may be classified into the following four categories: biological or physiological or functional ageing; chronological ageing; psychological ageing or 'self-definition'; and socio-cultural ageing.

Gender Perspective of Approaches to Ageing

These approaches were laid down keeping in view the male life cycle. Prakash (1994) was, in fact, right in mentioning that "much of human psychology was psychology of man". This is hardly surprising, because for a very long time, social scientists were guided by the blind assumption that men are more representative of the human race than women are. "The failure 'to build' women into social science research has impaired the accuracy and comprehensiveness of conceptual models and empirical findings. Even in psychology, female of human species, specially the ageing variety, is a relatively new entrant on the research scene" (Prakash, 1994). Given below is an attempt to analyse the approaches to define 'the aged' or 'the old' in general, and also from the gender perspective.

Physiological or Biological or Functional Ageing

The passage of time leaves some imprints on the body and functional capability of the individuals. And these become the marker of the ageing process. Given below is an attempt to analyse these markers by way of biological or physiological or functional approaches to ageing.

Physiologically, a person is old when the signs of wearing out of the body appear (Gray and Mobery, 1962). Thus, "ageing is the deterioration of mature organism resulting from time dependent and irreversible changes intrinsic to all members of that species. With the passage of time, they are increasingly unable to cope with the stresses of the environment and head towards decay and eventual death" (Handler, 1960). Ageing consists of two simultaneous components: anabolic building-up and catabolic break down. The first two decades of life, according to Becker (1959), are predominantly anabolic, during which there is growth and development. In contrast, the last few decades are largely catabolic, during which antrophy and degeneration dominate. In the middle years, there is essentially a balance between expansion and decay. In other words, while growth predominates in youth, degenerative changes, which originate in early life, predominate in the later life span (Khan, 1997).

Although there is still considerable debate about the precise biological definition of ageing, Strehler (1977) suggests four criteria to distinguish ageing from the other biological processes. These are: universality (must happen to each member of the population), internality (must come from within the organism), progressiveness (must occur gradually over time) and harmfulness (must have a deleterious effect upon the organism and its ability to cope with its environment). All areas of the body are affected to some degree. But the various systems of the body do neither deteriorate at the same time and at the same rate, nor does the similar pattern of decline follow or occur for all persons. Furthermore, the age associated changes are also affected and enhanced by disease processes which inflict individuals and these contribute to what has been called as 'disease ageing' as distinct from 'normal ageing' (Sharma and Agarwal, 1996).

Though ageing is universal, some researchers consider ageing and old age as functional, and not chronological concepts. Functional ageing reflects the relationship between biological maturation or deterioration, and the way how an individual can perform physical, social and/or cognitive tasks (Kumar, 1999). Sharma (1998) opines that "in old age, person's competence—physical, mental and social is reduced and becomes dependent, to a great degree, on the environment".

The biological changes that seem to herald the onset of ageing are more apparent and occur earlier in women as compared to men. The popular image of an aged woman is often that of a frail, senile, hard of hearing and in need of help with routine activities of living: bathing, eating, dressing, etc. and gives the impression of ageing as a period of mal-adaptation, which is not true in the majority of the cases (Sharma, 1998).

Ageing is, generally, the post-reproductive phase in a person's life. And, menopause tells a woman in no uncertain terms that her reproductive function has come to an end. The physiological truth is more obvious in women than in men. In societies where a woman's reproductive function is overvalued, a post-menopausal woman is considered old. In cultures, where menopause is equated with loss of vitality, sexuality and feminity, this event may be taken as a marker of ageing (Prakash, 1994). Ganesh (1997) views that reproductive senescence sets in women at menopause, which is earlier than 60 years; and is the basis generally used to define the 'aged'. "Despite increase in longevity, the mean age for menopause has remained almost constant at 51 years in developed countries and a couple of years lower in developing countries. The average age of menopause is between 47–50 years" (Sahi, 1998). In the coming decades, "the average life span of females is expected to be over 80 years in developed countries and between 65–70 years in the developing world" (Iyer, 1998). Generally, an average woman would live one-third or more of her life after menopause (Iyer, 1998 and Sahi, 1998). And 76 per cent of post-menopausal women would be living in the developing countries (Iyer, 1998). However, menopause is experienced differently by women in different cultures. Yet, Bavadam (1999) emphasises that the women have a more complex phase of old age (i.e., the post-menopausal phase).

The ageing is more threatening for women than men because it has more negative implications. Men tend to report more decline in their hearing and greater hair loss than women, whereas women tend to report more decline in their eyesight and energy as well as in the quality of their skin and figure. Menopause markedly accelerates bone loss (Carolina et al., 1998). Women do also tend to be more obese.

The male-female perception of ageing are largely different because of the differences in the ageing process, and when all signs of ageing, viz., gray hair, dry skin, wrinkles and loss of energy are appeared, there is really not much difference between the sexes in recognizing the onset of old age. The impact of ageing, however, may be somewhat greater on women when it comes to special consequences and connotations of beauty and sexuality. But, the struggle against the irreversible change in one's looks most likely peaks about late middle age rather than in old age. Once women are old, there may be little or no difference about the effects of ageing on their appearance in comparison with old men. In fact, old age may be the time of life when looks matter the least.

However, no biological parameter has been found which will clearly indicate when an individual person has become old. Practically, except for certain limited purposes, it is not yet practicable to use any physical criterion as the basis for determining whether or not an individual is old.

Chronological Ageing

Chronology or calendar age is frequently used to define the onset of old age. This index has given increasing importance in modern society, specially where legal definitions couched in terms of chronology have become important in defining particular phases of life cycle, such as the age of legal responsibility, majority, marriage or retirement. Chronological age is, in fact, a good criterion for demarcating 'the aged' as it is an important indicator of health, functional capacity, labour force participation, life cycle stage and income.

But assigning a particular point of time at which a person becomes aged is a difficult proposition. It, according to Victor (1988), has two distinct dimensions: the first is based upon the cultural ascription of the society, and the second dimension relates to the response of the state to the perceived problems of old age. Also, the cut-off point to define the aged relates to the longevity of the people. When the life expectancy of the population was 40 years, a person aged 40 was considered as aged. In the least and less developed countries, the expectation of life at birth is hovering around 60 years while in the developed countries, it is around 65 years. And hence, the 60 years demarcation is accepted for the aged in the former (Devi et al., 1999) and 65 years in the later (Tyagi, 1996). Resultantly, divergent views exist regarding a particular age at which a person becomes aged. Most of the official documents, including the UN literature, define the aged as those 60 years and above. But, the available data in the USA term 'elderly' as those 65 years of age and above.

The retirement age, generally considered as a demarcation point for the aged, across and within the countries is not systematic. In Germany, it is 65 years. In USA, the retirement age of male and female is 65 and 60 years respectively. In India, the retirement age varies from 35 years (for soldiers), 55 years (for a few government employees, e.g., the state government employees of Kerala; and Jammu & Kashmir), 58 (in central and state governments), 60 (government employees including IAS, IPS, scientists and academicians), and 65 (for judges and a few professors). The age of Old Age Pension also varies (60; 65; or 60 for females and 65 for males) from state to state. But the senior citizen concessions and benefits given by Indian government are for those 65 years or above.

'The aged' is a relative term and generally used in relation to the young. There is no consensus about the cut-off point for the aged even among the researchers. For example, Sen (1991) indirectly pointed that senescence starts after 39 years of age. On the similar lines, Anuradha and Prakash (1991) considered the age of 40 years and above for the aged. Raigbai (1960), Jaten et al. (1991) and Devi and Bagga (1997) chose 50 years as the cut-off point for the elderly. But majority of the scholars considered 55 or 60 years as the lowest age to consider a person as aged. But Devi et al. (1999) and Rajkumar (1995) considered aged persons as those aged 65 years or above.

Most of the scholars have assigned same chronological age for demarcating aged men and women from the rest of the population. But there are others who opine that women become aged at a younger age than men. Just to quote, Mahajan (1987) used 60 years for defining 'aged men' and 55 years for 'aged women'. Hazan (1994) mentioned that "an old person is someone who has reached the age of sixty (if female) or sixty-five (if male)".

However, defining the aged as a single group, as is done in all the above definitions, say 55+, 60+ or 65+ is also not sufficient nor satisfactory because it ignores the heterogeneous nature of the aged population, covering a range of at least 25 years (in the case of a less developed country) or more (in the case of a developed country). Regrouping this population into smaller age categories, nonetheless, can solve this problem. Many authors have adopted this strategy of regrouping the aged population into smaller categories, viz., 58–65 or 60–65, 65–74, 74–85 and 85+. However, increasingly, there is a trend to differentiate between young elderly (between 60–74 years) and the 'old' elderly (75+years). Gradually, the term 'old old' has emerged to designate those who are 75 years or more.

Whatever may be the cut-off point for the aged, Victor (1987), rightly points out that "the use of this measure requires a society to be sufficiently well organized so that its members have an idea of their chronological age". Gray and Wilcock (1981) suggest that even as late as seventeenth century, people in Britain had only a very rough idea of their age". In India, even today, a large number of people, particularly the women, do not have any idea about their age. But, the Census of India does not include any category 'age not known' while categorizing the people on the basis of their age. Naturally, the investigators use indirect techniques (e.g., age of self-marriage, age of the eldest son, major national calamities or accidents in relation to life cycle stages, etc.) to find out the age of such persons.

In fact, ignorance about one's exact age by the members of a society poses a serious limitation to the 'chronological approach to ageing'. Also, this criterion is questionable because at a particular age, say 55 or 60 years, some people become fragile and result in loss of stamina, while there are others who are quite active even at 85 years of age. It is really questionable whether it is right to group all persons in one category on the basis of just their age, while avoiding their functional status and capabilities.

Psychological Ageing

Psychological ageing, among the various approaches, refers perhaps to the most ambiguous phenomenon. "Age is a state of mind", is a widely held notion. From the psychological viewpoint, ageing expresses itself in typical perception and awareness as of limitations, handicaps and problems, overall dissatisfaction and difficulties of adjustment on account of advanced age and typical strategies adopted by the aged to cope with them (Sinha, 1989). Bhatia (1983), on the similar lines, mentions that "the psychological changes in respect of an individual's conception of the self, his ideas about his worth as an individual and as a member of social groups, his feelings about the attitudes and behaviour of others towards himself and his general view of life and the world, including his own place therein, play significant part in the process of psychological ageing".

Thus, psychological ageing consists of a general decline in the mental abilities that accompany old age. Psychologists take various mental abilities such as memory, intelligence, changing emotional reactions and attitudes, etc., as the base for demarcating the aged (Tyagi, 1996).

Is psychological ageing voluntary or involuntary? Scientific evidence is convergent on the latter. The psychological perspective has it that the process of ageing sets early in age but it is not rapid or strong. This stage in one's life may be called 'senescence'. It is succeeded by the phase of rapid decline in mental and emotional health and is called 'old age' or senility (Khan, 1997). With ageing, fluid intelligence or ability to acquire new knowledge and to assimilate it decreases (Ramamurti and Jamuna, 1993). Comfort (1957) considers ageing as a change in behaviour of the organism which comes about with the increase in chronological age and which leads to a decrease in adjustment and hence in fitness, so to say, for survival (Khan, 1997).

Bernice Neugarten has described the major conflicts of old age as related to having to give up one's position of authority and evaluating one's former competence, achievements and pleasures. For both sexes, there is reconciliation with significant others: resolution of grief over the death of self, maintenance of sense of integrity in terms of what one has been rather than what one is (Sharma and Agarwal, 1996). Thus, it is assumed that ageing processes can be accelerated due to the stress and strain in life. A positive state of mind, interest in life and things around oneself help in reducing the ageing process. On the other hand, an unfavourable and negative attitude towards the changed physical and social conditions proves not only a hurdle in better adjustment in old age but brings about psychological ageing more quickly (Bhatia, 1983; Tandon, 1997).

Elderly women, especially in the Third World countries like India, suffer from malnutrition and debilitating symptoms as well as report higher psychological distress (Prakash, 1997). Due to neglect and discrimination in their younger age, women are more likely to develop negative attitude towards life and face depression and mental illness.

Just to illustrate, widowhood amongst Indian women induces psychological and physical distress (Prakash and Anuradha, 1988). Psychologically, rural women appear to be at a disadvantaged position compared to urban ones. Both the middle and old aged women from rural areas report multiple somatic complaints, display symptoms of emotional distress, report low satisfaction in several domains of life and consider themselves 'worse off ' than others. Rural conditions characterized by illiteracy, poverty, and the absence of material comforts act as an 'environmental press', leading to depression in older women (Prakash, 1994).

Menopause, the biological symptom of ageing among women, is also generally accompanied by various psychological problems. Neuro-endocrine symptoms like mood changes, anxiety, irritability, insomnia, cognitive deficit, depression, poor confidence and low self-esteem are common problems in a large majority of post-menopausal women (Dass, 1998; Khetarpal, 1998).

Since "the psychological causes of ageing when combined with the physical, accelerate the ageing process by speeding up the rate of decline of mental and physical capacities" (Bhatia, 1983: 5), the ageing process is likely to be faster or quicker for women as compared to that for men.

The above point gets strengthened if we analyse the 'self-definition' of ageing. One important way of defining 'the aged' is the seemingly unproblematic self-definition: an 'old person' is someone who regards himself or herself as such (Hazan, 1994). But, it is to be remembered that a woman's self-definition of 'the aged' is likely to be influenced heavily by her sex role stereotypes, her socialization, cultural practices, etc. Hence, one has to take into consideration all socio-cultural variables so as to analyse this 'self-definition' of women.

Society's standards of female beauty and physical appeal are, more or less, related to youthfulness. Therefore, women may be more aware of the ageing process than men are because the physical signs of ageing produce graver social consequences for women. Denial of ageing has therefore been considered more of a female trait. A double standard seems to exist in the popular culture also, in that elderly men may be thought of as 'handsome' or 'distinguished', but elderly women are not likely to be considered 'beautiful' (Cockerham, 1991). And women have been taught for centuries, to define themselves in terms of largely patriarchal beliefs and expectations.

Thus, there is a difference between men and women as to when they consider themselves 'old'. In terms of 'social age', women consider themselves old at a younger age than men. Some of the studies suggest that women consider themselves old at the age of 50 while for the men it is 60+. Similarly, as per the younger people's perception, a younger age was indicated as the 'threshold of ageing' for women (Prakash, 1994).

In sum, psychological ageing seems to occur earlier and appears to have more negative implications on women as compared to that on men. Yet, the indices of psychological age differ from woman to woman and from society to society. Thus, it is not practically feasible to use psychological criterion for determining who is old because the problems of measurements have not yet been surmounted. It is a phenomenon which is easy to intuit but difficult to define. And, as a basis of further research, it is not proper to consider it as a criterion because of its ambiguous nature.

Socio-Cultural Approach

The socio-cultural ageing, as distinct from biological or psychological ageing, refers to the stage in the life span of the individual who is regarded as old by the social group or community.

There are a number of social events in the life of an individual that also serve as bases of recognizing oneself as being old. These are: retirement from employment, marriage of children and birth of grandchildren, avoidance of sexual activity or decline in expression of interest in the opposite sex after a certain age due to social censorship, assuming new social responsibilities, deserving privileges and respect mainly on account of one's age, and the expectations of younger members in the family to share more and more responsibilities in the family affairs.

Some authors consider 'social ageing' and 'cultural ageing' as synonymous and interdependent and have used the term 'socio-cultural ageing' to describe the two. Just to illustrate, Tyagi (1996) states that according to socio-cultural viewpoint, a person is termed aged when he distances himself from those roles and statuses which he was performing as an adult. He becomes disengaged from his normal adult roles such as withering away from the family roles and constricting the community of friends, etc. On the other hand, other studies (like Victor, 1984; Khan, 1997; Tondon, 1998) narrate that 'social ageing' is different from the 'cultural ageing', for example, while there is much commonness between the cultural and sociological perspectives. The sociological perspective lays more emphasis on changes in behavioural patterns which surface with age. On the other hand, the cultural approach gives importance to life cycle. Accordingly, age is viewed as the progression of a person through different stages of life. For example, the family dimension of life cycle involves numerous transitions including newly married, new parents, parents of teenagers, 'empty nesters', retirees and widows.

However, in the Indian social context, starting of family life by one's progeny may herald the onset of one's old age. In the traditional societies, a woman is deemed old when her eldest son marries and brings home his wife. At this stage, there will be major changes in the roles and status of the elder woman. So is the case with her behavioural norms. She is supposed to hand over the responsibilities of the house to her daughter-in-law.

Thus, as per the socio-cultural approach to ageing, it is basically the socio-cultural events that mark the onset of ageing. And these events occur varyingly from individual to individual and society to society. Not everyone will experience all the phases of family cycle and there may also be enormous variations in the age at which individuals experience various transitions. And these characteristics render this approach inapplicable as a criterion of ageing for further research. Yet, it does give some very important insights about the ageing process.

The Political Economy Approach

It may be added that the socio-cultural view of old age in industrialized western countries is a little different. Victor (1987) has described it as 'the political economy approach to ageing'. According to this approach, old age is defined neither by chronology nor biology, but by the relationship between older people and the means of production. The social and economic status of elderly is supposed to be related to the institutions of society that are either partly, or entirely organized around the concept of production. The old age results in the individual being labelled 'old', and rejected by the productive economic market, simply on the ground of age. Policies for social security, retirement benefits and pension are fundamental to this approach, since they mark the boundary between independent and dependent status.

The aged are seen as a group separate from the wider social context, but as an integral part of society. Old age is often thought of as an extension of life during which paid employment and self-employment get shortened, and may eventually lead to total retirement (Khan, 1997). According to this approach, the aged should be seen as a reserve 'army' of labour. In times of slump, older workers (50–65 years) are encouraged to leave the labour force to make way for younger workers. Conversely, in period of labour shortage, the justification for retiring and becoming non-productive may be questioned, and the older workers will be encouraged to remain in the labour force as long as possible.

The political economy approach to ageing was derived keeping in view the industrially active populations. And, perhaps, this is the limitation this approach has. This approach seems to be of little use if we try to apply it to agrarian or non-industrialized societies, that too from the gender perspectives. In a country like India, women have always been considered dependent on their male counterparts. They had never been directly or independently involved in production work of market economy. If we consider household work partly as a means of production, we can say that since women never retire from their household responsibilities, they never become old. On the other hand, if we do not consider household work as a means of production or part of labour economy, then too, this approach becomes inapplicable, since women will be considered dependent on the society or family or their male counterparts throughout their lives. Obviously, though this approach gives some useful insights into the status of the aged in the society, yet it seems inappropriate in defining the 'aged woman' particularly in societies where women do not directly participate in the labour market and economy.

To sum up, chronological age is the most popular criterion (for defining the aged) among the researchers. There are no definite biological or psychological or socio-cultural parameters which, individually or collectively, can demarcate the particular chronological age uniformly. Yet, from the 'operational' point of view, chronological age provides the easiest way of defining 'the aged'. And that may be the reason for the popularity of this criterion.

Even within the chronological approach, there is no uniform cut-off age for defining 'old age'. The criterion of regrouping the aged population into smaller age categories also varies from researcher to researcher. Though the cut-off age for the aged is usually considered equal for men and women, there is the general impression that women become aged at a younger age than men.

However, none of the approaches is conceptually viable or free from limitations. Also, neither of the approaches provides any uniform parameters that may clearly indicate when an individual becomes old. But each of the approaches helps us to gain some insights into the ageing process. As of today, for research or policy-making, chronological ageing has been given the first priority followed by socio-cultural ageing. Yet, for understanding ageing as a process, each approach is required to be taken into consideration.

Review of Literature

Interest in ageing among the western social scientists started in the early 1940s and 1950s. Linto (1942), Cottrell, Jr. (1942), Anderson (1960), Burgers (1960), Tibbitts (1960), Aries (1962), Maddox (1970) and Riley, Johnson and Foner (1972) have made remarkable contributions to the studies on ageing by covering many issues, for example, demographic aspect of ageing, health, income, changing roles, work patterns, retirement, leisure time activities, family life of the aged, ageing and the economy, living arrangements, special housing arrangements, psychological problems, morale, self-concept, isolation and loneliness, government and ageing, and ageing and voluntary association. But, gender ageing, as an area of research, did not get due recognition even in developed countries till late nineties and issues of the aged women had been dealt by the aforesaid scholars along with the aged men.

In India, researches in the field of ageing and the aged started in the sixties. Most of the researches identified have been conducted after seventies, which show the growing concern for the problems of the aged during this time. One of the reasons could be attributed to the demographic factors. The elderly population has been increasing at an alarming rate. As of now, there is a considerable amount of writing and research on gerontology in India. And they have been undertaken by various disciplines, viz., medical science, psychology, anthropology, sociology, demography and social work. A series of annotated bibliographies on 'Elderly in India' published by TISS (1999 and 2001), and a bibliographical study by Ruprail (2002) are significant contributions and give insights about the literature on gerontology.

However, the following is an attempt to cite a few important foreign and Indian studies conducted after eighties that have specifically dealt with the 'aged women'. Though, it is impossible to differentiate the studies dealing with the 'lifestyle' with those dealing with 'health' or 'social mobility', etc., the studies selected for present review have been put in different categories apropos of their main focus.

Lifestyle

According to Allen and Pickett (1984), the life course of women had undergone significant transformation during the past two centuries. They analysed the social, economic and demographic changes that had interacted with the lifestyle options of American females. These factors included the shift from the Victorian separation of spheres, to dual employment patterns, increased entrance of women into new fields of employment, expansion of educational careers, significant alterations in marriage and divorce patterns, prolongation of the life course, and a great imbalance in the proportion of males and females in the later years. By examining the lives of the elderly women from the long view of history, an awareness of variations in life patterns and choices was fostered.

Carlton (1992), considered elderly black women as a risk population while describing their productive lifestyles in South Eastern North Carolina, Charlotte. The focus of the study, however, was on the problems these women had been facing because of their advancing age, poor health, care-giving responsibilities and isolation, and the deterioration of traditional resources.

Dixon (1997) analysed gender differences in religiosity, health, self-esteem, lifestyle and life satisfaction by focusing on 513 adults in Riverside, Canada. The study revealed that there were no significant gender differences in religious affiliation. The church was seen as a good place for social relationship formation and the religion as a supplier of answers to ultimate questions. But compared with men, women found religion more important personally, and were more likely to be guided by religion and felt the presence of God. The sample could be described as the 'well elderly', regardless of gender, except that women visited doctors and went to hospitals more often. Women were more likely not to have smoked, or drunk alcohol. Men and women appeared to have similar lifestyles, but differed on only the dimension of self-esteem. There were statistically significant gender differences in all dimensions of life satisfaction, but theoretical reasons for these were not made clear.

Warren and Maltby (1998) have studied the lifestyles and health of older women in the United Kingdom. The findings highlight the link between social integration and health, covering topics such as education, employment, marriage, housing, leisure activities and attitudes toward ageing and older people. Discussed also are the aims to establish a basic set of questions that are effective in eliciting information from older women on how they perceived their well-being and needs, and, ultimately, to develop more proactive and empowering models of health assessment, intervention and support.

Daniels (2004) has drawn biographical sketches of "Three African American Elderly Women in Later Life". In the context of the familial and social issues that burden African American elderly in addition to the typical psycho-social issues (e.g., care-giving and widowhood), he presented qualitative interviews of African American women, aged 65+, to examine how these women had dealt with family traditions, lifestyle changes and growing old. Their perceptions of personal joys and frustrations, plus their views on how race was a significant factor in lives was highlighted.

McCallum (1992) has studied the Asia-Pacific Retirement Models for different countries. The co-existence of a traditional and modern sector in much of the Asia-Pacific region offers a traditional family lifestyle, as well as paid work and retirement choices. Results of the study demonstrate the importance of cultural and developmental factors within and among countries. There is less dependency on family in more developed countries: wealthier households in more developed countries depended on income of their own, while in developing countries they depended on families. In contrast, women in developed countries tended to retire along with their husbands to share retirement leisure.

Housing

Stavenuiter (1992) has investigated the composition of households of elderly women in Amsterdam, the Netherlands, during the period 1851–1891. Analysis reveals that elderly women's independence was related to their position within the household, that is, whether they were member of the household or heads of a household.

Voges and Pongratz (1988) analyses the lifestyles of older women with relation to their retirement. The impact of the move from a private household to a residential care facility on dimensions of lifestyle, and the success with which adaptation to the new setting is made, are analysed on the basis of interviews with female residents (aged 69–91) of residential care facilities in Munich (West Germany), supplemented by interviews with a close relative of each woman and a member of the care facility staff who knew the woman well. A positive relationship between continuity in lifestyle and contentment with life situation is indicated in general terms, though compensation for a lifestyle dimension disrupted by the transition with another dimension is often said to occur.

Reznikov and Rozhkor (1991) have investigated the lifestyle of elderly people living in special boarding houses. They obtained the data from unmarried, divorced or widowed respondents in and near Omsk, USSR, in 1989. About 37 per cent of the residents had adult children when they first came to the boarding houses. Men with adult children were three times as likely as women with adult children to seek admission to a boarding house. The most commonly cited reasons for wanting admission included loneliness, poor health and family conflicts. Suggesting improvements in maintaining the mobility and self-sufficiency among the elderly, the scholars opined that if services could be delivered to the elderly in their homes, the need for internment in old age homes could be averted.

Shah (1991–92) has analysed the needs and problems of the urban ageing women (55+ years) of low socio-economic status. Majority of the ageing women from low socio-economic status presented a real and very sad picture about their living conditions. Being illiterate and widowed, the majority of these poor women had to live with a son/daughter or alone in very poor housing conditions. They had been spending a major portion of their life either in front of or at the back place/space of the house, either in leisure or performing household work activities.

Audiarayana (1999), on the basis of a survey of the elderly widowed (274) and currently married (242) women, reveals that the elderly widowed are more likely to live with their children, (than their married counterparts particularly with their un married son(s)). Generally, both the widowed and married women are more inclined to live with their children when they belong to economically better households. Living in urban areas tends to increase significantly the likelihood of co-residence with children among the widowed elderly.

Health

General Health

Branigan and Cousins (1995) have examined, in case of older women, whether motherhood had got to do anything with beliefs about exercise risk. To identify socio-demographic and lifestyle explanations for variations in older women's perceptions for 6 fitness activities, women aged 52–73 in Alberta, Edmonto, responded to a survey questionnaire. Women who were mothers held lower levels of perceived risks for late-life exercise.

Shaul (1994) in the study, conducted in Texas, Austin, USA concluded that women are three times more likely to be diagnosed with rheumatoid arthritis (RA) than men (RA). RA affects all dimensions of a woman's life, resulting in the loss of work, social and recreational activities. Because women incur 40 per cent more chronic illness and live longer than men do, they require more health care and supportive services as they age. Women typically earn less money during their working lives than men do and are more likely to be economically impoverished in old age. Research is needed to identify the multidimensional impact of RA on older women and to explore treatment, lifestyle and work options that will help younger women prepare for their economic needs in old age.

As per Roberto (1993), the three common approaches used in the treatment and prevention of osteoporosis in older women are: hormone replacement therapies, nutrition interventions and exercise programmes. These strategies aim at maintaining or stabilizing bone mass and preventing further loss. Living with osteoporosis presents older women with a variety of physical, psychological and social challenges. To maintain a productive and healthy lifestyle, older women must recognize their physical limitations and make adjustments in their daily lives to cope with these changes successfully.

Collado (1989) analyses undesirable effects of the process of ageing. The consequences of greater longevity on the Spanish population distribution by age, gender and health in old age were addressed, using data from a 1987 national survey on disabilities, deficiencies and handicaps. The impacts of age, behavioural, environmental, lifestyle, hereditary, socio-economic and educational variables on health and infirmity were discussed. To conclude, though infirmity is not inevitable, the ratio of infirm-to-able population increases with age and women suffer with more disability than men do because of their longer longevity. The health condition of the elderly (aged 50+) has consequences for the population as a whole, as well as for the quality of life in old age.

Bagga (1994) has examined the health status of Maharashtrian Brahmin women residing in three old age homes in Pune, India. Blood pressure variation (52%) was found to be the most common complaint of those elderly women, followed by digestive disorders (44%) and arthritis (43%). A gradual increase was noticed in the frequency of blood pressure variations from sixth decade (35%) to seventh (45%), eighth (60%) and ninth decade (67%) respectively. Onset of memory loss and dullness in demeanour was noticed almost simultaneously towards the end of seventh decade with a marked increase in the subsequent years.

Disease and disability go hand in hand with old age, yet there are various individual and regional variations in epidemiological pattern. Devi and Bagga (1997), in their anthropological investigation that was carried out on the older women of Manipur, India, in the age groups of 60 to 96 years, also examined these variations in the prevalence of diseases and disability. The variables studied were: educational level, occupation, economic status, daily activities, etc. The most commonly reported health problems were: eye-ailments, arthritis, digestive disorders, blood pressure, diabetes, hearing impairment, urinary incontinence, cryptogenic drop attacks and fractures. A substantial increase in the frequency of urinary incontinence was noticed from 'young-old' to 'old-old' reaching an alarming high of 87 per cent in women in their 9th decade. Majority of subjects being illiterate, no association could be established between education and frequency and types of health complaints. The respondents who were from comparatively well off families registered more number of complaints than the ones from the weaker sections.

Using a sample of 480 men and women of Chittoor district, Ramamurti (1999) has investigated the importance of knowledge of and attitude to health as components of well-being in old age. Results showed that men had better knowledge and attitude towards health than women did. However, those belonging to higher social and economic classes were found to have better knowledge and more favourable attitude towards good health than others.

Manandhar (1999), in his study on aged women (N=639) living in slums of Mumbai, revealed high levels of undernutrition, anaemia and poor function, particularly in women over 65. Their undernourishment carried a significantly increased risk (over four times) of having poor handgrip strength independent of age, morbidity and other confounders. Nutrition vulnerability was found to be influenced by a variety of social, emotional, physical and economical factors. The study demonstrated the importance of identifying these factors and of addressing undernutrition to enhance the functional ability and quality of life of poor older women.

Using a sample survey of 1,209 elderly residents of Singapore (629 females), Yadav (1999) reveals that more than half of the aged had a disability, and the rate of disability was significantly higher among females as compared to males. More than one-third of the elderly had a handicap and the rate of handicap among females was twice as much as that among the males. Also, the females lived more years of disabled life than the males.

Jamuna (2001) has investigated the psychological factors including Quality of Life of very senior citizens (80+, N=250 male and 250 females) of different economic backgrounds from rural and urban areas of Chittoor, Cuddapah and Nellore districts of Andhra Pradesh. Women had poor memory for later span as compared to men. The gender groups did not differ with regard to functional capability, though women reported slightly high limitations in functional activities than men. As regards to physical and mental activities, women who were living with their spouses scored significantly low compared to those living by themselves.

However, all the persons with longevity were slender; had good eating habits; had long-lived parents and with deep faith in God and religion. Smoking and consumption of alcoholic drinks were not common for almost all of them.

Gynecological Health

'Genital Neoplasm in the Elderly Women of Himachal Pradesh, India' was examined by Gupta and Pal (1998) in their six-year study. According to the authors, "most of the genital tumours among women 60+ are malignant, quite often they are not detected because they do not interfere with physical and sexual activity. Among women, the cancer of cervix is the commonest gynecological malignancy. Early detection can help in treating the problem.

Literature regarding prevalence, etiopathogenesis, clinical manifestation and management problems pertaining to renal disorders in elderly females is very scarce in spite of voluminous research in the field of geriatric nephrology. Keeping in view these handicaps, Prakash (1998) has documented the experiences and concluded that nature of diseases occurring in the elderly are no different from those occurring in younger population except their prevalence rates. Hormone replacement therapy has proved that frequency, severity and recurrence of urinary transmitted infections among postmenopausal women can be dramatically reduced. Whether it will be effective when administered to elderly females above 75–80 years of age still needs to be researched.

Chetna (2001), in her study on ageing women (60+, N=152 Sabarkantha district, Gujarat and N=153 Chittor district, Rajasthan) has revealed that 95 per cent of women had attained menopause naturally, whereas the remaining had undergone hysterectomy. In Rajasthan, 23 per cent of women reached menopause at 36–44 years, whereas 38 per cent of them attained it at 45–49 years. Very few women attained menopause before 35 years (7%) and after 51 years (17%) of age.

In both the districts, 24 per cent of women became pregnant for 4–5 times, whereas 60 per cent became pregnant for 6–13 times. This included still birth, miscarriages, abortion and dead children too. The repeated pregnancies reportedly had adverse effect, such as becoming weak, becoming old early and having gynaecological problems, affecting their health. Interestingly, 49 per cent of the aged women of Sabarkantha district and 75 per cent of that of Chittor district were aware that a couple could decide when and how many children to have. The most widely used method of family planning in both the states was tubectomy (70%), followed by IUD (14%) and vasectomy (10%).

Social Mobility and Interaction

Synge (1994) has studied the pattern of companionship and sociability among older Canadian women. Data from a survey of middle-aged and elderly people were collected to explore the lives of older females, mostly widows, in the city of Hamilton, Ontario. A clear weekly pattern of the lives of females aged 70+ was noticed: family members are visited on weekends, usually on Sundays, while friends are on weekdays. Older widows eat most of their meals alone, even on weekends. Females, but not males, have several extended telephone conversations (30 minutes average) per day with friends and family members. Most of the older females go to church and social events alone rather than with family. Data show the importance to women of flat-rate telephone service and suggest the great value of church-sponsored sociability and conviviality.

Jerrome (1981) emphasizes the significance of friendship for women in later life. By interacting women aged 55–85 years and residing in Sussex, England, she concludes that as the middle class women enter retirement, through giving up a job or losing a spouse or dependent relatives, they adopt different friendship strategies. Some extend and deepen the existing relationships; some make new friends; some develop the role of the 'good neighbour'; some grow closer to siblings. One of the most popular ways of making friends is to join a voluntary association; but this strategy is not always successful. Among them, friends provide a variety of services, support and company. Old friends contribute something unique to the acceptance of ageing and adjustment to changing circumstances. Such friendships have a hedonistic quality that matches satisfyingly with the lifestyle of the middle class women in retirement.

Bambawala (1995 and 1997) has examined the television viewing habits of aged women living in Pune, India and retired from jobs. As per the findings, the aged women watch television regularly, but not for long hours. They watch television for entertainment; and not for education or awareness. Most of the viewing is planned. There is a distinctive preference for local news and programmes. Hence, television can very well be used as a medium of social change, especially for the aged women.

Family/Social Support and Life Satisfaction

According to Saraceno (1992), in traditional representations of the life cycle, old age has always been characterized by considerable ambivalence. On the positive side, old age is associated with wisdom, while on the negative side, this life stage can be characterized by physical decay and the approach of death. The increase in life expectancy and rise in material living standards have changed perceptions of old age: for many, retirement leads to a peaceful, relaxing lifestyle with new opportunities to enjoy life. The self-perception processes inherent in ageing depend not only on individual life histories, but also on historical and social circumstances. It is argued that the institutionalization of life course tends to complicate the delivery of social services to the elderly, which is especially true for women, for whom problems of self-realization can be particularly acute.

Troll (1994), in his study of white individuals aged 85+ in the San Francisco, California Bay Area, has revealed that most have 1+ surviving relative, but only 50 per cent have relatives available to them if they need help. The primary family resources are children, especially for women. The respondents seem to derive satisfaction from thinking about relatives now dead—men usually about their dead wives and women about their mothers and siblings. There is a sharp contrast in lifestyle and feelings between those who are most embedded in their families and those at the other extreme, the 'family deprived'; the embedded ones being much the better off.

O'Brien (1991) has analysed the life experiences of never married older women. Personal, social and economic factors influencing unmarried older women in everyday living and ageing were compared to stereotypes surrounding this lifestyle. In-depth interviews were conducted with 15 women aged 80+, on Prince Edward Island, Canada, covering the topics of early childhood and family life, education, career, retirement and attitudes towards marriage and children. Results were at odds with negative stereotypes about 'old maids', as most of these women felt they were better off than their peers, and reported satisfying relationships with family and friends. In older age, however, they needed more formal support than did those with husbands and children.

Singh, Singh and Sharma (1987) have examined the problems of the aged women of village Kidholi Pahladpur in Sonepat district of Haryana, India. Among the problems experienced were health and economic problems and the strained relationship with the young, especially the daughter-in-law.

Jamuna and Reddy (1991) have analysed the self-concept of women aged 50–79 years through a 30-item self-concept inventory. They found that widows had a considerably more negative self-concept than non-widows. The effect of widowhood was highest in the first year of widowhood than in the later years. Interventions directed to changing the self-concept have been suggested.

Jamuna (1994) has assessed the role of variables contributing to successful ageing in a sample of 300 women in the 60–69 years of age, from the semi-urban areas of Chittoor district, Andhra Pradesh, India. A step-wise multiple regression analysis showed that out of the ten variables studied, positive self-regard, satisfaction with role activity, satisfaction in husband-wife relationship, and subjective assessment of general health were found to be the significant determinants of successful ageing.

Kabir (1999) in her study on aged (60+, N=701) living in Bangladesh has found that a high proportion of widowed women and married men. Elderly women reported lower income than men did. A high proportion of women reported no income at all due to almost exclusively being involved in household work. The combination of widowhood and low or no income pointed at the vulnerability of elderly women.

Bambawale (2004), in her empirical study on 864 women aged 60+ of Pune, Maharashtra, has examined the kind and pattern of elder abuse. Describing abuse as covert (hidden) and overt (direct), she revealed that 40 per cent women felt totally neglected by the family and considered it as abuse. Economic deprivation and religious abuse was also rampant, specially in the case of aged widows.

Panda (2005) examines the levels and correlates of life satisfaction among aged women (N=350; 60–96 years) residing in metropolitan South Delhi. It was inferred that life satisfaction is an intrinsic variable and is not affected by increasing age, education, religion, caste and material achievements. However, those married; living with their family; having a sense of security, maintaining good health; optimistic about future and continuing their preferred active lifestyle by involving in household chores generally had a higher satisfaction level compared to their counterparts. Contrary to this, those living with their unmarried children (having tension and anxiety related to vocational settlement and marriage of children); and those feeling lonely scored low in life satisfaction.

Adjustment Pattern

Menopause is a very significant event in a woman's life bringing in its wake a number of physical and psychological changes that affect the day-to-day adjustments of the middle-aged women. There are not many Indian studies on the psycho-social effects of menopause. Keeping this in view, Jamuna (1987) has analysed 'adjustment patterns among pre- and post-menopausal rural women' (n = 300). It was found that the menopausal group was significantly more maladjusted than the pre-menopausal group. The post-menopausal group was also more maladjusted than the menopausal group but to a lesser extent.

In yet another study on 'Role-activity and General Adjustment Pattern of Middle-Aged and Older Women' Jamuna (1988) examines the role activity of 300 workers from 20 villages in Chittor district of Andhra Pradesh, India, belonging to the age groups 40–49, 50–59 and 60–69.

Arora and Saxena (1997) try to highlight the pattern of adjustment of 50 retired working and 50 non-working women from Jaipur and Moradabad cities. It was found that the retired working women showed higher scores in vocational and interest aspects than non-working women. Scores on certain other aspects such as physical conditions, institution for old people, etc.

reflected that retired working women scored more on these aspects than non-working women, but differences were negligible.

Jamuna and Ramamurti (1998) also analyse the 'adjustment patterns of middle-aged and older widows and non-widows' belonging to middle class families in the rural areas of Chandragiri taluk, Andhra Pradesh, India and between 40 and 70 years by using Ramamurti's Adjustment Inventory for older persons. The results of the study indicated poorer adjustment among widows than non-widows.

Asgarali and Broota (2000) in their study on the aged (N = 30 male and 30 female aged 50–82 years with a median age of 63) of Coimbatore district, Tamil Nadu noticed no significant gender difference in the experience of loneliness and death anxiety.

Iecovich (2005) has investigated differences between the general elderly population and elderly new immigrants from former Soviet Union countries in regard to the incidence of elder abuse and neglect, victims' characteristics, and perpetrators' characteristics. In addition, the study sought to examine predictors of various types of abuse and neglect. Both groups significantly differed in terms of victims' and perpetrators' characteristics. A new immigrant was found to be a significant predictor of physical abuse and neglect.

Care-giving Responsibilities

The perceptions of sons-in-law regarding parent care were analysed by Kleban, Brody, Schoonover and Hoffman (1989). Parents' families and the men's perceptions of the care-giving situation were compared with those of their wives. Many of the husbands reported the personal effects of parent care often cited by principal care-givers. Those sharing households with their mothers-in-law were more likely to report consequences such as interference in social lives, family vacation plans, time with wives and children, and relationships with other relatives. Even though husbands and wives disagreed on the extent to which relationships in the nuclear family were affected by care-giving, yet agreed about the occurrence of more objectively apparent lifestyle disruptions.

According to Siegel and Tacuber (1986), the US is currently experiencing significant population ageing, defined here as an increase in the number of persons aged 65+ in relation to the total population. This development, which can be expected to continue into the next century, will have a significant impact on the US society. The elderly are unevenly distributed geographically; they tend to remain in the same residence or at least the same area. Life expectancy is steadily increasing and the elderly are healthier than is commonly assumed; changes in lifestyles could benefit both health and longevity further. Elderly women far outnumber elderly men; and while men tend to live in family settings, women are more often divorced or widowed. The need to care for them imposes substantial burdens on their children, often themselves middle-aged or elderly.

Jamuna (1987) has assessed how the needs and problems of the aged women had been perceived. The perception of the aged women and the perception of their care-givers with regard to needs and problems were different. Appropriate counselling and interventions were suggested to mitigate their economic and other psycho-social problems and needs as well as to reduce the gap in the perception of the elderly and their caregivers.

A similar study was conducted again by Jamuna (1994). Reviewing 200 rural and urban households, in different wards at Tirupati of Andhra Pradesh, India, the study aimed at finding out the conditions of the elderly women. It attempted to find out the level of functionality of the elderly women, the attitude of the caregivers; to assess social support to the elderly and to the caregivers. The study also tried to find out views of the caregivers on future needs and problems of the elderly women in the 21st century.

Jamuna (2000) briefly discusses some of the pressing issues with regard to work status, dependency ratio, living arrangements, gender ageing, health and disability status, family and kinship relationships and availability of social security provisions for the elderly. She highlighted the increasing stress and strains on the primary caregiver, the fast pace of social change that is affecting traditional care-giving mechanisms for the elderly, as well as the need for a dynamic action plan to utilize the resources of the elderly and enhance their social status.

National Policy for Older Persons, 1999 (India): A Critical Appraisal

In India, the government has been slow in recognizing its responsibilities towards the aged, particularly the aged women. To our politicians, ageing seems to be the issue of the last priority. In such a situation, the National Policy on Older Persons (NPOP), 1999, is definitely a landmark.

The NPOP seeks to move away from stereotyped welfare programmes and looks at ways to empower the aged. The Ministry of Social Justice and Empowerment has been designated as the nodal ministry to co-ordinate all matters relating to the implementation of the Policy (Clause 92). The envisages setting up of a National Council for Older Persons (Clause 95), a separate Bureau of Older Persons to look into the problems of the elderly persons (Clause 92); an inter-ministerial committee to co-ordinate matters relating to implementation of the policy and monitor its progress (Clause 92); and preparation of five year and annual action plans by each ministry to implement the aspects which concern the aged (Clause 93). It provides the states to be encouraged to set up separate directorates of older persons as well as machinery for coordination and monitoring (Clause 92).

The policy also provides for setting up of a pension fund to ensure security and empowerment of those in the unorganized sector so as to cover all older persons below poverty line under the old age pension scheme (however, no details have been spelt out) (Clauses 59 and 63), construction of old age homes (Clause 61) or day care centres(Clause 62) for every three or four districts, establishment of resource centres and re-employment bureau for the 60-plus population; and concessional fares for rail and air travel within and between cities (Clauses 68 and 71).

The policy aims also at subsidizing health care network with private sector involvement; increasing standard tax deductions for senior citizens; strengthening legislation on parent's rights to be supported by their children; easy access to housing loans and special provisions in the Indian Penal Code for the protection of the older persons.

The policy assures further that the education, training and information needs of older persons will be met (Clause 55). Discrimination, if any, against older persons for availing opportunities for education, training and orientation will be removed (Clause 56). Also, an educational (Clause 57) and media programme (Clauses 58, 88, 89) is planned to be launched for creating greater awareness and avoiding stereotype images of the older persons. Obviously, the policy discusses the importance of research and training of manpower as well as the use of media and NGOs to deal with the problems of the aged.

Limitations of the Policy

But the policy does not explain how the implementations of its suggestions are to be financed. No deadline has been set up for the ultimate objectives, whatsoever. The policy contains more references to the urban milieu and to the formal, organized sector of employment. Though it recognizes that three-fourths of the elderly reside in rural areas, many of the proposals, commitments and initiatives contained in the paper refer to the urban ageing population and their needs (Sujaya, 1999).

Regarding the educational needs of older persons, the policy talks about removing discrimination, if any, against older persons in availing various opportunities. But it does not analyse the existing scenario in this regard. Will the access of older persons to various resources and opportunities be tried by a piecemeal approach or will it be thoroughly planned with wide coverage? Will it be an optional exercise or mandatory one? Who owes the responsibility to plan and to implement: the University Grants Commission, Central Government, State Governments, universities or the school administration? The policy document is silent about these serious questions.

Gender Issues in Policy Statement

The National Policy Statement says: ... special attention will be necessary to older females so that they do not become victims of triple neglect and discrimination on account of gender, widowhood and age... and need for expansion of social and community services for older persons, particularly women (Clause 17).

However, the gender issues are not sufficiently highlighted. The overall proposed areas of intervention and action strategies are: financial security, health and nutrition, shelter, education, welfare, protection of life and property, other areas of action, non-governmental organizations, family research, training of manpower and media. However, the gender issues are not sufficiently highlighted. Out of the strategies mentioned, only three have some reference to women. These are:

- *Financial security*, which states that widows will be given special consideration in the matter of settlement of benefits accruing to them on the demise of husband.
- *Welfare*: It mentions that non-institutional services by voluntary organizations and other support services will provide some relief through sharing of the family's caring responsibilities. Obviously, there seems to be an underlying emphasis on the need to fill the gap caused by the *changing roles of women* (i.e., young women) and its impact on the care of the elderly (Sujaya, 1999).
- *Protection of life and property*: This provides that widow's rights of inheritance, occupancy and disposal, which at times are violated by their own children and relatives, will be protected. However, the policy paper does not discuss the property rights of women, especially the widows.

Under the section 'Implementation' elaborate administrative and policy-making mechanisms have been planned. Again, there is practically no reference made anywhere in the section to whether the aged women will be adequately represented in these bodies, bureaus, councils, associations, etc.

Keeping in view our scarce resources and the apathetic attitude of the society, it is yet doubtful whether there will be a drastic change in the status of the aged, particularly the aged women, because whatever policies and programmes we have, are not free from the gender bias, and do not give due consideration to the special needs of the aged women.

The above review brings into light the following points:

As far as the studies on feminization of ageing all over the world are concerned, they are still in their infancy. 'Aged women' is the area which has started receiving some attention of the researchers just one or two decades back (in the 80s and 90s only); and it is yet to be recognized by the policy makers as a thrust area. Although a few serious attempts have been made to analyse issues relating to the aged women, the efforts have been scanty and sporadic.

Studies of gerontology in India are of recent origin. It is the post-independence period that saw the emergence of gerontology

Table 2.1

Yearwise Growth of Studies on Gerontology

Year/s	*No. of Studies*
1889	1
1896	1
1925	1
1932	1
1951–53	1
1954–56	2
1957–59	7
1960–62	9
1963–65	25
1966–68	50
1969–71	140
1972–74	91
1975–77	72
1978–80	103
1981–83	220
1984–86	261
1987–89	394
1990–92	511
1993–95	597
1996–98	939
1999–2000	1,243
Total	4,669

Source: Ruprail, 2002: XI.

as a branch of study. Till now, 'ageing' is not an established field of Sociology or Social Work in India, scattered evidences have been provided only by a handful of Indian workers. Social gerontology and community geriatrics have also been dealt with rather scarcely. Yet India has witnessed a rapidly growing interest in ageing in the last three decades. Attempted with different analytical perspectives and varied methodologies, the studies reflect a wide spectrum of thinking and insightful reflections on the subject. Year wise growth of studies (shown in the Table 2.1) shows that the writings and studies on gerontology in India have been continuously increasing. And, it may be predicted that in the next two or three decades, gerontology will be established as a full-fledged discipline in India also.

The subject analysis (Ruprail, 2002) reveals that the most scholars focused on welfare services, followed by health/medical problems, aged and ageing in general, their psychology, their socio-economic status, women, government, family and demography. The least researched aspects are religion, crime and law. Subject break up of studies is shown in the Figure VII. The description makes it clear that like most other disciplines in India; 'ageing' is also suffering from gender bias. And during the period of 1889–2000, only 6 per cent studies were on issues related to women.

Figure VII
Subject Break-up of Studies on Gerontology

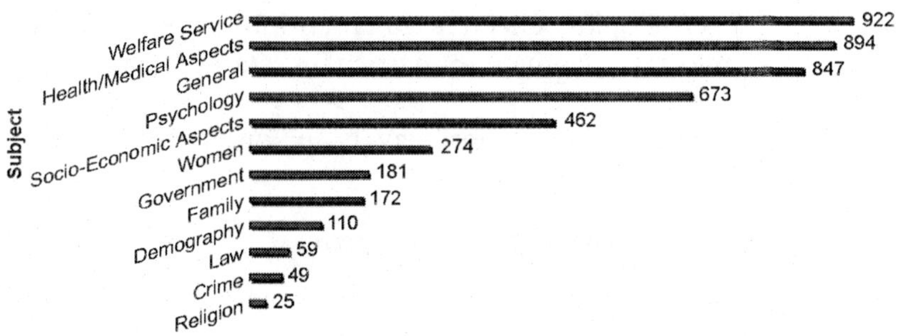

Several scholars have documented the fact that data on elderly women in India are hardly enough and never unbiased. It should not look strange as female gender has always been a victim of discrimination at the hands of policy-makers, health care providers and research workers--it may be children, adolescent, adult, post-menopausal or geriatric females.

Otherwise, generally, the issues and problems of the aged women have been examined with those of their male counterparts. And it has been consistently demonstrated that compared to the old men, old women are more in number, poorer, older, sicker, have less adequate housing and access to private transport, and are more likely to experience widowhood, severe disability and economic crisis.

The above description strongly highlights the need to undertake serious researches on various aspects of the life of the aged women; and also to sensitise policy-makers so as to protect their interests.

As it is not possible to altogether remove the factors that have contributed to the problems of the aged women, coping mechanisms could be developed both by the aged women and their family members or caregivers for mitigating their problems. In this context social work intervention may prove to be of immense value.

Certain categories of the aged women experience more problems than the others. Therefore, there is a need to explore the problems of the aged women in relation to their marital status, type of family, economic status, occupational background, physical mobility, etc. This exploratory exercise is intensely required for developing effective intervention-strategies in the interest of the aged women in particular, and the society in general.

The following observations may be in order in the above context.

Theoretical Perspectives

Gerontology is the study of ageing. It is a multidisciplinary area of investigation with three core components: the biological, the psychological and the social. The third aspect of ageing is usually referred to as social gerontology, which incorporates three distinct aspects. These aspects include: ageing as an individual experience; ageing in the social context, which seeks to understand the position of the elderly within the society; and the social consequences of ageing (Sati, 1996). Social gerontology is a new field that marked its beginning in the late 1940s (Cockerham, 1991). The term 'social gerontology' was first used by Clark Tibbits in 1954. This field has grown with the recognition of the extent to which ageing differs across cultures and societies (Hooman and Kiyan, 1988).

However, the development and testing of theoretical statements (in social gerontology) have largely taken place only since the 1960s (Cockerham, 1991). Nevertheless, a considerable amount of theoretical work has been accomplished to provide the field with a variety of theories and a solid foundation for future studies. Yet, Victor (1987) avers, "social gerontology does not possess an extensive theoretical framework in its own right. The systematic development of theory and its subsequent application are activities, which have been absent from many social scientific studies of ageing. Frequently, researchers have been content simply to describe aspects of behaviour in later life or the characteristics of various sub-groups of the elderly population, without trying to organize the findings into a coherent theory of social ageing".

Actually, the notion of developing and verifying a theory of ageing may seem unnecessary or purely academic. We all grow older. Our bodies change with age, and so do our interests and lifestyles—not just theoretically, but in fact. Yet, in very informal and often unconscious way, we all develop theories from our own experiences. We observe older people in our families and communities and make generalizations about them. In a sense, the stereotypes of older people (for example, to assume that most elderly people are unintelligent, unemployable, non-productive, senile and asexual) are not supported by facts. These stereotypes, sometimes labeled as 'ageist', are the result of unconscious theorizing about the meaning of growing old (Hooman and Kiyan, 1988).

Theory: Nature and Importance

But the scientific approach to theory-making is different in that it is a conscious and systematic attempt to explain why an event or set of events occurs. A scientific theory is based on a logically related set of statements, called 'propositions' and 'hypotheses', each of which is subjected to testing through empirical research (Hooman and Kiyan, 1988). The usefulness of any theory depends on how it functions: (1) to explain past events; (2) to predict future events; and (3) to generate new theory. One function of theory is to provide explanations of what facts already exist about some phenomenon (Bond and Coleman, 1990).

Another importance attributed to theory is that it has strong relationship with research in social sciences. Theory and research are symmetrically interrelated. In the process a theory guides the research and helps to arrive at a given appropriate finding. On the same way research tests the theory and helps in constructing a new theory (Kumar, 1999).

Theories are of great intellectual value in as much as they encapsulate a great variety of facts and complex processes, and help us make sense of the world and see more coherently and logically what we would have done otherwise. Theories guide research further.

The theories of ageing should expectedly point to unanswered questions or potential changes; for example: what makes for successful ageing? Are the criteria of successful ageing similar for men and women or do they differ? Are the ageing experiences similar for men and women in various cultures and in different societies? Are our elderly helpless, senile and rejected? Why do some of the elderly remain healthy and happy and get respect and reward while others do not? What should our society be doing with regard to the elderly?

Social Gerontology and Theoretical Construction

Fisher (1978) rightly remarked that social gerontology has not succeeded in creating a body of theory. Probably, gerontology will never be a theoretical discipline in its own right, but rather a consumer of theory from other sciences. Coleman (1990) also strengthens the view while pointing that "the study of ageing has as yet generated little theory of its own, and even less has percolated through to influence ordinary attitudes". Expressing somewhat similar opinion, Kumar (1999) points out that "to understand the 'ageing in old age' certain theories have to be explained because, as Marshall (1981) said, one perspective cannot explain all social phenomenon associated with ageing or the aged. Hence, it is necessary to derive theories from sociology, psychology, anthropology and biology". The failure to formulate a systematic theory of social ageing is perhaps not surprising, given the complexity of the field and its relatively recent development as a substantive area of study (Victor, 1987; Sati, 1996).

Yet, gerontologists have been successful in deriving various micro, intermediate and macro level theories to explain ageing as a social experience. The theories at the *micro level* are: Role Theory, Disengagement Theory, Activity Theory and Continuity Theory. The theories at the *intermediate level*, which reflect interactionist perspectives, are: Symbolic-Interaction Theory, Labeling Theory, Theory of Social Breakdown and Social Reconstruction and Social Exchange Theory. And, the theories at the *macro level* are: Marxist Theories including Conflict Theory and Political Economy of Ageing, and Non-Marxist Theories including Age Stratification Theory, The Subculture of Ageing or The Aged as a Minority Group and Modernization Theory or Socio-Environment Theory. The ensuing analysis of these theories will pursue the linkage between meaning and control among the macroscopic level of social structure; intermediate level of interaction between environment (social structure) and person (self); and the microscopic level of self. One area in which these three levels meet is the identification of old people as a social problem.

Theories at the Micro Level

Role Theory

One of the earliest attempts by social gerontologists to explain how individuals adjust to ageing involved an application of role theory (Cottrell, 1942). Status and role are the two basic concepts associated with the role theory, and the two concepts were first introduced by Linton (1942). Generally, social status refers to a socially defined position within a given social structure that is separate from but related to other positions. Role is a pattern of behaviour, structured around specific rights and duties and associated with a particular status within a group or social situation. A person's role in any situation is defined by the set of expectations from his behaviour had by the others and also by the person himself. A woman may play a variety of social roles in their life time, e.g., as student, mother, wife, daughter, businessman, grandmother, and so on. Such roles identify and describe her as a social being and are the basis of self-concept.

In most societies, chronological age is used to determine eligibility for various positions, to evaluate the suitability of different roles, and to shape expectations of people in social situations. Some roles have a reasonable biological basis related to age, e.g., the role of a mother and the role of a voter, but many roles as well could be fulfilled by the individuals of a wide age range, e.g., the role of a volunteer. Age alters not only the roles expected of people, but also the manner in which they are expected to play them. For example, a family's expectations of a 32-year-old mother are quite different from their expectations of her at an age of 62. Age norms—the assumptions of age-related capacities and limitations; the beliefs that a person of a given age can and ought to do certain things—serve to open up or close out the roles that people of a given chronological age can play. Every society conveys age norms to its members through socialization—a lifelong process (Hooman and Kiyan, 1988).

As many changes in roles are linked to chronological age, social scientists and gerontologists have used role theory to understand the ageing phenomenon. In fact, role theory is an important tool to understand social behaviour of an elderly person in a given situation. And, the role theory, in return, also guides the aged learn how to perform new roles, adjust to changing roles, and relinquish old ones. In other words, this theory provides some directives about role learning, role change and role transition for the aged.

Role Dilemmas/Role Conflicts of the Aged

With age, people are more likely to lose the roles that have been played in the past than to acquire new ones. The most common role losses are irreversible; for example, the loss of role of a spouse with widowhood or loss of role of a worker after retirement. Although some older widows remarry and some retirees return to work when they find it satisfying, the majority do neither, nor do they replace those roles they have lost. Furthermore, many older people who are unwilling to take on the diminished status and 'usefulness' of the retiree role face a lack of desirable role options and models. Others, particularly women and ethnic minorities, may lack the resources to move into new roles or to emulate the young, with more physically attractive role models.

The aged, specially women face lack of appropriate role models particularly due to the fact that whatever role models have been existing till now, tend to be oriented for the youth in appearance and behaviour, maintaining middle age standards which can actually hinder socialization at old age.

With age, roles also tend to become more ambiguous. Guidelines or expectations about the requirements of roles, such as that of family authority or nurturing parent, become less clear to the elderly themselves as well as to the others (Rosow, 1985).

Further, the role transition (transition from one role to other, say, for example, from the worker role to that of the retiree) is characterized by role discontinuity whereby what is learned at one age level may be useless, conflicting or contradictory at the next age level. For example, learning to manage time or be highly productive in the workplace may be antithetical to adjusting to leisure time in retirement.

In fact, in modern societies, the aged lack a consensus about societal rules to guide their behaviour, which serves to exclude them from socially meaningful activity and reinforces stereotypes about old age.

By and large, the role conflicts/dilemmas have an impact on the individual's identity, self-image and social behaviour. Since roles are the basis of an individual's self-concept, role loss can lead to an erosion of social identity and self-esteem (Rosow, 1985). Many researchers found that role losses with widowhood or retirement were related to depression, feeling of uselessness or non-importance and maladjustment. Burgess (1960) mentioned the paradox that the role of a retired person is rolelessness, to have no role at all.

However, the proponents of this theory would agree to the view that in future, the situation of the elderly can be improved by using a number of intervention strategies; for example, counselling, pre-retirement as well as post-retirement, widows' support groups, involving the elderly in community services, etc. These strategies, if adopted, especially by social workers, may help the elderly to deal with the situations of role loss, role change or transition and even rolelessness. If due to these strategies or otherwise, the number of active, happy and healthy elderly persons grows, the 'ageist' stereotypes will automatically get diminished. In old age, role loss of one type (e.g., spouse, worker, daughter-in-law), if balanced with the role gains of the other types (since role losses are generally irreversible), for example that of a volunteer, part-time worker, grand parent, role of neighbour with greater intensity and participant or coordinator of community welfare programmes, it will ensure a better future to the elderly. Obviously, the various social institutions including health, social work, welfare and policy-making institutions have a major role to play in this regard. Facts explained by the Role Theory, as experienced by the elderly, underlie two of the most widely debated theories of successful ageing: Activity Theory and Disengagement Theory. Both were based on the Kansas city study of adult life (Havighurst, 1968), but they reached fundamentally different conclusions about successful ageing.

Activity Theory

Activity Theory was developed by Robert Havighurst (1963) by analysing the Kanas city study of 300 people—primarily white, middle class, healthy and ranging from 50 to 90 years' of age—who were interviewed at regular intervals over a six years' period (Hooman and Kiyan, 1988).

This theory maintains that normal and successful ageing involves preserving as long as possible, the attitudes and activities of middle age. And any exhibition of behaviour by older persons that would not be appropriate in middle-aged persons is considered maladjustment. Since, the norms for old age are the same as those for middle age; ageing is conceptualized as a continuous struggle to remain middle-aged. The theory assumes that aged people who are active will be more satisfied and better adjusted than less active elderly persons. To be happy in old age, individuals need to be active in old age. So, if existing roles or relationships are lost on account of retirement, poor health or otherwise, it is important to replace them by some adaptable or feasible ones.

The empirical support for Activity Theory is mixed. In a longitudinal study carried out at Duke University over a period of ten years, Erdman Palmore (1968) found that the older men tended to show almost no overall reduction in their activities or in life satisfaction, whereas the older women tended to have a small but statistically significant reduction in both—activities and life satisfaction. He pointed out that his data were obtained from people who were relatively healthy, and therefore, disengagement may be more typical of the less healthy. It was also found that activity was strongly related to high morale, life satisfaction and happiness (Cockerham, 1991; Dhillon, 1992; Hooman and Kiyan, 1988 and Victor, 1987).

Lemon, Bengeston and Peterson (1972) have examined the variables 'social integration' and 'role losses such as widowhood or retirement' in relation to life satisfaction but found no evidence to establish any correlation. Activity was found to be strongly related to high morale and life satisfaction by Fontana (1977) and Knapp (1977).

Other researchers have concluded that active people have better physical and mental health and take greater satisfaction in life than do the inactive, such people are generally better educated and have more money and options than those who are less active (Havighurst et al., 1969; Palmore, 1974; Thurmond and Belcher, 1980–81). A negative association between formal group activity and life satisfaction was also indicated by Longing and Kart, 1982. Therefore, Hooman and Kiyan (1988) seem to rightly argue that socio-economic conditions, lifestyle, and generational variables may be more important than maturational ones in the association found between activity and life satisfaction, health and well-being.

On the basis of the above findings, the Activity Theory can be modified by stating that keeping the other variables controlled, the activity is strongly related to high morale, life satisfaction and happiness. But besides the ambiguity observed in the empirical support, Activity Theory is also open to various other criticisms. One may question the value judgment inherent in the theory that activity in old age is a 'good thing'. As many aged persons derive happiness by staying inactive, for they prefer what may be called a 'rocking chair approach' to old age.

Also, some authors, for example Dhillon (1992), argue that it may not be role activity that determines high morale, rather it may be that those with high morale who can form friendships and have a greater probability of staying active than those with low morale. Havighurst (1968) himself later acknowledged the importance of personality in predicting the association between activity levels and life satisfaction (Hooman and Kiyan, 1988). Some sociologists argue that rather than remaining active, good adjustment to the ageing process requires/involves disengagement. A further difficulty with this approach is that it says little about those who lose the battle to remain active as those who are middle-aged.

Disengagement Theory

Diametrically opposed to the notion of activity is Disengagement Theory. Disengagement Theory, one of the most widely known and controversial theories in social gerontology, was first formulated by Elaine Cumming and William Henry in 1961. Through a survey conducted in Kansas City (USA) of two samples of men and women aged 50 to 70 years and aged over 70 years, the authors aimed at finding out disengagement between the individual and the society. For this, they adopted three measures: 'Role Count' (measures number of active roles a person has); 'Interaction Index' (measures density of interaction in social intercourse); and 'Social

Life Space' (which measures the number of discrete contacts of the respondents with others). And, in all the aforesaid measures of social involvement, a fairly abrupt decrease was found in the age group of 70+ years. Also, this decrease occurred five years earlier among women than among men (Sati, 1988).

According to its proponents, the theory has three basic assumptions: that the process of mutual withdrawal of ageing individual and society from each other is natural, inevitable and necessary for 'successful' ageing, and the orderly continuation of the society (Cockerham, 1991; Dhillon, 1992). Victor (1987) points out the core aspects of this theory as under: disengagement is a life-long process rather than an abrupt or sudden one as throughout the life course of life; the individual is continuously acquiring and dropping particular social roles.

Because of the inevitability of death, because of the probable decrement in the ability as one ages, because of the value placed on the youth and because of the need to ensure that the tasks are efficiently completed and, the roles are adequately played, both the individual and the society demand disengagement (Kumar, 1999). Whether voluntary or imposed, this theory provides a mechanism whereby the youth can enter and advance in the labour force, roles are taken up generally by more competent and energetic people and the death of an individual is not disruptive to the functioning of the social systems.

Even for the individual, withdrawal may mean relaxation from social pressures, which insist on productivity, competition and continued achievement. Thus, being adapted as well as beneficial, the Disengagement Theory is more relevant to the modern capitalist societies.

But every coin has the other side also. So is the case with this theory. It suffers from many limitations. There is little evidence that old people take the initiative in 'disengaging', and there is a good deal of evidence to suggest that they dislike loss of roles and relationships. Even when 'disengagement' appears to be gradual, as when an elderly housewife gives up first the shopping, then the heavy cleaning and washing, and only last of all, the cooking, there is evidence of marked unwillingness to surrender these functions.

Even very old women would like to retain important roles as of the housewife, mother and grandmother (Sati, 1988).

The Disengagement Theory fails also to account for variability in individual preferences. Not everyone in our culture disengages, as evidenced by growing number of older people, many in their eighties, who are employed, healthy, and politically and socially active. The extent to which a person disengages may also vary with the individual's position in the social structure. A retired college professor, for example, has more opportunities to remain professionally involved than a retired steel worker. Disengagement also does not appear to be uniform amongst individuals. A person may disengage socially (e.g., attend fewer social events) but remain fully engaged psychologically (e.g., continue to read about and discuss current events). In addition, what may appear to be disengaged behaviour to an outsider may have a very different meaning for the ageing person. An older person who sits by a window for hours may not necessarily be disengaged, but may fully enjoy the changing street scenes. Disengagement Theory has also tended to ignore the part that personality plays in the way a person adjusts to ageing (Hooman and Kiyan, 1988).

Convincingly enough, disengagement seems bad, since some of the most knowledgeable and experienced members of society are being removed either by voluntary or mandatory methods, and are replaced by less competent younger people. When they have disengaged, this may not represent personal preference but rather the failure of our society to provide opportunities for continued engagement.

However, disengagement theory has formed the intellectual basis for policies of segregation of people in terms of age that foster the separation of the elderly from others in society (Victor, 1987). Fisk (1986) suggests that this theory has further enabled the professionals dealing with the elderly to rationalize their negative stereotypes.

A potential danger of both the theories—Disengagement and Activity—is that the individuals as well as the society may interpret them as more prescriptive or philosophical recommendations about how to live during the later years rather than explanations of the ageing process. More variables need to be examined before we can explain why some people are happy in an active old age while others are content to narrow their activities and involvement.

Continuity Theory

The evident shortcomings of the Disengagement and Activity Theories led to the emergence of a third social-psychological theory of adaptation in old age. The Continuity Theory, comparatively a recent one, is based on the premise that people retain a high degree of consistency in their personality over the various stages of the life cycle. "That people, whether young or old, have different personalities and lifestyles, and that personality plays a major role in adjusting to ageing. People who have always been passive or withdrawn are unlikely to become activists upon retirement. Similarly, those who have always been active, assertive, and socially involved are unlikely to sit quietly at home in their old age. Basically, this perspective states that with age, we become more of what we already were when younger. Core values become even more salient with age. An individual ages successfully if she or he maintains a mature, integrated personality while growing old" (Hooman and Kiyan, 1988).

In other words, Continuity Theory starts with the premise that the individual will try to maintain as long as possible, his or her preferred lifestyle, and then holds that adaptation can go in several different directions depending on how the individual perceives his or her changing status and attempts to adjust to this change. Continuity Theory does not assert that one must be disengaged or active in order to be well adjusted in the later years, but rather that the decision regarding which roles are to be discarded and which are to be maintained, will in large measure be determined by the individual's past history and preferred style of life (Dhillon, 1992).

Continuity Theory, therefore, has the advantage of offering a variety of adjustment patterns from which an individual can choose (Victor, 1987). The theory contributes to our understanding of the ageing process by showing that the personality of people in the old age tends to be much the same as it was in the middle age. This finding is of great use in predicting the behaviour of old people and provides both practical and theoretical insight into researchers' studying how ageing is experienced (Cockerham, 1991). But Hooman and Kiyan (1988) doubt that the lifestyle observed in the old age may be a response to growing old rather than the reflections of lifelong patterns.

The Continuity Theory is not a complete formulation in the literature on ageing, it is concerned with only one particular and limited aspect of ageing, that of personality effects. It presents a micro, rather than a macro orientation. Micro views allow us to see how individuals, not the wider society, construct their own behaviour.

Another disadvantage is the problem of testing it empirically. Each individual's pattern of adjustment in the old age or during retirement becomes a case study in which the researcher attempts to determine how successfully the individual was able to continue in her previous lifestyle. Building a generally applicable theory on this basis is, therefore, difficult (Victor, 1987).

However, the Continuity Theory provides an important perspective on behaviour among the elderly.

Theories to Explain Ageing at the Intermediate Level: Reflecting the Interactionist Perspectives

Recent efforts among social gerontologists have focused on the person-environment transactional process. The environment is a complex variable and its impact on human behaviour and well-being is widely recognized in diverse disciplines. "Lewin's Field Theory (1935, 1951) emphasizes that any event is the result of multiple factors, individual and environmental; or more simply stated, B = f(P,E) (i.e., behaviour is a function of personal and environmental characteristics). A change in either the person or the environment produces a change in behaviour" (Hooman and Kiyan, 1988).

The person experiences optimal well-being, when his or her needs are in equilibrium with characteristics of the environment. Kahana's Theory of Person-Environment Fit (1973, 1975) is the first congruence model developed and empirically tested with the elderly. Kahana hypothesized that incongruence between specific individual needs and environmental press along parallel dimensions produces stress, which in turn requires adaptation, and ultimately affects the older person's well-being. Such stress is compounded for older people whose cognitive and functional capacities are severely impaired, because they are less likely to be able to modify the environment or to leave the situation. Therefore, this (Interactionist) perspective, which incorporates within it various Person-Environment Theories of Ageing may be even more useful for understanding older people's behaviour than for other populations.

Relocation, or moving from one setting to another, for example, disturbs the person-environment configuration. Let us take the example of a widow to understand it further. The widow had four sons. None of the sons wanted to take the responsibility of the mother solely. So, she had to live with all of her sons by turns. She used to get all facilities and comforts everywhere. But she was not at all happy or satisfied. It was just because of person-environment incongruence. She reportedly expressed her situation to be very painful. By the time, she got adjusted at one place (in one environment), she was made to leave that place so as to be shifted to the other place (in the other environment). She could not change the situation by getting settled at one place because of scarcity of resources and lack of social support.

The greater the change, the longer it takes to adapt. Thus extensive changes in lifestyle, though may be towards betterment, result in greater stress and require greater adjustments. This perspective can explain why many old people want to live unto death in their own old houses even without much facilities, rather than shifting to a new one with better facilities and environment.

The following is an analysis of a few theories, which reflect or are based on the person-environment transaction process. These theories are: Symbolic Interaction Theory, Labelling Theory, Social Breakdown Theory and Social Exchange Theory—all emphasize the dynamic interaction between older individuals and their social world. These theories implicitly assume that older people must adjust to ongoing societal requirements. Here is an attempt to explain these theories:

Symbolic Interaction Theory

Symbolic Interaction Theory is one among the major theories in sociology. It has considerable potential for ageing research, specially with regard to explaining the self-concepts and social relationships of the elderly. This theory views society from the micro level stand point of the individual person, specially in context of the interaction that person has with other people. It regards the individual as a creative and thinking entity able to choose his or her behaviour instead of reacting more or less mechanically in order to the influence of large-scale social forces, as implied by functionalist theories. The assumption underlying this theory is that the individual and the surrounding social environment continuously act and react towards each other, and during the course of this interaction symbolic meanings are shared, communicated and manipulated and ultimately condition the individual to self-direct his or her behaviour.

George Herbert Mead's (1863–1931) book *Mind, Self and Society*, based upon student notes from his courses and unpublished manuscripts, is considered to be the foundation stone of this theory. Herbert Blumer (1969), one of Mead's students, explained Mead's analysis of social action by denoting its five control features:

1. *Self* of a person which is formed and developed as a result of social interaction and experience with other people. Thus, the human being (self) is able to perceive, have conceptions of, communicate with, and act toward himself or herself as a social object in relation to other people.
2. *Act* for which the individual has to identify what he wants, establish an objective or goal, map out a prospective line of behaviour, note and interpret the actions of others, figure out what to do at other points, and frequently spur himself on in the face of dragging dispositions or discouraging settings.
3. *Social interaction* which is of two forms: non symbolic (a non-thinking response to a certain stimulus or the reflex action, e.g., spontaneously raising a hand to catch a base ball) and symbolic (a thinking response in which an individual

interprets and defines actions and objects based upon symbolic meanings shared with other people).

4. *Object* which does not define inherent meaning but become what they are defined as by human beings interacting with each other. For example, gold may not have anything intrinsic which makes it valuable. But it is considered valuable because human beings define it as valuable and act towards it accordingly.
5. *Joint act* is an instrument to judge group behaviour. By fitting separate individual acts in line, it is possible to ascertain the overall direction of group behaviour.

Thus, the group activities are socially constructed by individual people coming together and interacting with each other in respect of the overall group enterprise. Once started, joint actions may be interrupted, abandoned, modified or continued as expected. What happens depends upon what those involved decide to do and how they act upon their decisions. The stability in social situations may, thus, be attributed to joint acts because these joint acts require a participant to identify that activity and orient him or herself in that direction prior to engaging in behaviour that is appropriate to the scene. And, the human behaviour is thus regarded as an ongoing process of definition, interpretation of and calculated response to the actions of others and the conditions of the environment.

The symbolic interactionist view of ageing argues that the interaction of such factors as the environment, individuals, and their encounters with it can significantly affect the kind of ageing process people experience (Hooman and Kiyan, 1988). Thus, an understanding of the impact of ageing requires an understanding of the meaning and interpretation of the events that accompany the old age (Victor, 1987). There are, as yet, a very few empirical examples of use of this perspective in the study of old age (see Fairhurst, 1976; Rossell, 1981).

A limitation of the Symbolic Interaction Theory, however, lies in linking individual and small-group behaviour to the larger social order. Micro-level theories like symbolic interaction often do not adequately acknowledge the influence of larger social structures and organizations on account of the relationship between them. The strength of this approach, on the other hand, lies in the capability of explaining how people perceive situations, events and people, and define a course of action. It also helps to explain individual variations and the role of culture in providing symbolic meanings (Cockerham, 1991). Thus, the theory emphasises that low morale and withdrawal from social involvement are not inevitable to ageing, but are one possible outcome of an individual's interactions that can be altered. Policies based on the symbolic interactionist framework optimistically assume that both environmental constraints and individual needs can be changed. An environmental intervention, for example, is the elimination of age discrimination in employment, whereas the individual's decision to pursue leisure rather than paid employment is an attempt to modify personal needs (Hooman and Kiyan, 1988).

Labelling Theory

Labelling Theory has been derived from the Symbolic Interaction Theory. This theory has, traditionally, been used by sociologists to explain criminal behaviour and mental illness. Kuypers and Bengtson (1973) are the first social gerontologists to suggest that this theory can be used to explain some of the behaviour of the aged, because in a youth and health conscious society, the old age is socially defined or labelled as a deviant condition (Victor, 1987).

The basic assumption of the Labelling Theory is that people derive their self-concepts from interacting with others in their social milieu. We often think of ourselves in terms of how other social actors define and react to us. This may result in changes in the way we think and act. Thus, according to this theory, the behaviour of the older people is seen to depend largely on the reactions of significant others in their immediate social world. The reactions of these significant others will depend upon how they define and classify the elderly. In essence, the behaviour of the elderly is seen as being socially determined as through the processes of labelling, individuals are forced into acting out specific roles (Victor, 1987; Dhillon, 1992; Kumar, 1999).

The theories of Social Breakdown and Social Reconstruction, which are the outgrowths of the Labelling Theory, will help us in further understanding it. These theories are being described below:

Social Breakdown and Social Reconstruction

Zusman (1966) formulated the social breakdown model by identifying its major components as: (1) the individual's susceptibility to psychological breakdown; (2) the labelling of the individual as incompetent or deficient; (3) the adoption by the individual of this label and thereby learning of the behaviour associated with it; and (4) the identification of the individual with this role (Victor, 1987). Just for illustration, this labelling process occurs when someone who is about to retire starts to behave as others have defined retirees: non-productive, useless and inactive (Hooman and Kiyan, 1988).

From this basis, Kuypers and Bengtson (1973) suggest that with suitable inputs, the model can be used to foster a more positive image of ageing for social reconstruction. These inputs include: the liberation of individuals from an age specific view of status; avoiding use of economic or productive positions as the means of defining status; improved services to the aged which may enhance their adaptation; and dealing with their problems of inadequate housing, poor health care, low income or poverty; and providing the elderly with opportunities which can develop in them greater self-confidence and autonomy, e.g., involving them in planning or giving them some measures of self-determination in the development of social care programmes (Victor, 1987; Hooman and Kiyan, 1988). Thus, the Social Reconstruction Theory suggests that with the assistance of significant others within various social systems, the aged could increase their level of competence, adaptive capacity and coping skills and thereby could gain greater control and power over their own social lives.

Social Exchange Theory

Social interactionism concentrates upon the nature of the individual-society relationship; Exchange Theory, on the other hand, provides a more detailed explanation of why individuals behave as they do in particular situations. The notion of social behaviour as exchange can be traced back to the anthropological work of Mauss (1954). The sociological studies by Homans (1961) and Blau (1964) have also studied the exchange relationship. The centrality of exchange in the social relationships of older people has been recognized since the writings of Simmons (1945), who argued that the ability of the older person to maintain reciprocal relationships was the key to the status of the aged. It is, however, only fairly recently that Dowd (1980) has proposed an explicit theory of ageing as Social Exchange which seeks to explain the decreased social interaction of later life (Victor, 1987).

The theory states that the society consists of social actors, who interact to pursue common goals. In order to achieve their goals (or get rewards or gains), the actors do pay some cost (e.g., time, energy or money). And, the interaction among the actors (individuals or groups) is an attempt to maximize rewards and minimise cost. Interaction is sustained because, and only as long as, it is profitable for the participating actors. Power derives from the imbalance of the exchange, i.e., when one actor values the rewards to be gained from interaction more than the other. Thus, one participant achieves power through the inability of the other to reciprocate (Victor, 1987; Dhillon, 1992).

Disengagement and Activity Theories are criticized for not addressing the question of why social interaction and activity often decrease with age. But, the Social Exchange Theory, besides predicting this decrease in interaction (with advanced age), also analyses the associated reasons. The reasons identified by its proponents are: (1) In the present social system, the aged are systematically deprived of valued resources needed for favourable social exchanges. (2) All the power resources, for example, personal characteristics such as beauty, strength and intelligence; relational characteristics such as influential friends or caring children; and generalized reinforcements such as respect, approval, recognition and support—all tend to favour the young. Thus, where the young worker was able to exchange skill and knowledge in return for wages in her old age, she has to comply with statutory retirement in return for a subsistence welfare income. The older worker has to cope with the outdating of her skills. This too can bring imbalance to the exchange relationship. In the context, loss of power or the ability to control one's environment is offered as the explanation of why the older people, left only with the capacity for compliance, disengage. According to this theory, the older people disengage not because it is mutually satisfying, but because society enjoys a distinct advantage in the power relationship. The difficulty for the older person is that the unbalanced power relationship becomes institutionalized, and then becomes the norm for future exchange.

The Social Exchange Theory is not confined to describe the behaviour of only the aged persons. In fact, the processes and outcomes identified could be relevant to any individual experiencing comparable changes in resources. Basically, this theory can also be used in explaining selected facets of social interaction between generations (young and old).

The great value of an exchange model study of ageing is the multidisciplinary origin of the model, its dynamic nature, and its ability to incorporate processes of both role and resource allocation. As yet there have been few empirical applications of this theory because of its relatively recent formulation. However, this may prove to be one of the more fruitful areas in the development of social gerontology theory in the future (Victor, 1987).

Theories at Macro Level

The theories at macro level may further be categorized as Marxist Theories including Conflict Theory and Political Economy of Ageing; and Non-Marxist Theories which include Age Stratification Theory, Sub-Culture Theory and Modernization Theory. Following is an attempt to explain 'ageing' with reference to these theories.

Marxist Theories

Conflict Theory

Karl Marx (1818–1883) was the classical theorist of social conflict. Touched by the evident human misery, which he perceived to be the result of private ownership, narrow concern of the employer for the employee, and the rapid social and technological changes of the nineteenth century, he felt deep concern about man's welfare.

Marx was against promoting the dissolution of the family by the absorption of women and children into the labour force. And, he considered individual and social problems as an outcome of economic system (Jesser,1975). This materialist outlook, that is the way people are used in production and the social relations of production, distinguishes one social system from another, and ultimately becomes the basis of transformation of a social system by way of organization of social classes and inter-class struggle.

A given social system reaches its terminus and will change when the social forces of production conflict seriously enough with existing property relations, and when material conditions necessary for change are already in embryo. Due to scarcity, which is omnipresent, conflict occurs, but more importantly, because and when, within the division of specialized labour different classes with dashing interests arise. The classes compete and seek to share out as much of the share of rewards or life chances, for themselves as possible. The exploited people in each stage will not necessarily be victorious over their exploiters; for this to happen, they must represent a mode of production that will dominate in the future.

Marx's contribution was that each system (thesis) contains within itself the seeds of its own destruction (antithesis), which become instrumental in the evolution of new forces as an outgrowth of the previous system (synthesis) (Jesser, 1975). Thus, Marx's Theory of Social Change is two-fold. First, it contains the concept that property relations, backed by the laws of the state, are rigid. Therefore, the class that embodies the new productive force must destroy the outmoded relations. Second, economic conditions, generally in addition to property relations, in the long run determine the other aspects of the social structure (other institutions such as policies, education, religion, etc.), so that as the former change, the latter change as well.

The Marxist Theory of Social Conflict, as described above, was as such, adopted by the gerontologists so as to explain the situation of the aged in the society. Since, social relationships between people are determined by their relative positions in regard to the means of economic production common in their society; and since the aged do not have that much important position in the market economy, owing to their poor health, outdated technology, knowledge and like factors, they are bound to be marginalized and disadvantaged. Being less in demand as workers, their status as unemployed or retired, places them in a pitiable devalued position in a capitalist society. Among the aged, women become the worst victims in this context.

Consequently, a conflict theory explanation grounded in Marxism has serious limitations and appears confined to the manner in which work affects the elderly. For instance, being socially and economically disadvantaged when old is not peculiar just to capitalism, but is found throughout human history in various types of societies.

But lastly, Marx "took the bull by the horns". If a system can be created which master and victimize man, the same system can be changed so as to serve man. Marx's optimism and humanism is appealing (Jesser, 1975). It also indicates that if the aged (women included), as a social class, become aware and conscious, struggle against the forces victimizing them; they can very well change the situations. The capability of the aged to mobilize political action in capitalist nations and bring reform may prove to be strong evidence in support of the view. But, as per the notions of the Marxist Theory, the stereotypes about the aged (women) only will change until and unless they take concertive, organized and continuous efforts and represent a mode of production in which they themselves have an important role to play.

Political Economy of Ageing

The Political Economy of Ageing is based on the basic presumption that social class is a structural barrier to older people's access to valued resources, and that dominant groups within society try to sustain their own interests by perpetuating class inequalities (Walker, 1981; Minkler and Estes, 1984). It is less a theory of individual attributes and processes than a macro analysis of structural properties that determine how people adapt in old age. Its proponents believe that social, political and economic conditions affect the way social problems, including those of the elderly, are defined and treated. Therefore, the major problems faced by the elderly are socially constructed as a result of the societal conceptions of ageing and the aged. The process of ageing, in itself, is not the problem; the problems are societal conditions facing the older people, e.g., inadequate income, health care, or housing needs that a capitalist society has created. Secondly, national, social and economic policies are the key determinants of life conditions of the aged. Social policies are also directly influenced by the state of the economy. In a time of shrinking resources, for example, the federal governments generally reduce their roles in addressing problems faced by the elderly.

Old age has been considered as a time of inevitable physical decline; and hence, the elderly have tended to set them apart to be a dependent group with needs requiring special policies and programme. More recently, the problems of old age have been defined as a crisis which is the result of declining birth rates, increased longevity, and earlier retirement, and not the outcome of prior social inaction or economic policy. This definition has resulted in 'scapegoating' of the elderly, blaming them for rising health care and social security costs.

The theory proposes that fundamental policy changes are necessary in order to shift perceptions and structural alignments. For this purpose, policy solutions should tend to focus on integrating and socializing the elderly to adapt to their status, rather than effort to fundamentally alter social and economic conditions. Instead, policies should alter both objective conditions of the aged as well as the social processes by which policies are made and implemented.

The major contribution of Estes's work has been her critical analysis of the larger socio-political conditions that generate the necessity for separate social policies for groups such as the elderly. The major limitation of her radical critique to date is the lack of empirical research (see Hooman and Kiyan, 1988).

Non-Marxist Theories

Age Stratification Theory

Age Stratification Theory is a relatively recent theory based largely on the work of Matilda White Riley (1971 and 1985) and Riley,

Johnson and Foner (1972). The proponents maintain that an approach similar to that used in sociological analysis of class stratification is useful in understanding the position of age groups and the meaning of age within a particular social context.

Society is often conceptualized as being stratified or divided, along a number of dimensions, such as social caste or ethnic status. Age stratification theory uses chronological age as the defining variable. This age stratification reflects and creates differences in capacities, roles, rights and privileges related to age. Thus, the elderly, teenagers, and the middle-aged are seen as distinctive status groups. Each stratum consists of individuals with similar characteristics because they are at the same stage in the life cycle. Further, each stratum consists of those who have had similar experiences because they have shared a common history.

Age stratification model suggests that the link between age and a social individual will play in society, may be either formal or informal (formal, e.g., age of marriage, voting right, etc., and informal which may originate in tradition, factual regularity or negotiation, e.g., age of admission of a child to a school, etc.). Age stratification models are obviously flexible. This approach may be used to look at a variety of age groups, not just the elderly. Also, these models are culturally and historically specific. However, mobility across the strata in the age stratification model is inevitable, universal and irreversible owing to the natural progression of time (Victor, 1987). As per the Age Stratification Theory, socialization is a lifelong process as people move through a sequence of roles as they age. And this system of age stratification in society influences, and is influenced by the changing social, political and economic fabric of the society.

Secondly, the Age Stratification Theory does offer a method by which most characteristics of age cohorts can be analysed. An age cohort can be seen as a particular generation in relation to other living generations and one that brings its own attitudes, beliefs and values to bear on situations held in common (Cockerham, 1991).

Ageing is not passive, the individual's ageing process is influenced at the 'macro' level by the wider society and at the 'micro' level by other people and the person's own characteristics and personality. The Age Stratification Theory is attractive because it is logical, appears comprehensive and points the way towards which a researcher can analyse the interplay between macro and micro-level social processes as they relate to ageing (Cockerham, 1991). Yet, basically, the Age Stratification Theory is very much a macro-scale approach to the study of ageing, for, whilst it tells us about the attributes of different cohorts, it is of limited value in explaining individual behaviour. This approach can often be seen as being deterministic and allowing little freedom of action for the individual social actor (Victor, 1987).

The Age Stratification Theory has also been criticized for assessing age too narrowly, primarily in terms of chronology or life stage, with little consideration of the importance of physical appearance, length of time that a person has been in a given position, and level of physical, mental and social functioning. And, the researchers opine that functional differences in physiological and social ageing must be taken into account in any successful theory. Another limitation of this theoretical perspective is that family background, sex, ethnic minority status, social class and the political and economic structure may all be more salient in defining people's roles than age stratification itself. In fact, some social gerontologists contend that we are moving towards an 'age irrelevant' society, with age based constraints weakening and socio-economic status becoming more salient (Hagestad and Neugarten, 1985, also see Hooman and Kiyan, 1988)

This theory is also somewhat difficult to operationalize for testing and empirical research because of its complexity. Gordon Streib and Carroll Bourg (1984) seriously question whether age stratification theory actually qualifies as a theory of stratification, because it hardly accounts for social inequality. Rather, they maintain that differences within age cohorts, especially those pertaining to socio-economic differences, can be as great or greater than differences between age cohorts. Streib and Bourg also reject the notion that a person's experience of historical events is as strongly determined by age as the theory suggests (see Cockerham, 1991).

Sub-culture Theory

The sub-culture is broadly characterized by a unique set of beliefs, attitudes, values, norms, customs and language. Rose believes that a subculture among age groups emerges when the group members interact among one another more significantly than they interact with persons in other age categories. This, he asserts, occurs when the members (a) have a positive affinity for each other due to factors such as long-standing friendship or common problems, interests or concerns, and (b) are excluded from interaction with the members of the other groups in the population to some significant extent

Rose and Peterson (1965) proposed that the aged form a subculture (or a minority group) and that it is this sub-culture that defines and gives direction to their behaviour. According to Rose and Peterson (1965), both the above mentioned circumstances apply to the elderly of most societies in varying degrees. Features such as exclusion of older people from the employment market, their dependence upon others for their income, and marginality to the mainstream of life have been used to support the view that the elderly constitute a subculture. The aged may or may not engage in face-to-face interaction, yet they begin to influence the lifestyle of those who identify themselves with their sub-culture.

The proponents of this theory do recognize that many of the distinctive behaviour of the aged result from factors other than the ageing sub-culture such as biological changes, social norms and generational changes. However, of all the subcultures, to which an aged individual belongs, the age sub-culture is the most powerful. In other words, the ethnic, religious, gender, social class or occupational sub-cultures are overridden by age sub-culture (see Dhillon, 1992; Hooman and Kiyan, 1988; Victor, 1987).

Although the concepts of the elderly as a sub-culture or minority group provide descriptive guides for understanding the role and status of older people in our society, these have limited power to predict behaviour. The obvious weakness of this view is that the concept of a disadvantaged sub-culture does not apply universally, for the elderly are a highly diverse group. Some older people weild considerable power and prestige in areas as of law and politics. Many older people are financially well-off; most live in age integrated neighbourhoods; and most interact across generations within their families. There are forces contrary to the formation of a cohesive subculture (see Hooman and Kiyan, 1988; Victor, 1987).

Streib (1965), the most vocal critique of the view of the elderly as a minority group, maintains that compared to ethnic minorities, most older people are not systematically deprived of power and privileges, nor do they regard themselves as objects of collective discrimination by a hostile, controlling out group. Moreover, the membership among the elderly population is neither exclusive nor permanent, but rather awaits all who live long enough (Hooman and Kiyan, 1988).

In a nutshell, this perspective is of only limited utility as a conceptual framework.

Modernization Theory

As a theory of social change, the Modernization Theory takes the position that underdeveloped societies will gradually be transformed by industrialization to resemble North America and Europe. The theory depicts the world as divided into either wealthy industrial nations or poor pre-industrial countries, with poor countries in various stages of evolution towards modernity. According to Walt Rostow (1978), there are four stages to modernization: (a) the traditional stage, in which mortality and population growth decline and life expectancy increases as a result of improved health care and living conditions; (b) the take-off stage, consisting of growth in a market economy and an increased achievement orientation among the population; (c) the drive to technological maturity, which includes a growing industrial economy, urbanization and mass education; and (d) the high mass consumption stage, in which a wide range of consumer goods and services appear. The Modernization Theory seems to be in consistence with the foreign policy of industrial nations with respect to providing assistance for economic development and introducing Western culture. However, the theory attracts some severe criticisms: (i) it tends to view technological advances as positive only; (ii) it has only one path and that is towards modernization; (iii) the causes of poverty in developing nations are not found just in underdeveloped regions of the world, nor are solutions to these problems found only among industrialized countries. Many nations have experienced modernization as suggested by modernization theory, but the theory remains controversial because it seems to favour a privileged position for developed societies as a model in the world economy and overlooks issues of conflict and exploitation.

Modernization Theory is a macro-level theory of global social change in sociology that has been accepted by Donald Cowgill (1986) to explain ageing (Cockerham, 1991). For the first time, this theory was proposed by Cowgill and Homes (1972) in a cross-cultural study that analysed the status of the aged in fourteen different societies. These societies ranged in degree of modernization from gerontocratic tribe in Ethiopia to the highly industrialized country such as United States. The major hypothesis of this theory was that the role and status of the aged varies inversely according to the degree of modernization in a society. As social change occurs and society becomes more modernized, the elderly people lose functional roles, become devalued, and ultimately lose status and security.

Thus, the aged have relatively high status in developing societies where they are able to continue useful and valued functions, but have low status in technologically advanced societies where the most important work is done by the younger people. Retirement and dependency prove to be the contributory factors in their status being low. Even modern education appears to promote devaluation of the elderly. According to Cowgill, "the specialized institutions of formal education, along with libraries, voluminous printed material and recent revolutionary techniques for storing and retrieving information have all but completely abolished a formerly highly significant role of older people as of repositories and transmitters of vital information to the younger generation". One consequence of all the developmental efforts, educational, economic, and technological, is that very shortly the younger generation has command of more information, especially technical information, than the elderly. Certainly, the aged no longer have a monopoly on such information, as they have in non-literate societies, and with the loss of that monopoly, they loose a vital status according role.

With a lessened position in education and the workplace, combined with urbanization and the decline of the extended family, modernity appears to have adversely affected the status of the aged. Therefore, modernization would seem to be an especially negative process for the status of old people. Yet Cowgill suggests that this is not necessarily the case in the mature modern state. Among modern nations, the most advanced accord greater esteem to the elderly than do the less advanced. The most modern societies, according to Cowgill (1986), "are now beginning to come to terms with their aged populations and are achieving appropriate cultural and institutional adaptations". Hence, the status of the older persons is higher in modern societies than it is elsewhere.

Modernization Theory on ageing has been criticized for its not adequately accounting for differences in gender and socio-economic status in the ageing of modern populations (Down, 1980; Williamson, Evans and Powell, 1982). Furthermore, when it comes to the effects of modernization on ageing, culture appears to be an important intervening variable. Japan is one of the most modern and industrialized nations in the world, yet the status of the aged has remained quite high. The Japanese tend to remain strongly integrated into both family and community life in a manner consistent with Japanese culture in particular, and Asian culture in general. The effects of modernization on the status of the aged may, therefore, be strongly influenced by culture as well (Cockerham, 1991).

However, the theory highlights some changing trends regarding the status ascribed to the elderly in various societies.

The intention behind these theories has been the design of interventions either to help individuals age successfully. No one theory is a completely faithful representation of the reality, but some provide better insight into a particular phenomenon than do others. Thus far, none of these theories adequately explains social ageing, but rather describe different aspects of the roles of the elderly in our society. Also, none of these theories is universal. Nor does any of these theoretical perspectives fully account for the wide variations or multiple dimensions in ageing experiences.

The above analysis of the theories at the micro, intermediate and macro level makes it clear that successful and happy ageing incorporates in it the elements of individual perception and activities; the social treatment to the aged in terms of attitude reflected through policies, provisions and practices; and the interaction between the two (individual and social environment). Just for the sake of understanding the process of ageing, these theories have been discussed severally. But satisfactory ageing is a resultant of various micro and macro level factors in interaction with each other. And human beings have the ability to change their environments. So attempts are required to be made at all the levels, micro (individual), intermediate (interactionist) and macro (environmental) levels, so as to make ageing a satisfactory phenomenon.

Theoretical Framework of the Study

Because of methodological difficulties, pre-experimental biases, and lack of multidisciplinary focus, there is no one theory that unifies the biological, psychological and social perspective on ageing. Yet the growth of these theoretical models has laid the framework for future research. These theoretical approaches to ageing, in fact, have the potential for refinement, enhancement and synthesis. In particular, we need to develop cross-classes, cross-cultural and cross-national perspectives in the study of ageing in order to increase the power of any future theoretical development in social gerontology.

The present study aims at developing cross-class (economic) perspectives on ageing. The study focuses mainly at the individual level, keeping the interactionist and environmental level at the secondary level, so as to deal with the problem of the aged women. So it was thought best to select micro level theories for testing, and as compared to the other micro level theories, viz., Role Theory and Continuity Theory, the author considered the Activity Theory and Disengagement Theory because of their practical applicability, availability of empirical evidences and easy testability. Thus, the study attempts to test the Activity and Disengagement Theories of ageing, though only partially.

The Activity Theory maintains that the aged who are active will be more satisfied than the less active elderly. And, to be happy in old age, individuals need to be active in old age. The Disengagement Theory, based on three measures [Interaction Index (measures density of interaction in social intercourse), 'Role Count' (measures number of active roles a person has) and 'Social life space' (which measures the number of discrete contacts of the respondents with others)] maintains that the disengagement is beneficial both for the individual and the society.

In order to test the above mentioned theories, the following study has developed three indicators: Physical Mobility, Ability in Household Work and Social Interaction.

Physical Mobility

The points of measure of mobility of the individual in performing the activities of daily living (ADL), viz., standing up and sitting down, walking without aid, getting in and out of bed, going up and down the stairs, combing one's own hair, self-feeding, reading (proper eye-sight), attending to own toilet and washing or bathing without help. All these are called the basic level of competence–BaCo (Prakash, 1988).

A composite scale was constructed for measuring the level of physical mobility. The urban aged women were asked nine questions which concerned the activities mentioned above. (The general question put up was: Do you have difficulty in the activity?) Each response was analysed. Accordingly, numeric value 'one' was assigned to a 'no difficulty' response, 'two' to a response 'difficulty but can do of my own', and three to a 'difficulty, cannot do of my own' response.

Thus total score acquired by a respondent ranged from 9–27. On the basis of the acquired score, all the respondents were placed in any of the four levels as shown below:

Levels of Physical Mobility

Level	*Score Value*
Perfect	9
High	10–12
Moderate	13–15
Low	16–27

Ability in Household Work

Ability and competence of the urban aged women in performing household work was assessed with regard to the following activities: light household work like washing up, dusting, tidying; heavy cleaning like washing floors and cleaning windows; light kitchen work like making a cup of tea; heavy kitchen work, for example, preparing a hot meal; shopping and heavy washing. A composite scale was developed to judge the competence in household work and accordingly all the respondents were placed in either of three categories of competence: low, moderate and high.

The respondents were asked, "Here are some activities which you may or may not do for yourself, but could you do without difficulty?" The responses regarding each of the six activities mentioned above were obtained from every respondent on a three point scale: 'no difficulty', 'difficulty but can do', and 'difficulty, cannot do'. Accordingly, the numerical values 'one', 'two' and 'three' were allotted respectively to the three responses. Thus, the total score acquired by a respondent ranged from 6–18. On the basis of the acquired scores, all the respondents were placed in any of the three levels as mentioned below:

Levels of Ability in Household Work

Level	*Scores*
Low	6–9
Moderate	10–14
High	15–18

Social Interaction

Social Interaction is a measure of density of interactions one gets involved in with other human beings. This measure has been based on five types of social interactions that occur during the course of paid work/occupation/employment; shopping, playing with children/grandchildren; seeing or visiting relatives and seeing or visiting neighbourhood persons. Prakash (1998) discussed more or less a similar variable called expanded level of competence (ExCo), which was a measure of the skills needed for leisure and social activities.

The urban aged women were asked questions about the frequency of their involvement in each of the above-mentioned activities. And the responses for each of the questions were collected on a five-point scale: daily, often, sometimes, rarely and never. The numerical value 'one' was assigned to a 'daily' response, 'two' to an 'often' response, 'three' to a 'sometimes' response, 'four' to a 'rarely' response and 'five' to a 'never' response. Thus, the total score value acquired by an aged woman ranged from 5–25. On the basis of the acquired score values, all the aged women were placed in any of the three levels mentioned as below:

Levels of Social Interaction

Level	*Score Value*
High	5–11
Moderate	12–18
Low	19–25

Thus, scaling technique was used to judge the levels of physical mobility, competence in household work and Social Interaction of the urban aged women.

Satisfaction in Old Age

Life satisfaction has been identified as a multi-dimensional measure having several correlates, for example, self-acceptance of ageing changes, self-perception of health, self-rating of abilities in activities of daily living and satisfaction with familial and social interaction (Ramamurti, 1970); level of activity (Palmore and Luikart, 1972); adjustment, morale and happiness, and mental health (Lawton, 1975; Poon, 1992; Ramamurti, 1989a, 1989b, 1990; Ramamurti and Jamuna, 1992; Thomae, 1993). Erickson (1982) asserts that old people review their past life and if they feel that most goals of their life have been fulfilled, they feel satisfied. On the similar lines, Thomae (1993) indicated that the exposure to life experiences may be related to health and life satisfaction. The negatively perceived events, particularly, have been contributed negatively to health and satisfaction. Life satisfaction among the aged was found to be positively associated with multiple roles and psychological well-being (Adelmann, 1994); and wisdom (defined as a composite of cognitive, reflective and affective qualities) (Ardelt, 1997). Panda (2005) inferred that the aged women who continue to maintain their preferred active lifestyle by involving themselves in household chores generally have a higher life satisfaction.

In this study, to identify the parameters of satisfaction in old age, the respondents were asked to express their satisfaction level about their old age at a three-point scale: satisfactory, neither satisfactory nor dissatisfactory (so-so) and dissatisfactory.

And, the three indicators described above were analysed in relation to the satisfaction level of the aged women in the direction of the following hypotheses:

1. Higher the level of physical mobility, higher will be the level of satisfaction among the urban aged women.
2. Higher the level of ability in household work, higher will be the level of satisfaction among the urban aged women; and
3. Higher the level of social mobility, higher will be the level of satisfaction among the urban aged women.

If these hypotheses prove to be true, it will be an affirmation of the activity theory, and de-affirmation of the disengagement theory. The conclusions could be seen in the chapters to follow.

3

Urban Aged Women

Personal Profile and Resource Endowment

The changing trends in the proportion of India's aged population indicate that the emerging scenario will comprise more females, with one-fourth of the population living in urban areas. Gender and locational variations will add to their misery. Though some rapid changes are underway, the socio-economic profile will have serious implications on the circumstances under which the aged women live. Their lifestyle, socio-economic and psycho-cultural needs and appended problems are presumed to be highly influenced by their socio-economic background. This chapter aims at examining the socio-economic and occupational background of the urban aged women, specifically their social and economic resource endowment that plays a significant role in framing attitudes and values and somehow affects the way a woman responds to the unjust social systems or the problematic conditions.

Personal Profile

The present section deals with the age, religion, caste, mother tongue, marital status and occupational profile of the urban aged women. An analysis of these variables will help in understanding the similarities and differences in the personal characteristics with respect to the income group.

The 225 respondents belonged, in equal proportion, to the three income groups: lower, middle and higher.

Age

Age greatly influences the physical and social mobility and the health status of the aged. The needs and problems of the aged are found to be largely associated with their age.

Amongst the urban aged women, a large proportion, i.e., 44 per cent belonged to the 60–64 years age group, followed by 28 per cent in the 65–69 years age group. The respondents of 70+ years depicted comparatively a lower percentage (Table 3.1).

Table 3.1

Age and Income Group

Age	*Income Group*			*Total*
	Lower	*Middle*	*Higher*	
60–64	33	36	30	99
% within income group	(44.0)	(48.0)	(40.0)	(44.0)
% of grand total	(14.7)	(16.0)	(13.3)	(44.0)
65–69	23	21	19	63
% within income group	(30.7)	(28.0)	(25.3)	(28.0)
% of grand total	(10.2)	(9.3)	(8.4)	(28.0)
70–74	10	7	13	30
% within income group	(13.3)	(9.3)	(17.3)	(13.3)
% of grand total	(4.4)	(3.1)	(5.8)	(13.3)
75+	9	11	13	33
% within income group	(12.0)	(14.7)	(17.3)	(14.7)
% of grand total	(4.0)	(4.9)	(5.8)	(14.7)
Total	75	75	75	225
% within income group	(100.0)	(100.0)	(100.0)	(100.0)
% of grand total	(33.3)	(33.3)	(33.3)	(100.0)

Pearson Chi-square Value = 3.454 at df = 6; Assymp. sign (2-sided) = 0.750.

It is clear that there is no considerable difference in the distribution of the respondents of different age groups in the three income groups. In all the income groups, the 60–64 years age-group respondents were in large number. In the lower and middle income group, it was followed by 65–69 age group. The 70+ age group was comparatively small in these income groups.

On the other hand, the 70+ age group constituted a larger proportion in the higher income group. And, it leads to the hypothesis that life expectancy of the 60+ women is comparatively high in the higher income group. Further research is required to test it.

Religion and Caste

An overwhelming majority of 90 per cent respondents was Hindu. The Jains constituted 5 per cent, while the remaining 5 per cent of the respondents belonged to the other religions, viz., Islam, Sikhism and Christianity. The dominance of Hindus was observed in all the three income groups. It is representative of the general population in the state/country.

There was no significant difference in the religion-wise distribution of the urban aged women by the three income groups. But, on the other hand, caste-wise distribution highlighted a marked difference in the three income groups. The Scheduled Castes (SCs), Scheduled Tribes(STs) and other backward classes (OBCs) predominated the lower income group, while the middle and higher income groups were sequentially predominated by the general castes. For example, in the lower income group, there were 41 per cent aged women, who belonged to either the OBC or the SC/ST category. The percentage of the OBC and SC/ST aged women was only 8 in the middle income group and this percentage was further declined to 7 in the higher income group (see Table 3.2).

The data clearly indicate that, even now, the majority of the lower castes and tribal people has found it hard to overcome the negative social forces imposed on them, and hence, still belongs to the lower income group. Only a minute percentage of them could raise their income level so as to be included in the middle or the higher income groups.

Mother Tongue

India is known for its linguistic diversity. About 4,000 languages are spoken in India. Each region, is characterized by some specific languages. The language and the region—both may be taken as an indicative of the lifestyle of the residents. Though, it is very

Table 3.2

Religion, Caste and Income Group

Religion	*Income Group*									*Total*
	Lower			*Middle*			*Higher*			
	OBC	*SC/ST*	*Gen.*	*OBC*	*SC/ST*	*Gen.*	*OBC*	*SC/ST*	*Gen.*	
Hindus	4	27	40	3	3	61	4	1	59	202
% within income group	(5.3)	(36.0)	(53.3)	(4.0)	(4.0)	(81.3)	(5.3)	(1.3)	(78.7)	(89.8)
% out of grand total	(1.8)	(12.0)	(17.8)	(1.3)	(1.3)	(27.1)	(1.8)	(0.4)	(26.2)	(89.8)
Jains	—	—	2	—	—	4	—	—	6	12
% within income group			(2.7)			(5.3)			(8.0)	(5.3)
% out of grand total			(0.9)			(1.8)			(2.7)	(5.3)
Muslims/Christian/Sikhs	—	—	2	—	—	4	—	—	5	11
% within income group			(2.7)			(5.3)			(6.7)	(4.9)
% out of grand total			(0.9)			(1.8)			(2.2)	(4.9)
Total	4	27	44	3	3	69	4	1	70	225
% within Income Group	(5.3)	(36.0)	(58.7)	(4.0)	(4.0)	(92.0)	(5.3)	(1.3)	(93.3)	(100.0)
% out of Grand Total	(1.8)	(12.0)	(19.6)	(1.3)	(1.3)	(30.7)	(1.8)	(0.4)	(31.1)	(100.0)

difficult to highlight this association in very specific terms, but the experienced and ageing people can well have an idea about the lifestyle by knowing the mother tongue of the people concerned.

Hindi was the mother tongue of majority (60%) of the respondents in all the three income groups, and was followed by Mewari (local dialect of the study area) (25%). None of the 4 per cent respondents, having Marwari as the mother tongue, belonged to the lower income group. In fact, the Marwari is the language spoken mainly in Gujarat by the business community. And, a fraction of this community had migrated to Rajasthan either for job or business purposes. Blochi/Sindhi, Punjabi, Urdu, Arbi and Malvi languages were the other mother tongues prevailing in the area of study.

Education

Education cannot be confined within the four walls of schools, because education is too wide a concept to include just the literary skills or acquired degrees. Yet, formal education is an important indicator of social status.

The level of education of the urban aged women was quite low; with a literacy rate of 64 per cent which is comparable to that of the official literacy rate (68%) of Udaipur city. About 70 per cent of them had no education (36%), had developed only the literary skills or had education up to the primary level. And, only about one-tenth had education up to graduate or post-graduate levels (see Table 3.3).

In the lower income group, 79 per cent women were illiterate whereas the proportion of illiterate women in the middle and higher income groups was 20 and 8 per cent respectively. Clearly, it can very safely be concluded that the level of education and the level of income group have a significant association and a positive correlation. Better accessibility of the resources to the higher income groups may be the obvious reason.

Professional Qualifications

About three-four decades back, professional education for women was not very common in India. So, in a small district of a backward state like Rajasthan, one can very well imagine the dismal

Table 3.3
Educational Status and Income Group

Educational Status	*Income Group*			*Total*
	Lower	*Middle*	*Higher*	
Illiterate	59	15	6	80
% within income group	(78.7)	(20.0)	(8.0)	(35.6)
% out of grand total	(26.2)	(6.7)	(2.7)	(35.6)
Literate/Primary	13	34	29	76
% within income group	(17.3)	(45.3)	(38.7)	(33.8)
% out of grand total	(5.8)	(15.1)	(12.9)	(33.8)
Middle/High School/Inter	3	20	23	46
% within income group	(4.0)	(26.7)	(30.7)	(20.4)
% out of grand total	(1.3)	(8.9)	(10.2)	(20.4)
Graduate/Post-graduate		06	17	23
% within income group	—	(8.0)	(22.7)	(10.2)
% out of grand total	—	(2.7)	(7.6)	(10.2)
Total	75	75	75	225
% within income group	(100.0)	(100.0)	(100.0)	(100.0)
% out of grand total	(33.3)	(33.3)	(33.3)	(100.0)

Pearson's Chi-square Value = 104.390 at df = 6; Assym. Sig. 2-sided = 0.000.

situation. Only 9 per cent of the aged women had some or the other kind of professional qualification. Out of these, 8 per cent had qualifications (B.Ed., M.Ed., M.Phil. or Ph.D.) relating to teaching—the traditionally accepted profession for women.

Hundred per cent aged women of the lower income group, 95 per cent aged women of the middle income group and 79 per cent aged women of the higher income group had no professional qualifications. Five per cent respondents of the middle-income group had qualification related to teaching. And, such women comprised 19 per cent of the higher income group. The very limited fraction of respondents having the other kinds of professional qualifications (MBBS and Diploma in Fashion Designing) belonged to the higher income group.

Statistically, a high level of association was found between the professional qualifications of the respondents and the income groups they belonged to.

Marital Status

In India, marital status is also an important indicator of social status. Marital status, many a time, proves to be a determining factor in assessing the lifestyle, needs, problems, attitudes and worries of the aged.

In all the three income groups of our respondents, married respondents predominated, followed by the widowed. And unmarried and divorced/separated respondents were found to be in a minority in all the income groups (see Table 3.4). A comparison of the census data (2001) with that of our sample survey concludes that our sample is a preferable figure. The majority (57%) was married compared to 47 per cent at the all India level. The incidence of widowhood was only 40 per cent compared to 51 per cent at the national level. But, the proportion of unmarried and divorced/separated respondents was also slightly more (3%) than that at the all-India level (2%).

Table 3.4

Marital Status and Income Group

Marital Status	*Income Group*			*Total*
	Lower	*Middle*	*Higher*	
Unmarried	1	1	3	5
% within income group	(1.3)	(1.3)	(4.0)	(2.2)
% out of grand total	(0.4)	(0.4)	(1.3)	(2.2)
Married	40	46	42	128
% within income group	(53.3)	(61.3)	(56.0)	(56.9)
% out of grand total	(17.8)	(20.4)	(18.7)	(56.9)
Widowed	33	26	30	89
% within income group	(44.0)	(34.7)	(40.0)	(39.6)
% out of grand total	(14.7)	(11.6)	(13.3)	(39.6)
Divorced/separated/deserted	1	2	—	03
% within income group	(1.3)	(2.7)	—	(1.3)
% out of grand total	(0.4)	(0.9)	—	(1.3)
Total	75	75	75	225
% within income group	(100.0)	(100.0)	(100.0)	(100.0)
% out of grand total	(33.3)	(33.3)	(33.3)	(100.0)

Pearson Chi-square Value = 4.869 at df = 6; Asymp sig. (2-sided) = 0.561

Occupational

An overwhelming majority of 87 per cent respondents was not employed. Among those employed, the majority belonged to the lower income group. Only one respondent from the middle income group and only two (1%) from the higher income group were engaged in one or the other occupation.

In the lower income group, 35 per cent of the respondents were working women and 30 per cent were earning just less than Rs 1,000 per month. Most of them were engaged in low-paid jobs, like those of house maid, home nurse, book binder, physical labourer in factories or farm houses, vegetable vendor or laundry worker. The working women of the middle/higher income group were teachers, while only one was a business entrepreneur. Excluding those belonging to the higher income group, all the aged working women had a monthly income of less than Rs 2,000.

Even at this age (60+), when health problems generally result in the loss of stamina, 5 per cent of the lower income group respondents had to work for 10–12 hours a day. And, the rest of the working women had usually been devoting 4–10 hours daily to their paid work. The monthly wages of the lower income group respondents seem to be in proportion to their working hours per day.

Obviously, the majority of the aged women was not employed. The employed ones had to work out of economic compulsions and were engaged in low-paid jobs.

To conclude, the majority of the urban aged women belong to 60–69 years age group. There are no striking differences in age-wise distribution of the respondents in the three income groups. The Hinduism is found to be dominating in all the income groups. The lower income group constitutes largely of those respondents who belong to SCs, tribes and OBCs. Education and income group are found to be highly associated in a positive correlation. The data regarding professional qualification further strengthen this finding. The majority of the respondents (57%) are married, followed by the widowed (40%). There is no striking difference in the distribution of the respondents by marital status in the three income groups. Only 13 per cent of the total respondents are employed. Those employed are found to be concentrated in the lower income group, indicating the economic compulsions being the compelling reason behind their taking up jobs.

The social and economic resource endowment of an individual determine, to a great extent, her lifestyle, needs and problems. The quality of life of the aged women, the standard of facilities available to them, the nature of care they get and their access to aid or help during emergency, all these are influenced by their resource endowment.

Social Resource Endowment

The social resources of the aged women are characterized by their living arrangements, interpersonal relations and status in the family. Living arrangement of the aged women, that is where they live and with whom they live, makes a considerable difference to a variety of factors that may directly or indirectly contribute to the quality of their lives. While the living arrangement, which includes housing conditions, household composition and family pattern, is a visible thing and can easily be observed and judged; satisfaction with this arrangement, however, is not easily observable. The latter depends a great deal on the nature of interpersonal relations in the household, which encompass attitudes, emotions and sentiments. Hence, it is necessary to distinguish between the living arrangement of an aged woman in a household and the quality of her life—food security, nutrition, medical care, familial/peer company, etc., in that household, leading to an overall satisfaction of the aged.

Many of the studies on the aged have examined their living arrangements also. But, the efforts have been sporadic and superficial. There are only a few deep and rigorous studies on the satisfaction of the aged from their living arrangements, their food, clothing, medical aid, etc. In the absence of such studies, one has to depend on personal and general observations and on insights derived from the micro-studies. The present study is a humble attempt to fill the gap. The following section will be concerned with the housing conditions, family pattern and children and their support. The food, health, physical mobility, leisure time activities and social interaction are dealt in the next chapter.

Living Arrangement

Housing Conditions

The study of housing needs of elderly persons has sociological importance. The real objective of housing for an aged woman goes far beyond the provision of providing suitable independent housing and living arrangement. It must be seen in the context of suitability for interaction with the family members, for her privacy and for maintaining and developing friendship with neighbours and relatives. The housing condition of the urban aged women with relation to their income group; and the kind of accommodation available to the aged women with relation to size and ownership of the house, as found in our study, is described below.

Type of House

Approximately, one-third (32%) of urban aged women were living in *kothis* or bungalows (bungalow refers to a house with garden, porch, servant's quarter and various other facilities). About one-fourth of the aged women was living in spacious *pucca* houses (*pucca* house refers to a house either single storied or multi-storied where the residents enjoy the ownership of the roof also). Almost the same percentage (24%) was residing in compact, comparatively less spacious houses, constructed on the single floor where the residents do not enjoy independent ownership of the roof. The remaining 18 per cent of the aged women were living in *kaccha/pucca* mixed houses. Some of these respondents had got their houses constructed on very big residential plots. They had been using *kaccha* area of their houses for running a dairy, a laundry or for agriculture. Most of them had a big *pucca* building for themselves and a small *kaccha* quarter for the servants (Table 3.5).

Table 3.5
Type of House and Income Group

Type of House	*Income Group*			*All*
	Lower	*Middle*	*Higher*	
Kaccha-Pucca Mixed House	21	14	6	41
% within income group	(28.0)	(18.7)	(8.0)	(18.2)
% out of grand total (225)	(9.3)	(6.2)	(2.7)	(18.2)
Flat (compact, less spacious house, constructed on a single floor, with no independent ownership of the roof)	43	9	3	55
% within income group	(57.3)	(12.0)	(4.0)	(24.4)
% out of grand total (225)	(19.1)	(4.0)	(1.3)	(24.4)
Spacious Pucca House (either single storied or double storied, with independent ownership of the roof).	4	23	29	56
% within income group	(5.3)	(30.7)	(38.7)	(24.9)
% out of grand total (225)	(1.8)	(10.2)	(12.9)	(24.9)
Kothi/Bungalow (with garden, porch, servant quarter, etc.)	7	29	37	73
% within income group	(9.3)	(38.7)	(49.3)	(32.4)
% out of grand total (225)	(3.1)	(12.9)	(16.4)	(32.4)
All	75	75	75	225
% within income group	(100.0)	(100.0)	(100.0)	(100.0)
% out of grand total (225)	(33.3)	(33.3)	(33.3)	(100.0)

Chi-Square Value—97.093 at df = 6; Asymp. sig. (2-sided) = 0.000

Statistically, a very close association was found between the 'type of house' and 'income group'. Obviously, the urban aged women of the higher income group have access to better houses as compared to their counterparts who belong to a comparatively lower income group.

Ownership Pattern

The 92 per cent of the respondents were living in houses owned by the family. Out of them, a substantial number of 38 per cent of the urban aged women owned the house either independently or jointly with some other member/s of the family. Only 8 per cent were living in the rented houses (see Table 3.6). The finding is

Table 3.6

Availability of Exclusive/Shared Room, Number of Rooms in the House and Ownership of the House

Exclusive/Shared Room Available in the House	Ownership of House											All I+II+III
	Rented/Government Allotted Accommodation			Owned by Respondent Independently or Jointly				Owned by Other Members of the Family				
	Rooms in the House			Rooms in the House				Rooms in the House				
	1–2	3–5	All I	1–2	3–5	6–11	All II	1–2	3–5	6–11	All III	
Room exclusively for the aged woman	5 (2.2)[1]	7 (3.1)	12 (5.3)	9 (4.0)	36 (16.0)	15 (6.7)	60 (26.7)	4 (1.8)	45 (20.0)	25 (11.1)	74 (32.9)	146 (64.9)
Room shared with spouse or children or grandchildren	3 (1.3)	3 (1.3)	6 (2.7)	6 (2.7)	15 (6.7)	3 (1.3)	24 (10.7)	10 (4.4)	33 (14.7)	3 (1.3)	46 (20.4)	76 (33.8)
No exclusive/shared room but corridor/kitchen, etc.	—	—	—	—	1 (0.4)	—	1 (0.4)	2 (0.9)	—	—	2 (0.9)	3 (1.3)
All	8 (3.6)	10 (4.4)	18 (8.0)	15 (6.7)	52 (23.1)	18 (8.0)	85 (37.8)	16 (7.1)	78 (34.7)	28 (12.4)	122 (54.2)	225 (100.0)

Note: 1. Percentage out of Grand Total 225

substantiated by Chetna (2001) which revealed that 91 per cent of the aged women (Chittor, Rajasthan) had family owned property.

All the rented private houses or government allotted accommodations had at the most five rooms. About one-fifth of the total respondents had 6–11 rooms in their houses. It is interesting to note that a vast majority of 65 per cent of the urban aged women had got a room in the house exclusively for themselves. About one-third (34%) of the aged women had been sharing their rooms with some or the other member/s of the family. And 1 per cent of the aged women had somehow to spend their time either in the kitchen or in the corridor of the small house. It is really disappointing to note that one respondent could not get even a corner in any of the four rooms of her self-owned house. Otherwise, most women who owned a house occupied a separate room.

Family versus Household

The distinction between 'household' and 'family' is not merely a matter of words but has a deeper meaning and substance in Indian society. For example, in India, a son's household may be separate from that of his parents; and two or more brothers may live in separate households but they consider themselves as belonging to a single family. In such a situation, it would be confusing to use the word 'family' for the household.

The census has also brought out that it is not unusual to find husband and wife working in different places and children living with the relatives or in hostels. This only shows the elasticity of the domestic groups (Singh, 1996). To understand the situation of an aged woman, it is important to find out if she lives alone/independently in a household or not. It is not enough to know her status as the only member of the family.

The earning members of the families of the Himalayan region generally work out of the station. They send a fixed amount every month to their families. The families depend on the amount received by 'money order' for their survival. This shows that the sons may remain cordial from a distance. They may even provide money for parents' maintenance. But that is not sufficient. Hindu law has ruled since the ancient times that the members of the joint family are entitled to receive maintenance from joint family property. Financial support may thus be available to the old and disabled parents and it may even be enforced by law. However, the law cannot enforce the question of residence in a joint household. And, the quality of life of an aged woman depends not only on the financial assistance or security but also on her household composition and family pattern.

The following is an attempt to describe and analyse household composition, family pattern and related aspects of the urban aged women.

Household Composition

A limited but substantial proportion of 4 per cent of the aged women was residing all by themselves without company and support of anybody. One does not need to explain how difficult and painful it is to be lonely in old age. An additional 1 per cent of respondents had managed to keep servants with them. Only 4 per cent aged women lived with their distant relatives. The remaining 91 per cent of the aged women were residing with the members of families, for example, spouse, children and grandchildren, in different compositions (see Table 3.7).

Table 3.7
Household Composition

Household Composition	*No. of Respondents*	*Percentage*
Aged woman living alone	8	3.6
Aged woman and spouse	26	11.6
Aged woman and/or spouse + unmarried children	27	12.0
Aged woman + daughter's family	9	4.0
Aged woman and/or spouse + son's family	16	7.1
Aged woman and/or spouse + unmarried children + son's family	113	50.2
Aged woman and/or spouse + son's family + grandson's family	14	6.2
Aged woman+ relatives other than the children	9	4.0
Aged woman + servant/s	3	1.3
All	225	100.0

Note: Here family refers to the family of procreation including spouse and unmarried children.

Prakash (1998) has analysed the household composition of the urban aged women and arrived almost at the same results as found in our study. According to her, 9 per cent of them were living alone, 4 per cent were living with their relatives and the remaining 87 per cent were living in different combinations of members of family.

It was noticed that 4 per cent of the aged women of our sample were living with their daughters' families. In Indian Hindu culture, it is not customary to live with married daughters. Yet, 4 per cent of the sampled women were living with their married daughters, may be only out of compulsion. Such women either had no son or were getting no support from the son/s. As long as the spouse is alive, such a Hindu aged woman does manage to live independently. But, as and when she becomes a widow, she has to join the daughter's family. It is ironical that in most of the cases, in India a woman living with her married son feels proud of her household composition, while if living with her married daughter feels morally down.

Generation-wise Household Composition

A majority of 56 per cent of the aged women had a composition of three-generation members living together (they themselves, their children and grandchildren or they themselves, their parents and children) in the household. About one-fourth (23%) of them was living in households where the members were belonging to two generations. And the remaining one-fifth (20%) was living in the households with members belonging just to their own generation (e.g., spouse, relatives or servants of their age) (see Table 3.8).

A comparison of household composition of the three income group respondents reveals that though the composition of three-generation-combination-household predominates in all the income groups, it is however more popular in the higher income group (69%) compared to that of the middle (60%) and the lower (40%) income groups respectively. The prevalence of one-generation-combination-household was maximum (33%) in the lower income group, followed by 17 per cent in the higher income group and 11 per cent in the middle income group. Thus, one-generation-combination-households (11%) were least

Table 3.8
Household Composition and Income Group

Household Composition	*Income Group*			*All*
	Lower	*Middle*	*Higher*	
(A combination of one generation people) Respondent without children—alone or with spouse, relatives or servants	25	8	13	46
% within income group	(33.3)	(10.7)	(17.3)	(20.4)
% out of grand total	(11.1)	(3.6)	(5.8)	(20.4)
(A combination of two generation people) Respondent with married and unmarried children and/or spouse	20	22	10	52
% within income group	(26.7)	(29.3)	(13.3)	(23.1)
% out of grand total	(8.9)	(9.8)	(4.4)	(23.1)
(A combination of three generation people) Respondent with children and grandchildren or parents	30	45	52	127
% within income group	(40.0)	(60.0)	(69.3)	(56.4)
% out of grand total	(13.3)	(20.0)	(23.1)	(56.4)
All	75	75	75	225
% within income group	(100.0)	(100.0)	(100.0)	(100.0)
% out of grand total	(33.3)	(33.3)	(33.3)	(100.0)

Pearson Chi-square value = 22.047 at df=4; Assymp. sig. (2-sided) = 0.000

prevalent among the middle income group respondents while for those belonging to the lower and the higher income groups, the composition of two-generation-combination-household was the least prevalent composition (27% and 13% respectfully) (see Table 3.8).

The 'household composition' had statistically a strong association with the 'income group'. The joint property and resources, many a times, pull the members of the joint family to live under one roof. And obviously, the higher income groups have more of joint property and resources as compared to the lower income groups. Also, for maintaining and continuing big joint families, more resources are required. Contrary to this, it can also be stated that when children find it difficult to maintain their living standard while living with their physically and/or economically dependent parents, they opt for nuclear families. And, it is more often a phenomenon of the lower income group. That may be the reason why the single-generation-combination-households were more prevalent and the three-generation-combination-households were the least prevalent among the lower income group respondents, compared to the middle and the higher income group respondents. Also, the aged belonging to the middle income group are presumed to be better off than their counterparts belonging to the lower or the higher income group. In any society, it is the middle income group, which is considered to be the repository of values, and ethics. Hence, it is natural that the children of this group may be feeling more responsible towards their elderly. And again, that may be the reason why one-generation-combination-households were the least prevalent households among the middle income group respondents.

Household Size and Family Pattern

The size of the household with relation to the family pattern will further help us in understanding the living arrangement of the urban aged women of different income groups.

A majority of 36 per cent of respondents had 6–8 members in their households, followed by 32 per cent of them who had 3–5 members in their households. The smaller households, with 1–2 members, (20%) or the bigger households, with 9+ members, (13%) were comparatively less prevalent (see Table 3.9).

The joint family pattern was most popular in the higher income group (43%), followed by the middle (28%) and the lower (11%) income group. As is obvious, the reverse was the trend of popularity of the nuclear families—the prevalence was 83 per cent in the lower income group, 68 per cent in the middle income group and 53 per cent in the higher income group. Those living all alone were concentrated mainly in the lower income group (see Table 3.9). It is obvious that due to lack of resources, the aged women of this income group who are the only members of their families have to spend their life while all alone. But, on the other hand, such aged women of the higher income group do manage to have servants and relatives for their aid and company.

Table 3.9

Family Pattern, Number of Members in the Household and Income Group

No. of Members in the Household (including aged woman)	*Income Group*												*All LT+MT +HT*
	Lower Family Pattern				*Middle Family Pattern*				*Higher Family Pattern*				
	Joint	*Nuclear*	*Living Alone*	*All LT*	*Joint*	*Nuclear*	*Living Alone*	*All MT*	*Joint*	*Nuclear*	*Living Alone*	*All HT*	
1–2	—	22	5	27	1	4	3	8	—	7	2*	9	44
% within income group		(29.3)	(6.7)	(36.0)	(1.3)	(5.3)	(4.0)	(10.7)		(9.3)	(2.7)	(12.0)	(19.6)
% out of grand total		(9.8)	(2.2)	(12.0)	(0.4)	(1.8)	(1.3)	(3.6)		(3.1)	(0.9)	(4.0)	(19.6)
3–5	3	19	—	22	3	28	—	31	1	17	1*	19	72
% within income group	(4.0)	(25.3)		(29.3)	(4.0)	(37.3)		(41.3)	(1.3)	(22.7)	(1.3)	(25.3)	(32.0)
% out of grand total	(1.3)	(8.4)		(9.8)	(1.3)	(12.4)		(13.8)	(0.4)	(7.6)	(0.4)	(8.4)	(32.0)
6–8	4	16	—	20	13	18	—	31	14	15	—	29	80
% within income group	(5.3)	(21.3)		(26.7)	(17.3)	(24.0)		(41.3)	(18.7)	(20.0)		(38.7)	(35.6)
% out of grand total	(1.8)	(7.1)		(8.9)	(5.8)	(8.0)		(13.8)	(6.2)	(6.7)		(12.9)	(35.6)
9+	1	5	—	6	4	1	—	5	17	1	—	18	29
% within income group	(1.3)	(6.7)		(8.0)	(5.3)	(1.3)		(6.7)	(22.7)	(1.3)		(24.0)	(12.9)
% out of grand total	(0.4)	(2.2)		(2.7)	(1.8)	(0.4)		(2.2)	(7.6)	(0.4)		(8.0)	(12.9)
All	8	62	5	75	21	51	3	75	32	40	3	75	225
% within income group	(10.7)	(82.7)	(6.7)	(100.0)	(28.0)	(68.0)	(4.0)	(100.0)	(42.7)	(53.3)	(4.0)	(100.0)	(100.0)
% out of grand total	(3.6)	(27.6)	(2.2)	(33.3)	(9.3)	(22.7)	(1.3)	(33.3)	(14.2)	(17.8)	(1.3)	(33.3)	(100.0)

*Aged woman living with servant/s.

Migration from native places while leaving their families back at home may be thought of as one of the reasons behind the low prevalence of joint families in the lower income group. But this was reportedly not true for the respective lower income group. Rather, setting up independent households by the children with an intention to pool maximum resources for their spouses and children was the reason mentioned by the aged women of the lower income group. According to them, the joint family was thought to be a barrier to the freedom and a threat to the standard of living of the children.

Here, it is worth having some details given by Shah (2000) so as to support the findings: "Although the ancient ideal joint household was prevalent throughout the Indian society—the idea that all the sons after their marriage should continue to live together with their parents was basically a *Sanskritic* ideal, prescribed by Hindu scriptures and practiced mainly in a small section of society composed of upper castes and classes. It was practiced to a lesser extent among the lower castes and classes and tribal groups, which constituted the overwhelming majority of the Indian society. Consequently, taking the society as a whole, the average household was small and simple or nuclear. Most of the joint households were also small, composed of one or both parents and only one married son. The main reasons for such households were three; one, life expectancy was low. Two, massive poverty meant lower level of household assets and thus lower tendency to live in joint households. If there was much poverty, how could there be much joint property to become an economic base for joint household? The third reason was: the lower level of sanskritization among lower castes and classes and tribal groups meant a weak emphasis on joint household among the masses".

The point to note is that the lower income group of our study was predominated by the lower castes, while the middle and higher income groups were mainly composed of general or higher caste people.

In all the income groups, most of the respondents—who belonged to the joint families—had six to eight members in their households. At the same time, most of the households with nuclear families had less than eight members therein. There were only very limited respondents in the middle and the higher income group, each who had nine or more members in their nuclear family household. But, the respondents of the same category constituted 7 per cent in the lower income group. The general assumption that in the lower income group, families/women are not aware of family planning measures and opt for more children compared to those of the middle and higher income groups, seems true in the light of the above findings.

Children and Their Support

The household composition and family pattern of an aged woman is definitely influenced by the number of male and female children she has, and the support she gets from them. If a woman has no children, she will have to reside all by herself with spouse and/or relatives. Similar will be the case of a woman having children but getting no support from them. Though Hindu customs do not favour an aged woman to reside with her married daughter, yet a woman having only daughter/s is left with no other alternative than to take shelter in the daughter's family. And if she, in any case, joins daughter's family, she will face continuous mental trauma because of difference in her normative and practised standards and the attitude of the society.

There is one more popular belief in the Indian society that sons are superior to daughters because they give support to parents in the old age. Daughters get married and go to live with their in-laws. There is the belief in Hindu religion that a son is a must for acquiring a place in heaven. It is the son who performs the 'last rites' after the death of a person. So, a woman in India, under the pressure of the family or her own belief or value system, goes on taking chances unless and until she gives birth to a male child. And, it results in the birth of a number of unwanted female children.

The data highlight that in all the income groups, the percentage of respondents with no daughter is quite high than those with no son. And, the difference between the two categories is also found to be continuously increasing with the level of the income group (see Table 3.10). To illustrate, in the lower income group, the urban aged women with no daughter constituted 57 per cent compared to those 16 per cent with no son. In the middle

Table 3.10

Number of Male and Female Children and Income Group

Number of Sons	*Income Group*																		*All 225 (LT +MT +HT)*
	Lower						*Middle*						*Higher*						
	No. of Daughters						*No. of Daughters*						*No. of Daughters*						
	0	*1*	*2*	*3*	*4+*	*All (LT)*	*0*	*1*	*2*	*3*	*4+*	*All (MT)*	*0*	*1*	*2*	*3*	*4+*	*All (MT)*	
Nil	9 (12.0)[1]	—	3 (4.0)	—		12 (16.0)	4 (5.3)	1 (1.3)	1 (1.3)	—	—	6 (8.0)	6 (8.0)	1 (1.3)	—	—	—	7 (9.3)	25 (11.1)[2]
One	14 (18.7)	1 (1.3)	2 (2.7)	—	3 (4.0)	20 (26.7)	18 (24.0)	3 (4.0)	—	5 (6.7)	1 (1.3)	27 (36.0)	31 (41.3)	2 (2.7)	3 (4.0)	2 (2.7)	—	38 (50.7)	85 (37.8)
Two	10 (13.3)	6 (8.0)	5 (6.7)	1 (1.3)	1 (1.3)	23 (30.7)	18 (24.0)	8 (10.7)	2 (2.7)	2 (2.7)	—	30 (40.0)	13 (17.3)	1 (1.3)	—	—	1 (1.3)	15 (20.0)	68 (30.2)
Three	6 (8.0)	6 (8.0)	3 (4.0)	—	—	15 (20.0)	6 (8.0)	4 (5.3)	2 (2.7)	—	—	12 (16.0)	11 (14.7)	2 (2.7)	—	—	—	13 (17.3)	40 (17.8)
Four+	4 (5.3)	1 (1.3)	—	—	—	05 (6.7)	—	—	—	—	—	—	1 (1.3)	1 (1.3)	—	—	—	2 (2.7)	07 (3.1)
All	43 (57.3)	14 (18.7)	13 (17.3)	1 (1.3)	4 (5.3)	75 (100.0)	46 (61.3)	16 (21.3)	5 (6.7)	7 (9.3)	1 (1.3)	75 (100.0)	62 (82.7)	7 (9.3)	3 (4.0)	2 (2.7)	1 (1.3)	75 (100.0)	225 (100.0)

Note: 1. Percentage within Income Group (75), 2. Percentage out of Grand Total (225)

income group, 61 per cent respondents had no daughter while only 8 per cent of the respondents had no son. And, in the higher income group, a still remarkable of 83 per cent of respondents had no daughter compared to 9 per cent of respondents with no son. Hence, it can very safely be concluded that the number of sons and daughters has a strong association with the income group of the respondents. And that the higher income group people being more educated, having more resources and enjoying better access to sex determination (of foetus) and family planning techniques are in an advantageous position to enjoy choice as far as the sex of the child is concerned. And, the superiority of the male child, over the female one, is a very well accepted proposition all over the society.

Again, the respondents with three or more sons constituted a larger proportion as compared to those with three or more daughters in general and in all the three income groups. The overall trends depicted in the table and cited as above clearly indicate a strong preference for a male child in all the income groups. The finding is strongly supported by Chetna (2001) who revealed that 82 per cent of the young adults (N=308) preferred to have a son to support them in old age.

The following is an attempt at analysing the following hypotheses: (1) the lower the income group, the higher will be the number of children, (2) the higher the income group, the greater will be the support from the children, and that (3) the higher the number of the children, the greater will be the support to the urban aged women.

The data (of the Table 3.11) show that the proportion of the respondents having four or more children constituted 32 per cent in the lower income group followed by 21 per cent in the middle and 9 per cent in the higher income group. This data is enough to prove the hypothesis one as mentioned above.

Now, let us examine the data about 'support from the children' in relation to the income group. The data show that 95 per cent of the respondents of the middle income group were getting support from all or few of their children. In the higher income group, the percentage of such respondents was 83, and that in the lower income group, it was 72 per cent. Also, not even a single respondent of the middle income group was such who had

Table 3.11

Number of Children, Support Therefrom and Income Group

No. of Children	*Income Group*															*All T_1+ T_2+ T_3*
	Lower					*Middle*					*Higher*					
	Support from Children					*Support from Children*					*Support from Children*					
	N.A.	*From All*	*From Some*	*From None*	*All (T_1)*	*N.A.*	*From All*	*FromS ome*	*From None*	*All (T_2)*	*N.A.*	*From All*	*FromS ome*	*From None*	*All (T_3)*	
Nil	9 (12.0)[1]	—	—	—	9 (12.0)	4 (5.3)	—	—	—	4 (5.3)	6 (8.0)	—	—	—	6 (8.0)	19 (8.4)[2]
One	—	10 (13.3)	—	4 (5.3)	14 (18.7)	—	19 (25.3)	—	—	19 (25.3)	—	28 (37.3)	—	4 (5.3)	32 (42.7)	65 (28.9)
Two	—	7 (9.3)	3 (4.0)	4 (5.3)	14 (18.7)	—	19 (25.3)	3 (4.0)	—	22 (29.3)	2* (2.7)	10 (13.3)	2 (2.7)	1 (1.3)	15 (20.0)	51 (22.7)
Three	—	6 (8.0)	7 (9.3)	1 (1.3)	14 (18.7)	—	12 (16.0)	2 (2.7)	—	14 (18.7)	—	9 (12.0)	6 (8.0)	—	15 (20.0)	43 (19.1)
Four	—	3 (4.0)	8 (10.7)	3 (4.0)	14 (18.7)	—	10 (13.3)	1 (1.3)	—	11 (14.7)	—	4 (5.3)	1 (1.3)	—	5 (6.7)	30 (13.3)
Five+	—	3 (4.0)	7 (9.3)	—	10 (13.3)	—	3 (4.0)	2 (2.7)	—	5 (6.7)	—	1 (1.3)	1 (1.3)	—	2 (2.7)	17 (7.6)
Total	9 (12.0)	29 (38.7)	25 (33.3)	12 (16.0)	75 (100.0)	4 (5.3)	63 (84.0)	8 (10.7)	—	75 (100.0)	8 (10.7)	52 (69.3)	10 (13.3)	5 (6.7)	75 (100.0)	225 (100.0)

Note: *Dependent children (mentally sick/paralytic). 1. Percentage within income group (75). 2. Percentage out of grand total (225).

been getting no support from any of their children. The percentage of this category of disadvantageous respondents constituted 7 and 16 per cent in the higher and the lower income group respectively. The trends cited above force us to reject the hypothesis that the higher the income group, the greater will be the support from the children. On the country, it leads to the conclusion that regarding support from the children, the respondents belonging to the middle income group are in an advantageous situation than their counterparts belonging to the higher and the lower income groups respectively.

Among the lower income group, 4 per cent respondents had four children each but they had not been getting support from anyone of them. On the other hand, the respondents having only one child constituted 19 per cent, 25 per cent and 43 per cent in the lower, the middle and the higher income groups respectively. And, in all the income groups, the majority of such respondents were getting the support of their children. In all the income groups, there were significant number of respondents who had two or more children, but only a few of them were getting support from their children. In the light of these facts, it is safe to drop the hypothesis that the more the number of children, the greater will be the support there from in favour of the null hypothesis that more children do not ensure greater support to the aged (women included).

The finding is substantiated by Chetna (2001), since as per 95 per cent of young adults, more number of children did not mean more comfort for the parents in later years of the life, as the children would tend to pass the responsibility of taking care of their parents on each other. However, those having the contrary view reasoned that if there were more children, at least one would take care of their parents.

Obviously, most of the aged women have satisfactory housing conditions. About 92 per cent of them have family owned houses. Amongst these, 38 per cent own house in their own name. Most of them have a room exclusive or on sharing basis. But, a negligible proportion of them have to spend life in the kitchen or corridor of the house. As it is clear, the aged women belonging to the higher income group have access to better houses as compared to those belonging to the lower income groups.

Children are the most important resources for the aged women. Approximately 80 per cent of them have the household composition of aged woman and/or spouse and married/unmarried children. Only a small fraction of the aged women (4%) is living all alone.

The support of joint family was available mainly to the middle income group respondents, followed by those of the higher and the lower income group. In India, it is the son who is supposed to give shelter and support to the aged parents. And, this may be the reason why more sons than daughters is the case observed very frequently and in an increasing order, in the three income groups—lower, middle and higher. Also, the lower the income group, the higher have been the number of the children. It is interesting to find that more children do not ensure a greater support to the urban aged women. To conclude, regarding social resources, the aged women of the middle income group are better off, followed by those belonging to the higher and the lower income group.

Economic Resource Endowment

One can easily have a rough idea about the economic resource endowment of an individual. But to know the exact economic condition is not easy. In the complex Indian society, it becomes even more difficult. The social relationships around a person play a prominent role in generating the ambiguity. There may be so many factors that contribute to and influence economic resource endowment, for example, employment status, property, savings, regular/irregular source/s of income and expenditure pattern. Below given is an account of the economic resource endowment of the urban aged women by analysing the mentioned factors.

The Indian aged woman is unique in some respects. She has been under the protective influence of male members of her family—father, husband, brother or son. If married, she considers, perhaps falsely, her husband's income as that of her own income. She is used to find her identity—whether social or economic—through her male partner. She does not directly handle money matters of her family and is largely ignorant of them. This is true even of educated women, because monetary management is considered a male prerogative. In case, she loses the male protection on widowhood or any other reason, she finds herself high and dry with lack of skills to handle economic resources left to her. She has to lean heavily on her adult children or relatives and even depend on them for economic help. Obviously, the role and status of her family plays a prominent role in determining her economic status. Hence, the economic condition of an aged woman cannot be studied in isolation but only in relation to her family.

The misery that attends an aged woman is due to her powerlessness, lack of financial assets and a regular source of income. This combined with existing social prejudice towards her, makes her position precarious. Therefore, what is needed to rectify the situation is social and economic empowerment of the aged women. An analysis of the financial condition, be it salary/wages, income, expenditure, savings, housing facility, medical facility or inheritance of property, is pertinent. It focuses on such issues as whether they are compelled to work for their livelihood or not; or whether something can be done to redeem their position by making them economically more viable so as to avoid economic distress in the later years. In this regard, the following is an attempt to thoroughly assess the economic aspects of the urban aged women in relation to their income group.

Employment Status

Generally, the employment status of a person is considered to be the strongest factor in determining ones economic condition, all over the world. But, for an Indian aged woman, employment status may not be a true indicator of her economic condition. Because, out of those working, many remain involved in informal employment like helping the family business. Though working, they do not get regular wages or salary. And, for those who are not employed, the employment status of the spouse and/or children determines their economic conditions. To be specific, it can be stated that the higher the employment status of spouse (and/or children), the better may be the economic condition of an aged woman. Obviously, it is not only the employment status of the aged woman herself but also that of her spouse and children, which together determine her economic condition. No doubt, the employment status plays an important role in determining the economic condition, but many a time, the economic condition becomes instrumental in deciding the employment status. This fact becomes clear from our findings.

The majority of 69 per cent of sampled respondents had never been in any kind of job/occupation. The remaining 18 per cent of them were retired, and only 13 per cent were in job (see Table 3.12).

Table 3.12
Employment Status and Income Group

Employment Status	*Income Group*			*All*
	Lower	*Middle*	*Higher*	
Never employed	31	65	60	156
% within income group	(41.3)	(86.7)	(80.0)	(69.3)
Retired	18	9	13	40
% within income group	(24.0)	(12.0)	(17.3)	(17.7)
Presently employed	26	1	2	29
% within income group	(34.7)	(1.3)	(2.7)	(12.9)
All	75	75	75	225
% within income group	(100.0)	(100.0)	(100.0)	(100.0)

Pearson chi-square Value = 57.287 at df = 4; Asymp. sig. (2-sided) = 0.000

In the National Sample Survey (1991), about two-thirds of the elderly females was stated to be fully dependent in economic terms, which might be due to invisible household economic activity. The residential background did not make a striking difference in this regard. In all, 86 per cent of the urban females were fully dependent, 5 per cent were partially dependent and the remaining were independent (Rajan et al., 2000).

However, an extremely high association was found between the employment status and income group. Our data show that the lower the income group; the higher is the percentage of those engaged in waged/salaried jobs or some occupations. And, in the middle and the higher income groups, the percentage of such employed/salaried respondents is negligible (see Table 3.12).

Consequently, the urban aged women of the lower income group have to work because of their livelihood concerns. Because of illiteracy, lack of skills and resources, they have to engage themselves in low paying jobs. The analysis shows that the only working woman of the middle income group was involved in teaching profession. The limited proportion of the aged women among the higher income group was involved in jobs like teaching and *batik* business. But, the working aged women of the lower income group were employed in the low-paid jobs like that of house maid (9%), home nurse (1%), factory worker (7%) and piece rate worker (4%) or were involved in small-scale individual or family business like laundry, press, dairy, fruit or vegetable selling (13%).

Similarly, Rajan et al. (2000) also concluded that despite the difficulties in their daily life, the elderly persons in India continue to work after 60 years of age. That the aged women, especially those residing in urban areas, are the most dependent (Dandekar, 1993). And that the financial worries are related to social class.

Monthly Income from Self-Employment/Occupation

Most of the respondents, who had been employed (13%), belonged to the lower income group and were earning less than Rs 2,000 per month.

Monthly Income from Different Sources

This monthly income basically refers to the money the aged women monthly get and enjoy control over it. It includes the monthly income of these women from all sources including their own earnings, contributions from their children, spouses, etc. The data clearly indicate that the individual earnings of the aged women have little to do with their monthly income from all sources (see Table 3.13).

It is noted that 15 per cent aged women had no income as such as they had been totally dependent on their families. Amongst the aged women of the lower, the middle and the higher income group, 64 per cent, 24 per cent and 8 per cent respectively were

Table 3.13
Monthly Income from All Sources and Income Group of the Urban Aged Women

Monthly Income from All Sources (Rs)	*Income Group*			*All*
	Lower	*Middle*	*Higher*	
Nil	13	7	13	33
% within income group	(17.3)	(9.3)	(17.3)	(14.7)
% out of grand total	(5.8)	(3.1)	(5.8)	(14.7)
1–1,000	24	9	2	35
% within income group	(32.0)	(12.0)	(2.7)	(15.6)
% out of grand total	(10.7)	(4.0)	(0.9)	(15.6)
1,001–2,000	24	9	4	37
% within income group	(32.0)	(12.0)	(5.3)	(16.4)
% out of grand total	(10.7)	(4.0)	(1.8)	(16.4)
2,001–4,000	10	18	6	34
% within income group	(13.3)	(24.0)	(8.0)	(15.1)
% out of grand total	(4.4)	(8.0)	(2.7)	(15.1)
4,001–10,000	4	19	12	35
% within income group	(5.3)	(25.3)	(16.0)	(15.6)
% out of grand total	(1.8)	(8.4)	(5.3)	(15.6)
10,001–20,000		13	14	27
% within income group		(17.3)	(18.7)	(12.0)
% out of grand total		(5.8)	(6.2)	(12.0)
20,001–46,000	—	—	24	24
% within income group			(32.0)	(10.7)
% out of grand total			(10.7)	(10.7)
All	75	75	75	225
% within income group	(100.0)	(100.0)	(100.0)	(100.0)
% out of Grand Total	(33.3)	(33.3)	(33.3)	(100.0)

having a monthly income of less than Rs 2,000. Out of those getting Rs 2,001–10,000 per month, a majority of 49 per cent was from the middle income group, followed by 24 per cent from the higher income group and 19 per cent from the lower income group. About 17–19 per cent of aged women from the middle and higher income group had been getting Rs 10,001–20,000 per month. And, approximately one-third of the respondents of the higher income group were getting Rs 20,000–46,000 per month from all of their sources.

From the analysis, it is emerged that the employment status of the aged women cannot be considered as the sole indicator of their economic status. And that most of the women, who were employed, belonged to the lower income group and were getting comparatively a smaller amount of money per month (from all the sources) compared to what their unemployed counterparts were getting. Also, a considerable percentage of the middle and the higher income group were having an income of Rs 10,001–46,000 per month, though only one respondent of the middle and only two respondents of the higher income group were employed.

Sources of Income

These aged women were getting almost a fixed amount per month from their spouses and/or children or they themselves were earning. Thus, the main sources of income/subsistence were that of their: spouses (30%), children (22%) and self (21%). About 14 per cent respondents had no income as such. They used to get no money to be handled. They were co-residing with their families/children and were just getting their basic or other needs fulfilled through them. Rent and agriculture proved to be the main sources of income for 9 per cent respondents while the remaining 4 per cent were dependent on the interest of their fixed deposits (see Table 3.14). About half of the respondents had just one source of income while only 13 per cent respondents had three or more sources of income (see Table 3.15).

Bambawale (1996) also found that 44 per cent of the aged women were dependent on their husbands, 14 per cent on their children and 18 per cent on their relatives while 23 per cent were independent.

The Ageing Survey (1993) reported multiple means of subsistence, and the prominent among them were: current work (29%), support by children elsewhere and not residing with them (22%) and dividends from past work such as pension (17%). Very few elderly females were found to be supported by relatives (2%), others (2%) and charitable organizations (1%) (Rajan and James, 2000).

The analysis of our data highlights that in the lower income group, a significant number of 44 per cent of the urban aged women was dependent mainly on own earnings, followed by 17

Table 3.14
Main Source of Income/Subsistence and Income Group

Main Source of Income	*Income Group*			*All*
	Lower	*Middle*	*Higher*	
Occupation (self)	33	7	7	47
% within income group	(44.0)	(9.3)	(9.3)	(20.9)
% out of grand total	(14.7)	(3.1)	(3.1)	(20.9)
Occupation (spouse)	12	28	28	68
% within income group	(16.0)	(37.3)	(37.3)	(30.2)
% out of grand total	(5.3)	(12.4)	(12.4)	(30.2)
Children	13	20	16	49
% within income group	(17.3)	(26.7)	(21.3)	(21.8)
% out of grand total	(5.8)	(8.9)	(7.1)	(21.8)
Interest on F.D.	1	2	6	9
% within income group	(1.3)	(2.7)	(8.0)	(4.0)
% out of grand total	(0.4)	(0.9)	(2.7)	(4.0)
Rent/Agriculture, etc.	3	12	6	21
% within income group	(4.0)	(16.0)	(8.0)	(9.3)
% out of grand total	(1.3)	(5.3)	(2.7)	(9.3)
Co-residing with family/children; No income as such	13	6	12	31
% within income group	(17.3)	(8.0)	(16.0)	(13.8)
% out of grand total	(5.8)	(2.7)	(5.3)	(13.8)
All	75	75	75	225
% within income group	(100.0)	(100.0)	(100.0)	(100.0)
% out of grand total	(33.3)	(33.3)	(33.3)	(100.0)

Pearson Chi-square value = 51.246 at df = 10; Asymp. sig. (2-sided) = .000

Note: White in first five cases aged women get some money regularly to handle it of their own, in the last case as mentioned in S.N. 6, they get no money as such. They just get their needs and requirements fulfilled by the families/children.

per cent and 16 per cent respondents being dependent on their children and spouses respectively. As is obvious, since the lower income group is characterized by less of savings and property, only a few respondents (5%) of this income group had rent/agriculture or interest on fixed deposits as the main source/s of their income. However, in the middle and the higher income groups, almost similar trends were observed regarding the main source of income. Spouses serve as the main source of income for the majority,

Table 3.15
Number of Sources of Monthly Income and Income Group

Number of Sources of Income	*Income Group*			*All*
	Lower	*Middle*	*Higher*	
One	46	45	25	116
% within income group	(61.3)	(60.0)	(33.3)	(51.6)
% out of grand total	(20.4)	(20.0)	(11.1)	(51.6)
Two	23	24	32	79
% within income group	(30.7)	(32.0)	(42.7)	(35.1)
% out of grand total	(10.2)	(10.7)	(14.2)	(35.1)
Three or more	6	6	18	30
% within income group	(8.0)	(8.0)	(24.0)	(13.3)
% out of grand total	(2.7)	(2.7)	(8.0)	(13.3)
All	75	75	75	225
% within income group	(100.0)	(100.0)	(100.0)	(100.0)
% out of grand total	(33.3)	(33.3)	(33.3)	(100.0)

Pearson Chi-square value = 18.707 at df=4, Asymp. sig. (2-sided) = 0.001

followed by the children and they themselves. Savings and property were reported as the main sources of income by 19 per cent and 16 per cent respondents of the middle and the higher income group respectively.

Hence the spouses, children or family members serve as the most prominent sources of income/means of subsistence for the urban aged women in India. Comparatively, a smaller proportion of them (say 20–30%) depends on their current work. The 'main source of income' of the urban aged women has some links with their 'income group' also. And, this association is strong. Also 'the number of sources of income' and the 'income group' are positively associated. Expectedly, the higher income group respondents have more sources of income compared to those belonging to the comparatively lower income groups.

Savings and Property

Income and savings are, generally, thought to be positively correlated. The aged (women included) who have saved enough for their later days or invested that on their children, landed property or cash savings will naturally have adequate financial security in old age. Since the persons who are proposed to inherit the property will look after their aged well. Those who fail to save for their old age in any of these forms will have difficulty and will have to continue to toil in life, till the end. Having all this in consideration, an enquiry was also made about the savings and the property of the respondents.

Savings

It is found that about 60 per cent of the respondents had no savings or no bank accounts. The proportion of about 7 per cent and 2 per cent respondents from the lower and the middle groups had small savings of Rs 100–5,000. No respondent of the higher income group was found to make such a small investment. Rather, a negligible proportion of the lower income group and a limited proportion (2–6%) of the middle and the higher income groups had reportedly deposited Rs 1–7 lakh. A very small fraction of the

Table 3.16

Bank Savings and Income Group

Bank Savings (Rs)	*Income Group*			*All*
	Lower	*Middle*	*Higher*	
Nil (no bank account)	49	44	41	134
% out of grand total	(21.8)	(19.6)	(18.2)	(59.6)
100–5,000	17	4	—	21
% out of grand total	(7.6)	(1.8)		(9.3)
5,001–25,000	6	13	9	28
% out of grand total	(2.7)	(5.8)	(4.0)	(12.4)
25,001–1,00,000	2	7	7	16
% out of grand total	(0.9)	(3.1)	(3.1)	(7.1)
1,00,000–7,00,000	1	5	14	20
% out of grand total	(0.4)	(2.2)	(6.2)	(8.9)
Unwilling to disclose	—	2	4	6
% out of grand total		(0.9)	(1.8)	(2.7)
All	75	75	75	225
% out of grand total	(33.3)	(33.3)	(33.3)	(100.0)

Pearson Chi-square value = 46.371 at df=10; Asymp. Sig. (2-sided) = 0.000

respondents from the middle and the higher income group denied disclosing the details of their bank savings, but not even a single respondent of the lower income group did so. It is clear that the higher the income group, the more had been the savings of the urban aged women, and vice versa (see Table 3.16).

Property

Estimated Value of the Property

About 25 per cent of the sampled respondents had no property, 37 per cent had property worth less than Rs 5 lakh, and 31 per cent had property worth Rs 5–20 lakh. The remaining 7 per cent respondents who belonged either to the middle or the higher income group only, had property worth more than Rs 21 lakh (see Table 3.17). The higher the income group, the more is the proportion of the respondents that own familial property; and the higher had been the estimated value of the property owned by the family.

Table 3.17

Estimated Value of Family Owned Property and Income Group

Estimated Value of Property (Rs in lakh)	*Income Group*			*All*
	Lower	*Middle*	*Higher*	
N.A. (no property)	21	18	17	56
% within income group	(28.0)	(24.0)	(22.7)	(24.9)
Less than 5 lakh	49	27	7	83
% within income group	(65.3)	(36.0)	(9.3)	(36.9)
5–10 lakh	3	23	25	51
% within income group	(4.0)	(30.7)	(33.3)	(22.7)
11–20 lakh	2	3	13	18
% within income group	(2.7)	(4.0)	(17.3)	(8.0)
21–50 lakh	—	3	10	13
% within income group		(4.0)	(13.3)	(5.8)
51+ lakh	—	1	3	4
% within income group		(1.3)	(4.0)	(1.8)
All	75	75	75	225
% within income group	(100.0)	(100.0)	(100.0)	(100.0)

If we consider the property as an indicator of social security, it may well be concluded that the higher income group respondents enjoy greater social security as compared to their counterparts belonging to the comparatively lower income groups, and vice versa.

Type of the Property

The 'house' was the preferred type of property of the lower income group (71% owned a house), followed by the middle (60%) and the higher income group (56%). The higher income group respondents (21%) had a greater orientation towards business—property, for example, shops and vehicles, compared to those of the middle (16%) and the lower income group (1%) (see Table 3.18).

Table 3.18

Family Owned Property and Income Group

Type of Property	*Income Group*			*All*
	Lower	*Middle*	*Higher*	
No property	21	18	17	56
% within income group	(28.0)	(24.0)	(22.7)	(24.9)
% out of grand total	(9.3)	(8.0)	(7.6)	(24.9)
House	52	40	18	110
% within income group	(69.3)	(53.3)	(24.0)	(48.9)
% out of grand total	(23.1)	(17.8)	(8.0)	(48.9)
House and land/plot	1	5	24	30
% within income group	(1.3)	(6.7)	(32.0)	(13.3)
% out of grand total	(0.4)	(2.2)	(10.7)	(13.3)
Business property (shops,	1	12	16	29
vehicles, etc.)	(1.3)	(16.0)	(21.3)	(12.9)
% within income group	(0.4)	(5.3)	(7.1)	(12.9)
% out of grand total				
All	75	75	75	225
% within income group	(100.0)	(100.0)	(100.0)	(100.0)
% out of grand total	(33.3)	(33.3)	(33.3)	(100.0)

According to 1995–96 data (NSS 52nd round), about 60 per cent of the aged persons in our country were owners of property, with women owning less property (44%) than men (77%). Also, ownership of financial assets was larger among the aged males (70%) than the aged females (38%) (Sundari and Geetha, 1999). More or less similar trends were observed in our sampling. The 40 per cent urban aged women had saved money in bank accounts and 38 per cent owned some property in their names.

Monthly Expenditure

There may be cases where those having good amount of income and big assets—savings and property, spend a little in their day-to-day life. Hence, monthly expenditure may prove to be a truer indicator of living standard of the people as compared to their income and savings. Following is an attempt to analyse the pattern of monthly household expenditure of the urban aged women.

Total Expenditure of the Household

The average monthly expenditure of the lower income group was Rs 2,229 with a standard deviation of 1,593 and a range of Rs 6,500. For the middle income group, the average monthly expenditure was Rs 5,965 with a standard deviation of 3,085 and a range of Rs 19,000. On the extreme end, the average monthly expenditure of the higher income group was Rs 17,041 with a standard deviation of 9,923 and a range of Rs 38,000 (see Table 3.19). The point of interest is that 'the higher the income group, the higher had been the monthly household expenditure of the respondents'; and vice versa.

Expenditure on Food, Clothing, Medicine, Maintenance and Entertainment

In the lower income group, 32 per cent respondents were spending Rs 350–1,000 per month on food of the household members (see Table 3.20). Exactly one-third respondents were spending in between Rs 1,001–2,000 and about one-fourth were spending Rs 2,001–5,000 per month. In the middle income group, about one-fourth of the respondents was spending Rs 1,001–2,000 on food, while 53 per cent had a monthly expenditure of Rs 2,001–5,000. And, the expenditure of about one-tenth of the

Table 3.19
Total Monthly Expenditure and Income Group

Total Monthly Expenditure of Household (Rs)	*Income Group*			*All*
	Lower	*Middle*	*Higher*	
	Mean=2 229 S.D.=15 93	*Mean=5965 S.D.=3085*	*Mean=17041S. D.=9923*	*Mean=8411.7S. D.=8732*
Do not know	8	6	9	23
%within income group	(10.7)	(8.0)	(12.0)	(10.2)
% out of grand total	(3.6)	(2.7)	(4.0)	(10.2)
500–2,000	32	–	–	32
% within income group	(42.7)			(14.2)
% out of grand total	(14.2)			(14.2)
2,001–4,000	22	11	–	33
% within income group	(29.3)	(14.7)		(14.7)
% out of grand total	(9.8)	(4.9)		(14.7)
4,001–7,000	13	30	3	46
% within income group	(17.3)	(40.0)	(4.0)	(20.4)
% out of grand total	(5.8)	(13.3)	(1.3)	(20.4)
7,001–15,000	–	27	19	46
% within income group		(36.0)	(25.3)	(20.4)
% out of grand total		(12.0)	(8.4)	(20.4)
15,001–21,000	–	1	21	22
% within income group		(1.3)	(28.0)	(9.8)
% out of grand total		(0.4)	(9.3)	(9.8)
21,001–42,000	–	–	23	23
% within income group			(30.7)	(10.2)
% out of grand total			(10.2)	(10.2)
All	75	75	75	225
% within income group	(100.0)	(100.0)	(100.0)	(100.0)
% out of grand total	(33.3)	(33.3)	(33.3)	(100.0)

Pearson Chi-square value = 220.273; df = 12; Asymp. sig. (2-sided) = 0.000

respondents ranged from Rs 5,001–8,000. In the higher income group, the monthly expenditure on food, of about one-fourth respondents ranged from Rs 2,001–5,000. And for the rest others, it was Rs 5,001–14,000 (see Table 3.20).

Table: 3.20

Monthly Household Expenditure on Food and Clothes and Income Group

Total Monthly Expenditure On Food (Rs)	*Income Group*																		*All Total of Col. 5, 11 & 18 (% out of 225)*
	Lower					*Middle*						*Higher*							
	Monthly Expenditure on Clothes					*Monthly Expenditure on Clothes*						*Monthly Expenditure on Clothes*							
	(1) (Nil)	*(2) 50-500*	*(3) 501-2000*	*(4) Don't Know*	*(5) All*	*(6) (Nil)*	*(7) 50-500*	*(8) 501-2000*	*(9) 2001-5000*	*(10) Don't Know*	*(11) All*	*(12) Nil*	*(13) 50-500*	*(14) 501-2000*	*(15) 2001-5000*	*(16) 5001-12000*	*(17) Don't Know*	*(18) All*	
Do not know *	–	–	–	8	8	–	–	1	–	6	7	3	–	–	–	–	6	9	24
% within income group				(10.7)	(10.7)			(1.3)		(8.0)	(9.3)	(4.0)					(8.0)	(12.0)	(10.7)
350–1000	17	7	–	–	24	–	1	–	–	–	1	–	–	–	–	–	–	–	25
% within income group	(22.7)	(9.3)			(32.0)		(1.3)				(1.3)								(11.1)
1001–2000	13	11	1	–	25	2	7	8	2	–	19	–	–	–	–	–	–	–	44
% within income group	(17.3)	(14.7)	(1.3)		(33.3)	(2.6)	(9.3)	(10.7)	(2.7)		(25.3)								(19.6)
2001–5000	6	4	8	–	18	1	5	34	–	–	40	–	–	7	9	1	1	18	76
% within income group	(8.0)	(5.3)	(10.7)		(24.0)	(1.3)	(6.7)	(45.3)			(53.3)			(9.3)	(12.0)	(1.3)	(1.3)	(24.0)	(33.8)

Cont'd...

Cont'd...

5001–8000 % within income group	—	—	—	—	—	1 (1.3)	2 (2.7)	4 (5.3)	—	1 (1.3)	8 (10.7)	1 (1.3)	1 (1.3)	3 (4.0)	15 (20.0)	8 (10.7)	—	28 (37.3)	36 (16.0)
8001–14000 % within income group	—	—	—	—	—	—	—	—	—	—	—	3 (4.0)	—	—	7 (9.3)	10 (13.3)	—	20 (26.7)	20 (8.9)
All % within income group % out of Grand Total	36 (18.0)* (16.0)*	22 (29.3) (9.8)	9 (12.0) (4.0)	8 (10.7) (3.6)	75 (100.0 (33.3)	4 (5.3) (1.8)	15 (20.0) (6.7)	47 (62.7) (20.9)	2 (2.7 (0.9)	7 (9.3) (3.1)	75 (100.0) (33.3)	7 (9.3) (3.1)	1 (1.3) (0.4)	10 (13.3) (4.4)	31 (41.3) (13.8)	19 (25.3) (8.4)	7 (9.3) (3.1)	75 (100.0) (33.3)	225 (100.0) (100.0)

* Totally Dependent.

On clothes, about half (48%) of the lower income group respondents had not been expending any amount. These respondents were managing with old, donated or gifted clothes only. About one-third were spending less than Rs 500 per month. And, only 12 per cent respondents had been spending more than Rs 500 per month on clothes. Most of the middle income group households (63%) were spending Rs 501–2,000 per month. And, about one-fifth had a monthly expenditure of Rs 50–501. Only negligible households of this middle income group reported a monthly expenditure of Rs 2,001–5,000. In the higher income group, the range of monthly household expenditure for the two-third majority (67%) was Rs 2,001–12,000. Only 9 per cent of the respondents were such who had not been spending any amount on clothes (see Table 3.20).

It is clear that the lower income group spends a major fraction of their income on food and comparatively a much smaller fraction on clothes. The difference in the amount spent on these two items, food and clothes, is found to decrease with an increase in the level of the income group.

While the lower income group had been spending an average of Rs 1,479 on food, this amount was Rs 3,132 (just double) and Rs 6,232 (four times) in the middle and the higher income group respectively. On clothes, the lower income group had an average monthly expenditure of just Rs 190 compared to Rs 884 and Rs 3640 spent by the middle and the higher income group households. The lower income group had been spending a greater amount on the medicines (Rs 209 per month) compared to that spent on clothes (Rs 190 per month), but reverse was the case with the middle and the higher income group. It is evident that almost all the income of the lower income group is spent on the basic necessities, which include food, clothing, medicine and maintenance (electricity, water, etc.). And that may be the reason why the lower income group households had been spending, on an average, only a meagre amount of Rs 28 per month on entertainment. Compared to this, Rs 253 was the average monthly expenditure on

Table 3.21

Mean, Standard Deviation and Range of Monthly Expenditure on Different Items and Income Group

Items	*Income Group (No. of Respondents) (Monthly Expenditure)*			*All (225) (Monthly Expenditure in Rs)*
	Lower (75)[1]	*Middle (75)*	*Higher (75)*	
Food	Mean = Rs 1,479 (66.35%)[2] S.D. = 986 Range = 4,000 Minimum = Rs 350	Mean = Rs 3,132 (52.5%) S.D. = 1769 Range = 7,000 Minimum = Rs 350	Mean = Rs 6,232 (36.57%) S.D. = 3424 Range = 12,000 Minimum = Rs 2,001	Mean = Rs 3,614 (42.96%) S.D. = 3,021 Range—14,000 Minimum = Rs 350
Clothing	Mean = Rs 190 (8.52%) S.D. = 321 Range = 1,500 Minimum = 0	Mean = Rs 884 (14.8%) S.D. = 649 Range = 3,000 Minimum = 0	Mean = Rs 3,640 (21.36%) S.D. = 2,736 Range = 12,000 Minimum = 0	Mean = Rs ,1571 (18.68%) S.D. = 2,208 Range = 12,000 Minimum = 0
Medical	Mean = Rs 209 (9.38%) S.D. = 247 Range = 1,000 Minimum = 0	Mean = Rs 485 (8.13%) S.D. = 469 Range = 2,500 Minimum = 0	Mean = Rs 1,659 (9.74%) S.D. = 1,526 Range = 7,000 Minimum = 0	Mean = Rs . 784 (9.32%) S.D. = 1122 Range = 7,000 Minimum = 0
Maintenance	Mean = Rs 179 (8.03%) S.D. = 165 Range = 1,000 Minimum = Rs 50	Mean = Rs 709 (11.89%) S.D. = 321 Range = 1,250 Minimum =Rs 80	Mean = Rs 2,228 (13.07%) S.D. = 1,630 Range = 8,000 Minimum = Rs 500	Mean = Rs 1,039 (12.35%) S.D. = 1,295 Range = 10,000 Minimum = Rs 50

Cont'd...

Cont'd...

Entertainment	Mean = Rs 28 (1.26%) S.D. = 165 Range = 1,000 Minimum = 0	Mean = Rs 253 (4.24%) S.D. = 274 Range = 1,400 Minimum = 0	Mean = Rs 2,955 (17.34%) S.D. = 3,448 Range = 15,000 Minimum = 0	Mean = Rs 1,079 (12.83%) S.D. = 2,394 Range = 15,000 Minimum = 0
All	Mean = Rs 2,229 (100%) S.D. = 1,593 Range = 6,500 Minimum = Rs 500	Mean = Rs 5,965 (100%) S.D. = 3,085 Range = 19,000 Minimum = Rs 1,500	Mean = Rs 17,041 (100%) S.D. = 9,923 Range = 38,000 Minimum = Rs 4,000	Mean = Rs 8,412 (100%) S.D. = 8,732 Range = 41,500 Minimum = Rs 500

Note: 1. No. of respondents. 2. Percentage out of total expenditure within income group.

Note: To calculate the above measures, the 'do not know' responses were not taken into account.

entertainment of the middle income group household. And for the higher income group households, it was Rs 2,955 (see Table 3.21).

The proportion (of the total expenditure) spent on different items was also analysed so as to compare the expenditure pattern of the three income groups. And it was found that about 66 per cent, 53 per cent and 37 per cent of the monthly expenditure had been spent on food by the lower, the middle and the higher income group households respectively. However, the proportion spent on clothes by the same was 9 per cent, 15 per cent and 21 per cent respectively. On medicine and maintenance, the three income groups had been spending approximately the same proportion (8–10% and 8–13% respectively) of their total expenditure. However, 'entertainment' was the item about which striking differences in expenditure could be observed. Whereas the higher income group respondents were spending a significant proportion of 17 per cent on entertainment, the middle and the lower income group respondents had been spending just 4 per cent and 1 per cent respectively.

It is clear that the lower income group has to spend the major proportion of the monthly income on the basic necessities—food, medicine and maintenance. And they are left with only a little money to be spent on clothes and entertainment. The middle income group has a reasonable amount to spend on clothes and entertainment. But they prefer to spend more on clothes (18% of total income) compared to that on entertainment (4%). The higher income group spends a reasonably good proportion on both—clothes (21%) and entertainment (17%).

Satisfaction from Food, Clothing, Medicine and Entertainment

The urban aged women who had never been in any kind of employment, were most satisfied, followed by the 'retired' and the 'currently working' aged women respectively. This is found true for all the items mentioned above (see Table 3.22).

About 22–25 per cent respondents of the lower income group expressed their dissatisfaction with the various items, viz., food, clothing, medicine and entertainment. As far as the middle income group was concerned, all the respondents were satisfied with the

Table 3.22

Employment Status and Satisfaction about Various Issues/Items

Employm ent Status	*Issues/Items*														
	Fooding			*Clothing*			*Medical Aid*			*Entertainment*			*Wants held up due to scracity of money*		
	Satis-fied	*Dissatis-fied*	*Total*	*Satis-fied*	*Dissat-isfied*	*Total*	*Satis-fied*	*Dissat-isfied*	*Total*	*Satis-fied*	*Dissat-isfied*	*Total*	*No*	*Yes*	*Total*
Never employed	148 (94.9)[1] (65.8)[2]	8 (5.1) (3.6)	156 (100.0) (69.3)	150 (96.2) (66.7)	6 (3.8) (2.7)	156 (100.0) (69.3)	145 (92.9) (64.4)	11 (7.1) (4.9)	156 (100.0) (69.3)	144 (92.3) (62.2)	12 (7.7) (5.3)	156 (100.0) (69.3)	131 (84.0) (58.2)	25 (16.0) (11.1)	156 (100.0) (69.3)
Retired	35 (89.7) (15.6)	4 (10.3) (1.8)	39 (100.0) (17.3)	36 (92.3) (16.0)	3 (7.7) (1.3)	39 (100.0) (17.3)	34 (87.2) (15.1)	5 (12.8) (2.2)	39 (100.0) (17.3)	36 (92.3) (16.0)	3 (7.7) (1.3)	39 (100.0) (17.3)	24 (61.5) (10.7)	15 (38.5) (6.7)	39 (100.0) (17.3)
Presently employed	23 (76.7) (10.2)	7 (23.3) (3.1)	30 (100.0) (13.3)	21 (70.0) (9.3)	9 (30.0) (4.0)	30 (100.0) (13.3)	22 (73.3) (9.8)	8 (26.7) (3.6)	30 (100.0) (13.3)	24 (80.0) (10.7)	6 (20.0) (2.7)	30 (100.0) (13.3)	14 (46.7) (6.2)	16 (53.3) (7.1)	30 (100.0) (13.3)
Total	206 (91.6) (91.6)	19 (8.4) (8.4)	225 (100.0) (100.0)	207 (92.0) (92.0)	18 (8.0) (8.0)	225 (100.0) (100.0)	201 (89.3) (89.3)	24 (10.7) (10.7)	225 (100.0) (100.0)	204 (90.7) (90.7)	21 (9.3) (9.3)	225 (100.0) (100.0)	169 (75.1) (75.1)	56 (24.9) (24.9)	225 (100.0) (100.0)
Pearson Chi-square	Value = 10.986 df = 2 Asymp sig. (2-sided) = .004			Value = 23.390 df = 2 Asymp sig. (2-sided) = .000			Value = 10.389 df = 2 Asymp. sig. (2-sided) = .006			Value = 24.202 df = 2 Asymp. sig. (2-sided) = .000			Value = 23.382 df = 2 Asymp. sig.(2-sided) = 000		

Note: 1. Percentage within employment status. 2. Percentage out of grand total

Table 3.23

Income Group and Satisfaction about Various Issues/Items

Income Group	*Opinion About Various Issues*											
	Food			*Clothing*			*Medical Aid*			*Entertainment*		
	Satis-factory	*Dis-satisfactory*	*Total*	*Satis-factory*	*Dis-Satisfactory*	*Total*	*Satis-factory*	*Dis-satisfactory*	*Total*	*Satis-factory*	*Dis-satisfactory*	*Total*
Lower	57 (76.0)[1] (25.3)[2]	18 (24.0) (8.0)	75 (100.0) (33.3)	58 (77.3) (25.8)	17 (22.7) (7.6)	75 (100.0) (33.3)	56 (74.7) (24.9)	19 (25.3) (8.4)	75 (100.0) (33.3)	57 (86.0) (25.4)	18 (24.0) (8.0)	100 (100.0) (33.3)
Middle	75 (100.0) (33.3)	—	75 (100.0) (33.3)	75 (100.0) (33.3)	—	75 (100.0) (33.3)	73 (97.3) (32.4)	2 (2.7) (0.9)	75 (100.0) (33.3)	74 (98.7) (32.9)	1 (1.3) (0.4)	75 (100.0) (33.3)
Higher	74 (98.7) (32.9)	1 (1.3) (0.4)	75 (100.0) (33.3)	74 (98.7) (32.9)	1 (1.3) (0.4)	75 (100.0) (33.3)	72 (96.0) (32.0)	3 (4.0) (1.3)	75 (100.0) (33.3)	73 (97.3) (32.4)	2 (2.7) (0.9)	75 (100.0) (33.3)
Total	206 (91.6) (91.6)	19 (8.4) (8.4)	225 (100.0) (100.0)	207 (92.0) (92.0)	18 (8.0) (8.0)	225 (100.0) (100.0)	201 (89.3) (89.3)	24 (10.7) (10.7)	225 (100.0) (100.0)	204 (90.7) (90.7)	21 (9.3) (9.3)	225 (100.0) (100.0)
Pearson chi-square →	Value = 35.296 df = 2 Asymp sig. (2-sided) = .000			Value = 32.971 df = 2 Asymp sig. (2-sided) = .000			Value = 25.466 df = 2 Asymp sig. (2-sided) = .000			Value = 28.676 df = 2 Asymp sig. (2-sided) = .000		

Note: 1. Percentage within income group. 2. Percentage out of grand total (225).

food and the clothes that had been made available to them. And, a very limited proportion of the respondents expressed their dissatisfaction with the entertainment facilities and the medical aid. In the higher income group, the proportion of the dissatisfied respondents with different issues ranged just from 1 to 4 per cent only. The trends as cited above prove that the higher the income group, the greater had been the satisfaction level of the urban aged women; and vice versa (see Table 3.23).

Monetary Constraints and Requirements

The aged women of the lower income group were more prone to money constraints compared to their counterparts belonging to the middle and the higher income group respectively (see Table 3.24). About 57 per cent of the lower income group respondents reported that some of their requirements were not fulfilled due to money constraints, but such respondents constituted just 8 per cent in the middle and the higher income group each.

These requirements, as reported by the aged women, relate to proper food, medical aid, daughter/s' marriage, proper accommodation, building a house and the expenditure on religious discourses like *pooja, bhajan and kirtan.* Some of the respondents also expressed the wish to furnish their houses or offering gifts to relatives.

The amount expected to fulfil the requirements was also found to be influenced by the income groups of the respondents. Most of the lower income group respondents had wished for a small monthly income in addition to what they already had. To be specific, 28 per cent respondents of the lower income group wished for an additional monthly income of Rs 250–2,000. But, almost all of those belonging to the middle and the higher income group had wished for comparatively a bigger lump sum amount (Rs 1 lakh to 7 lakh).

Probability/Future Plans to Fulfil the Requirements

The respondents were also asked about the probability of and the plans for their requirements to be fulfilled. The lower income group was found to be more pessimistic and disheartened since most of the aged women (30%) saw no probability of their

Table 3.24

Monetary Constraints and Requirements, Proposals to Fulfil the Requirements and the Income Group

Money required to fulfil the requirements	*Income Group*															*Total (16) (Total of Columns 5, 10 & 15)*
	Lower					*Middle*					*Higher*					
	Proposals to Meet the Wants					*Proposals to Meet the Wants*					*Proposals to Meet the Wants*					
	(1) N.A.[1]	*(2) Not Possible*[2]	*(3) No Plans*[3]	*(4) Specific Plans*[4]	*(5) Total*	*(6) N.A.*	*(7) Not Possible*	*(8) No Plans*	*(9) Specific Plans*	*(10) Total*	*(11) N.A.*	*(12) Not Possible*	*(13) No Plans*	*(14) Specific Plans*	*(15) Total*	
No such wants	32	–	–	–	32	69	–	–	–	69	69	–	–	–	69	170
% within income group	(42.7)*				(42.7)	(92.0)				(92.0)	(92.0)				(92.0)	(75.6)
Rs 250–500 per month	–	5	5	–	10	–	–	–	–	–	–	–	–	–	–	10
% within income group		(6.7)	(6.7)		(13.3)											(4.4)
Rs 501–2000 per month	–	7	3	1	11	–	–	–	1	1	–	–	–	–	–	12
% within income group		(9.3)	(4.0)	(1.3)	(14.7)				(1.3)	(1.3)						(5.3)

Cont'd...

Cont'd...

Rs 20,000–75,000 Lump sum	—	1	2	—	3	—	—	—	—	—	—	—	—	—	—	3
% within income group		(1.3)	(2.7)		(4.0)											(1.3)
Rs 1–9 lakh.	—	2	3	—	5	—	—	2	—	2	—	—	—	4	4	11
% within income group		(2.7)	(4.0)		(6.7)			(2.7)		(2.7)				(5.3)	(5.3)	(4.9)
Can't Specify	—	7	2	5	14	—	—	1	2	3	—	1	—	1	2	19
% within income group		(9.3)	(2.7)	(6.7)	(18.7)			(1.3)	(2.7)	(4.0)		(1.3)		(1.3)	(2.7)	(8.4)
Total	32	22	15	6	75	69	—	3	3	75	69	1	—	5	75	225
% within income group	(42.7)	(29.3)	(20.0)	(8.0)	(100.0)	(92.0)	—	(4.0)	(4.0)	(100)	(92.0)	(1.3)	—	(6.7)	(100.0)	(100.0)
% out of Grand Total (225)	(14.2)	(9.8)	(6.7)	(2.7)	33.3	(30.07)	—	(1.3)	(1.3)	(33.3)	(30.7)	(0.4)	—	(2.2)	(33.3)	(150.0)
Chi-Square Value			—			116.667 at df=6 ; Assump. Sign. .000					105.0 at df=4 ; Assump. Sign. .000					

Note: 1. Not applicable. 2. Not possible, beyond limits/capabilities. 3. No plan at present. 4. Yes, some specific plans are in hand.

requirements to be fulfilled. Compared to this, the higher and middle income groups appeared to be more hopeful. Out of those 8 per cent aged women of the higher income group who had complained of money constraints, only one respondent expressed her helplessness, and the remaining aged women were reportedly having some specific plans to overcome their money constraints. Among such (8%) respondents of the middle income group, no one was found to be totally pessimistic.

It is clear that economic resources of the urban aged women include a complex combination of their own earnings and income from different sources. Only 13 per cent of these women are currently working. An overwhelming majority of currently employed women belong to the lower income group and has been earning less than Rs 2,000 per month. The individual earnings of the urban aged women has very little to do with their monthly income from all sources—from spouse, children, investment, rent, etc. The majority of the lower income group respondents depend mainly on their own earning. But for majority of the middle and the higher income group respondents, the spouse and then children serve as the main sources of income. Also, the higher income group respondents have more sources of income, more savings and property compared to the comparatively lower income group respondents.

The lower income group has an average monthly household expenditure of Rs 2,200 compared to Rs 6,000 and Rs 17,000 of the middle and the higher income group respectively. Evidently, the lower income group households have to spend a major portion of their income on the basic necessities of life, and are left with only a little money to spend on entertainment. But, this is not the case with the middle and the higher income group households. The urban aged women who had never been in any kind of employment, are most satisfied, followed by the 'retired' and the 'currently working' aged women respectively. And, the higher the income group, the greater has been the satisfaction among the respondents. The lower income group respondents are more pessimistic, and see little hope in fulfilling their requirements, due to the lack of money, compared to those belonging to the middle and the higher income group respectively.

Examination of the personal profile and social and economic resource endowment of the urban aged women leads to the conclusion that there is a vicious cycle in which the lower income group respondents have been trapped. They comprised mainly of lower castes and are mostly illiterate. They have to take up jobs out of economic compulsions and remain unsatisfied with the amenities available to them. The middle income group respondents enjoy better social resources as compared to their counterparts belonging to the higher and the middle income groups respectively. The higher income group respondents, having better educational level and comprising mainly the higher castes, enjoy best of economic resources and report highest satisfaction about various amenities.

4

Health, Mobility and Leisure Time Activities

The aged women tend to be less healthy than their male counterparts. Their living conditions are not conducive to good health. Compared to their wealthier peers, they are more likely to be living alone, to have inadequate diets, to have lesser access to information about how to maintain their health and to have fewer physician contacts per year (Van Mering, O'Rand, 1981; Hooman and Kiyan, 1988). Since the aged women predominate among the elderly poor, women's health status, as compared to the menfolk, is more frequently harmed by the adverse conditions associated with poverty. In turn, the cost of poor health can deplete their limited resources. The health and resources have a direct bearing on their leisure time activities. Leisure time activities and involvement in social organizations provide an ample index of their lifestyles and attitude towards the life.

The scientists all over the world are thus engaged in researches to make ageing a healthy experience despite the many things that may go against it. The people become more susceptible to chronic diseases, physical disabilities and mental incapacities in their old age. Factors such as routine habits, leisure time practices, social interactions and social attitudes play a vital role in the physical and mental well-being of the aged. An analysis is required to be made about the factors which are responsible for the maintenance of good health and mobility. This chapter is an attempt in this direction. It will specifically deal with food and addiction, state of physical senses, diseases and health facilities. Also, the physical mobility, ability in household work and social interaction of the urban aged women will be analysed. Besides, attempts to study the day-to-day habits and leisure time activities of the urban aged women will also be undertaken.

Food

The aged women, specifically those belonging to the lower income group, suffer from malnutrition. Malnutrition affects not only their general health but makes them more susceptible to diseases and infection. Therefore, it is important that they ensure the intake of nutritious and balanced food. But often the aged women may not or cannot eat such food on account of poverty, ignorance or values and/or taboos attached to some of the foods in our society. In most of the Asian countries, food taboos are imposed on women and the custom is for men to eat first followed by boys, then girls and in the last the elderly women. There is little awareness of and importance given to the type of diet suitable for an ageing person. All cultures attach some values to foods, which are locally available. For example, certain food items are nutritive and rich in protein and vitamins, but may be less accessible due to the low purchasing power. Poverty is an important factor that prevents people from eating good and nutritious food especially, in case of the lower income group. As a result, the family may not have or get a rich and balanced food. The women in general, and the aged women in particular, become the worst victims of the above-described values or factors.

Food Habits

The urban aged women had been consuming the same food as prepared for the other members of their families. Milk, tea, pulses, vegetables and *chapati* were the items of daily consumption for most of them. In a limited frequency, fruits, rice and *paneer* were also being consumed. Butter and bread, an outcome of metropolitan living, was not very common among them. It may be because of the weak digestive power, high costs involved or being vegetarian that most of the aged women had been avoiding the consumption of egg and meat. The food items that should be preferred in old age owing to the debilitating conditions and systematic disorders had also been less preferred. Naturally, there seemed to be little awareness about the food suitable in old age. And that might be the reason why most of the aged women had been avoiding intake of soups, *rab*, *salad*, *khichri* (a preparation of rice and *moong* pulse) and curd (see Table 4.1).

Table 4.1

Frequency of Intake of the Daily Diet Items

Food Items	*Frequency of Intake*			*All*
	Rarely	*Sometimes*	*Often*	
Soup	149 (66.2)	38 (16.9)	38 (16.9)	225 (100.0)
Milk/Tea	9 (4.0)	22 (9.8)	194 (86.2)	225 (100.0)
Butter/Bread	126 (56.0)	72 (32.0)	27 (12.0)	225 (100.0)
Egg	177 (78.7)	11 (4.9)	37 (16.4)	225 (100.0)
Dal	1 (0.4)	35 (15.6)	189 (84.0)	225 (100.0)
Paneer	97 (43.1)	53 (23.6)	75 (33.3)	225 (100.0)
Meat	188 (83.6)	26 (11.6)	11 (4.9)	225 (100.0)
Rice	27 (12.0)	129 (57.3)	69 (30.7)	225 (100.0)
Fruits	28 (12.4)	70 (31.1)	127 (56.4)	225 (100.0)
Rab/Salad/Khichri/Curd	169 (75.1)	20 (8.9)	36 (16.0)	225 (100.0)

Note: The figures in the brackets show percentage.

Monthly Expenses on Food

The living arrangement of most of the urban aged women was such that it was found almost impossible to collect data on their individual monthly expenses on food. There were aged women who had no idea about even the monthly income or who were totally dependent on their families and had no income as such. So, to have an idea about their expenses on food, the only option left was to study their monthly family expenditure on food. Though not exact, it can give a fairly good idea about the general expenditure on food of the aged women.

Expenditure on and Satisfaction from Food Consumption

Since the expenditure on food has been discussed in chapter 3 in detail, the description, here, is mainly being focused on the satisfaction level. Nearly one-tenth of the total respondents were

Table 4.2

Family Expenditure on Food and Satisfaction Therefrom

Monthly Family Expenditure on Food (Rs)	*View*		*All*
	Dissatisfied	*Satisfied*	
Don't know	1	23	24
% within monthly expenditure group	(4.2)	(95.8)	(100.0)
% out of grand total	(0.4)	(10.2)	(10.7)
350–1,000	13	12	25
% within monthly expenditure group	(52.0)	(48.0)	(100.0)
% out of grand total	(5.8)	(5.3)	(11.1)
1,001–2,000	7	37	44
% within monthly expenditure group	(15.9)	(84.1)	(100.0)
% out of grand total	(3.1)	(16.4)	(19.6)
2,001–5,000	5	71	76
% within monthly expenditure group	(6.6)	(93.4)	(100.0)
% out of grand total	(2.2)	(31.6)	(33.8)
5,001–8,000	—	36	36
% within monthly expenditure group		(100.0)	(100.0)
% out of grand total		(16.0)	(16.0)
8,001–14,000	—	20	20
% within monthly expenditure group		(100.0)	(100.0)
% out of grand total		(8.9)	(8.9)
All	26	199	225
% within monthly expenditure group	(11.6)	(88.4)	(100.0)
% out of grand total	(11.6)	(88.4)	(100.0)

Pearson chi-square value = 51.269 at df = 5 Asymp. sig. (2-sided) = 0.000

dissatisfied about the food they had been consuming. All those who had been spending more than Rs 5,000 monthly on family's food, were found to be satisfied. It is obvious that the poor aged women belonging to the lower income group find it difficult to have food of their own choice (see Table 4.2).

The analysis shows that the levels of income and satisfaction about food have strong positive correlation. It is really disturbing to note that 5 per cent respondents did not get even satisfactory quantity of food. Most of these respondents belonged to the lower income group and comprised about 11 per cent of the group. It is disheartening to note that some of these respondents, instead of their preference for wheat flour, were compelled to use *makki* (maize corn) flour because of its lower cost. On the other hand, the negligible fraction of the middle and the higher income group respondents, who expressed dissatisfaction about the quantity of the food made available to them, had been deliberately served a little quantity of food by the family just on the health grounds.

All the aged women belonging to the higher income group expressed satisfaction about the quality of their food. But about 3 per cent of the aged women of the middle income group and 30 per cent aged women of the lower income group were dissatisfied with the quality of food they had been consuming. They were of the opinion that the food items are too costly, and hence, it was difficult to purchase all the required food ingredients. The vegetable, cooked once, had to be used for two times. Those living alone were finding it difficult to cook properly. Largely, the aged women used to prefer liquid and light food and avoid oily, spicy food. But their choices and requirements had not been taken into account in their families. The food preferred by the young members of the family was of course used to be prepared

Due to lack of teeth, the aged women may not be able to munch and take hard and semi-hard foods. This restricts the quality and quantity of food intake. As the taste and smell sensitivity gets blunted, one may need stronger concentrations of salt and sour to satisfy the palate, which may in turn aggravate conditions like hypertension, heart disease and acidity.

Obviously, in lower income group, a considerable proportion of one-third of the aged women are dissatisfied about the quality and about one-tenth are dissatisfied about the quantity of food. But, the proportion of such women is negligible in the middle and higher income group.

Addiction

Health and addiction are generally presumed to be correlated. In India, addiction seems to be the characteristic feature of the male community. The aged women are considered to be far away from it. But this argument does not fare well in the present study. Exactly one-fifth of the aged women had one or the other kind of addiction. [As per Chetna (2001), one-tenth of the aged women of Chittor district had addiction. *Bidi, tobacco, pan, hukka* and *naska* were the preferred items of addiction. *Bidi* was the choice of only the lower income group women, while *tobacco* was popular among both the middle and the lower income group. In the higher income group, only 3 per cent of the aged women reported the addiction of *tobacco*. Comparatively less popular, *pan, naska* or *hukka* were preferred mainly by the higher and the middle income group respondents (see Table 4.3).

Table 4.3

Addiction among the Urban Aged Women and their Income Group

Type of Addiction	*Income Group*			*All*
	Lower	*Middle*	*Higher*	
Bidi	16 (21.3)*	—	—	16 (7.1)
Tobacco chewing	7 (9.3)	12 (16.0)	2 (2.7)	21 (9.3)
Pan/hukka/naska	1 (1.3)	3 (4.0)	4 (5.3)	8 (3.6)
No addiction	51 (68.0)	60 (80.0)	69 (92.0)	180 (80.0)
All	75 (100.0)	75 (100.0)	75 (100.0)	225 (100.0)

Note: *Percentage within Income Group.

Pearson chi-square value = 43.593 at df = 6; Asymp. sig. (2-sided) = 0.000

It is found that the levels of income and rate of prevalence of addiction are inversely correlated, and the type of addiction is also influenced by the income levels.

Health

The health of the urban aged women across the age and income groups has been analysed by way of the following variables:

State of Physical Senses

Ageing process brings about deteriorating changes in the health of the aged women. They reported the prevalence of vision impairment (62%) as the highest; followed by that of bone-joints (56%), sleep (43%), memory (36%) and hearing (15%) (see Table 4.4). The findings are quite similar to those of Chetna (2001) with 63 per cent reporting vision problems; 50 per cent orthopaedic problems and 15.7 per cent hearing problems. The following is an attempt to analyse the state of health of the urban aged women in relation to these physical senses.

State of Physical Senses across the Age Groups

It is found that the deterioration in vision continues across all the age groups of the aged women. Yet, it is at the peak for the 75+ age group as the three-fourth majority reports deterioration in their vision during the last five years. It is followed by the 65–69 years age group with 70 per cent reporting the deterioration. As is expected, the youngest age group (60–65) is in a better situation. Yet, in all the age groups, 53–75 per cent of respondents reported deterioration in their vision.

In total, 54 per cent of the aged women reported problems of bone joints with a range of 45 to 65 per cent across different age groups. The prevalence of problem of bone joints increases with an increase in the age group but only up to 74 years. The 75+ age group shows a decline in the prevalence of the problem. Almost similar trends were observed regarding deterioration in sleep. However, the prevalence rate was 43 per cent on an average with a range of 33 to 57 per cent across different age groups.

About one-third of the respondents reported deterioration in memory during the last five years, with a range of 28 to 40 per cent across different age groups. The proportion of these respondents was minimum in the 60–64 age group, and maximum in the 65–69 age group.

Loss of *hearing power* and the age group were statistically proved to be positively correlated. In all, 17 per cent aged women complained of deterioration in hearing with a range of 10 to 30 per cent across different age groups.

The analysis reveals that the 60–64 years age group observed lesser health deterioration as compared to the other age groups. With the increase in the age, the more cases of health deterioration were reported. The 65–69 years age group was the worst victim of vision and memory impairment while the deterioration in the state of bone joints and sleep were most prominently reported by the 70–74 years age group. The hearing problem was found to be increasing with age. And, the 75+ age group had the maximum proportion of those noticing loss of hearing.

The description given above and the statistical measures indicate that the aged women, in general, report deterioration in their health status. But, the age, as such, has no strong association with the deteriorative changes observed in various senses.

State of Physical Senses across the Income Groups

Since almost similar trends were observed with regard to the variables, viz., state of bone joints, sleep, memory and hearing across different income groups, it was thought better to avoid describing each and every variable independently. However, the analysis reveals that the higher the income group, the lower had been the prevalence of impairment reported with regard to all these variables (see Tables 4.5–4.9).

Just to have a more elaborated picture, let us specifically analyse the data regarding state of vision (see Table 4.5). We find that in the lower income group, only 16 per cent of aged women had normal vision, but in the middle and the higher income group, the proportion of such women was 41–43. The analysis makes it clear that the levels of income and state of vision are inversely correlated. It also seems that the aged women of the middle and the higher income group take better care of their eyes. (About 47% women of the middle and the higher income group each were

Table 4.4

Deteriorative Changes in Different Sense Organs/Joints and Age

Changes Observed in Last Five Years	*AGE*				*All*	χ^2 *value at df=3*	*Asymp. sig. (2-sided)*
	60–64	*65–69*	*70–74*	*75+*	*60+*		
	99	*44*	*30*	*33*	*225*		
	(100.0)[1]	*(100.0)*	*(100.0)*	*(100.0)*	*(100.0)*		
	(44.0)[2]	*(28.0)*	*(13.3)*	*(14.7)*	*(100.0)*		
Deterioration in vision	52 (52.5) (23.1)	44 (69.8) (19.6)	19 (63.3) (8.4)	25 (75.8) (11.1)	140 (62.2) (62.2)	8.104	.044
Deterioration in state of bone joints	46 (46.5) (20.4)	39 (61.9) (17.3)	19 (63.3) (8.4)	18 (54.5) (8.0)	122 (54.2) (54.2)	4.903	.179 N.S. 3
Deterioration in sleep	33 (33.3) (14.7)	32 (50.8) (14.2)	17 (56.7) (7.6)	14 (42.4) (6.2)	96 (42.7) (42.7)	7.631	.054
Deterioration in memory	28 (28.3) (12.4)	26 (41.3) (11.6)	11 (36.7) (4.9)	13 (39.4) (5.8)	78 (34.7) (34.7)	3.373	.338 N.S.
Deterioration in hearing power	10 (10.1) (4.4)	10 (15.9) (4.4)	8 (26.7) (3.6)	10 (30.3) (4.4)	38 (16.9) (16.9)	9.570	.023

Notes: 1. Percentage within age group.
2. Percentage out of grand total (225).
3. N.S.—Non Significant.

wearing glasses in comparison to one-third of women in the lower-income group). Due to the care, many of them save themselves from being partially or totally blind. But this is not the case with the lower income group as approximately half of the aged women of this income group reported partial or total blindness. The proportion of such women was just 8–9 per cent in the middle and the higher income group each.

In a nutshell, it can be concluded that the aged women belonging to the higher income group enjoy better health status as compared to their counterparts belonging to the comparatively lower income groups.

Since the three income groups include aged women of all the age categories with approximately the same mean age (see earlier

Table 4.5
State of Vision and Income Group

State of Vision	*Income Group*			*All*
	Lower	*Middle*	*Higher*	
Normal	12 (16.0)[1] (5.3)[2]	32 (42.7) (14.2)	31 (41.3) (13.8)	75 (33.3) (33.3)
Wear glasses/contact lenses	25 (33.3) (11.1)	35 (46.7) (15.6)	35 (46.7) (15.6)	95 (42.2) (42.2)
Blind of one eye; or other problems (but can see)	22 (29.3) (9.8)	4 (5.3) (1.8)	4 (5.3) (1.8)	30 (13.3) (13.3)
Partially or totally blind of both the eyes (cannot see properly)	16 (21.3) (7.1)	4 (5.3) (1.8)	5 (6.7) (2.2)	25 (11.1) (11.1)
All	75 (100.0) (33.3)	75 (100.0) (33.3)	75 (100.0) (33.3)	225 (100.0) (100.0)

Pearson Chi-square value = 44.505 at df = 6; Asymp. sig. (2-sided) = .000

Notes: 1. Percentage within income group. 2. Prcentage out of grand total of 225.

Table 4.6
State of Bone Joints and Income Group

State of Bone Joints	*Income Group*			*All*
	Lower	*Middle*	*Higher*	
Normal	23 (30.7)[1] (10.2)[2]	42 (56.0) (18.7)	35 (46.7) (15.6)	100 (44.4) (44.4)
Minute problems–pain, problem in walking etc.	15 (20.0) (6.7)	22 (29.3) (9.8)	32 (42.7) (14.2)	69 (30.7) (30.7)
Severe problem	37 (49.3) (16.4)	11 (14.7) (4.9)	8 (10.7) (3.6)	56 (24.9) (24.9)
All	75 (100.0) (33.3)	75 (100.0) (33.3)	75 (100.0) (33.3)	225 (100.0) (100.0)

Pearson Chi-square value = 39.138 at df = 4; Asymp. sig. (2-sided) = .000

Notes: 1. Percentage within income group. 2. Percentage out of grand total of 225.

Table 4.7
State of Sleep and Income Group

State of Sleep	*Income Group*			*All*
	Lower	*Middle*	*Higher*	
Normal	26	50	53	129
% within income group	(34.7)	(66.7)	(70.7)	(57.3)
% out of grand total	(11.6)	(22.2)	(23.6)	(57.3)
Abnormal (less, with interruptions etc.)	40	24	20	84
% within income group	(53.3)	(32.0)	(26.7)	(37.3)
% out of grand total	(17.8)	(10.7)	(8.9)	(37.3)
Sleeplessness through out the night (severe problem)	9	1	2	12
% within income group	(12.0)	(1.3)	(2.7)	(5.3)
% out of grand total	(4.0)	(0.4)	(0.9)	(5.3)
All	75	75	75	225
% within income group	(100.0)	(100.0)	(100.0)	(100.0)
% out of grand total	(33.3)	(33.3)	(33.3)	(100.0)

Pearson Chi-square value = 27.686 at df = 4; Asymp. sig. (2-sided) = 0.000

Table 4.8
State of Memory and Income Group

State of Memory	*Income Group*			*All*
	Lower	*Middle*	*Higher*	
Sharp	5	28	45	78
% within income group	(6.7)[1]	(37.3)	(60.0)	(34.7)
% out of grand total	(2.2)[2]	(12.4)	(20.0)	(34.7)
Normal	20	26	21	67
% within income group	(26.7)	(34.7)	(28.0)	(29.8)
% out of grand total	(8.9)	(11.6)	(9.3)	(29.8)
Weak	50	21	9	80*
% within income group	(66.7)	(28.0)	(12.0)	(35.6)
% out of grand total	(22.2)	(9.3)	(4.0)	(35.6)
All	75	75	75	225
% within income group	(100.0)	(100.0)	(100.0)	(100.0)
% out of grand total	(33.3)	(33.3)	(33.3)	(100.0)

Pearson Chi-square value = 65.250 at df = 4; Asymp. sig. (2-sided) = .000
*Out of 80 (35.6%), 5 (2.2%) had partially lost their memory.

Table 4.9
State of Hearing and Income Group

State of Hearing	*Income Group*			*All*
	Lower	*Middle*	*Higher*	
Normal	59	63	69	191
% within income group	(78.7)	(84.0)	(92.0)	(84.9)
% out of grand total	(26.2)	(28.0)	(30.7)	(84.9)
Use hearing aid (normal after using the aid)	2	7		9
% within income group	(2.7)	(9.3)	–	(4.0)
% out of grand total	(0.9)	(3.1)		(4.0)
Problematic strange voice, or other problems	2	2	5	9
% within income group	(2.7)	(2.7)	(6.7)	(4.0)
% out of grand total	(0.9)	(0.9)	(2.2)	(4.0)
Partially or stone deaf	12	3	1	16
% within income group	(16.0)	(4.0)	(1.3)	(7.1)
% out of grand total	(5.3)	(1.3)	(0.4)	(7.1)
All	75	75	75	225
% within income group	(100.0)	(100.0)	(100.0)	(100.0
% out of grand total	(33.3)	(33.3)	(33.3)	(100.0)

Pearson Chi-square value = 24.337 at df = 6; Asymp. sig. (2-sided) = 0.000

chapter), it is concluded that the age affects the ageing process, but it is only one among several secondary factors affecting the health of a woman. The main factor, however, is the income group. Here, it should be evident that the income group indirectly influences deteriorative changes by way of so many direct factors like intake of quantity and quality of food, health facilities etc.

State of Chronic Diseases

Presence or absence of diseases is also a strong indicator of the health status. Good health is also defined as a state of absence of any diseases. Among the urban aged women, the blood pressure (lower or higher) was found to be the most prominent disease (52%). Also, a considerable proportion of them was also suffering from cough (19%), stomach problems like diarrhoea, acidity and constipation (9%), diabetes (9%), headache, body-ache or fever (8%) and heart problems (7%) (see Tables 4.10–4.11).

Table 4.10

Type of Chronic Disease and Income Group

Type of Chronic Disease	*Income Group*			*All 225 (100.0) (100.0)*	*χ^2 Value at df=2*
	Lower 75 (100.0) (33.3)	*Middle 75 (100.0) (33.3)*	*Higher 75 (100.0) (33.3)*		
Blood Pressure	40	41	37	118	0.463
% within income group	(53.3)	(54.7)	(49.3)	(52.4)	< .793
% out of grand total	(17.8)	(18.2)	(16.4)	(52.4)	
Cough	23	11	9	43	10.235
% within income group	(31.1)	(14.7)	(12.0)	(19.2)	< .006
% out of grand total	(10.3)	(4.9)	(4.0)	(19.2)	
Stomach problems[1]	4	9	8	21	2.206
% within income group	(5.3)	(12.0)	(10.7)	(9.3)	< .332
% out of grand total	(1.8)	(4.0)	(3.6)	(9.3)	
Diabetes	3	11	6	20	5.378
% within income group	(4.0)	(14.7)	(8.0)	(8.9)	< .068
% out of grand total	(1.3)	(4.9)	(2.7)	(8.9)	
Headache/Bodyache/fever	13	1	4	18	14.130
% within income group	(17.3)	(1.3)	(5.3)	(8.0)	< .001
% out of grand total	(5.8)	(0.4)	(1.8)	(8.0)	
Heart Disease	7	4	4	15	1.286
% within income group	(9.3)	(5.3)	(5.3)	(6.7)	< .526
% out of grand total	(3.1)	(1.8)	(1.8)	(6.7)	
Miscellaneous[2]	13	8	9	30	1.615
% within income group	(17.3)	(10.7)	(12.0)	(13.3)	< .445
% out of grand total	(5.8)	(3.6)	(4.0)	(13.3)	

Notes: 1. Diarrhoea, acidity, constipation.
2. Jaundice, kidney/bladder problem, asthma, lungs allergy, dust allergy, TB, uterus problems skin-disease (eczema), pyorrhea, mums/tonsils, anaemia, psychological problems, bone problem, paralysis and problems due to accidents.

Chronic Diseases across the Income Groups

It seems that in general, the prevalence of the chronic diseases is the highest in the lower income group. And in the middle and the

Table 4.11
Type of Chronic Disease and Age

Type of Chronic Disease	*Age Group*				*All 60+*
	60–64	*65–69*	*70–74*	*75+*	*225*
	99	*63*	*30*	*33*	*(100.0)*
	(100.0)[1]	*(100.0)*	*(100.0)*	*(100.0)*	*(100.0)*
	(44.0)[2]	*(28.0)*	*(13.3)*	*(14.7)*	
Blood pressure	54	33	15	16	118
% within age group	(54.5)	(52.4)	(50.0)	(48.5)	(52.4)
% out of grand total	(24.0)	(14.7)	(6.7)	(7.1)	(52.4)
Cough	21	11	2	9	43
% within age group	(21.4)	(17.5)	(6.7)	(27.3)	(19.2)
% out of grand total	(9.4)	(4.9)	(0.9)	(4.0)	(19.2)
Diabetes	7	9	2	2	20
% within age group	(7.1)	(14.3)	(6.7)	(6.1)	(8.9)
% out of grand total	(3.1)	(4.0)	(0.9)	(0.9)	(8.9)
Heart disease	8	3	2	2	15
% within age group	(8.1)	(4.8)	(6.7)	(6.1)	(6.7)
% out of grand total	(3.6)	(1.3)	(0.9)	(0.9)	(6.7)
Stomach problems[1]	6	7	3	5	21
% within age group	(6.1)	(11.1)	(10.0)	(15.2)	(9.3)
% out of grand total	(2.7)	(3.1)	(1.3)	(2.2)	(9.3)
Headache/Bodyache/fever	6	5	5	2	18
% within age group	(6.1)	(7.9)	(16.7)	(6.1)	(8.0)
% out of grand total	(2.7)	(2.2)	(2.2)	(0.9)	(8.0)
Miscellaneous[2]	16	7	5	2	30
% within age group	(16.2)	(11.1)	(16.7)	(6.1)	(13.3)
% out of grand total	(7.1)	(3.1)	(2.2)	(0.9)	(13. 3)

Notes: 1 Diarrhoea, acidity, constipation.
2 Uterus problem, psychological problems, problems related to lever (jaundice), kidney/bladder, pyorrhea, mums/tonsils, weakness, bone problems, paralysis, asthma/lungs allergy, dust allergy, TB, skin disease, anaemia, eczema, problems due to accident.

higher income groups, these diseases occur, more or less, with a similar frequency. Yet, some trends can be traced with regard to specific diseases across different income groups. Across the three income groups, almost half of the women were suffering with the problem of high or low blood pressure with the slight difference that needs attention. Cough, headache, body ache and fever were reported as much more frequent in the lower income group as compared to the middle and the higher income group. Similarly, the prevalence of diseases related to lever (jaundice), kidney, gall bladder, lungs (asthma, lungs allergy, and dust allergy), skin diseases (allergy and eczema), dental problems (like pyorrhoea) and the problems like anaemia, psychiatric problems and handicaps occurring due to accidents etc. was also the highest in the lower income group. The lower income group also reported the highest cases of heart diseases, but the lowest cases of diabetes and stomach problems like diarrhoea, acidity etc. (see Table 4.10).

Chronic Diseases across the Age Groups

Across the age groups, almost half of the women were suffering from blood pressure with a difference that needs attention. The data reveals that age and the prevalence of diseases are inversely correlated. About one-fifth of the aged women were suffering from cough with the maximum concentration in the 60–64 years age group and the minimum concentration in the 70–74 age group. Though, the cases of heart problems reported were less (7%), yet more of such cases were concentrated in the lower age groups compared to the higher ones. The lower age group (60–64 years) was also found to be more prone to miscellaneous diseases compared to higher age groups (see Table 4.11). May be, the coming generation of women is more prone to these diseases, particularly blood pressure problem. And, the blood pressure, cough and diabetes are the diseases, which reflect some correlation with the age.

To conclude, blood pressure was the most prominent disease (52%) among all the age groups and income groups of the urban aged women. It is comparable with the national level estimates, i.e., 45 per cent (NSSO, 1995–96). Cough, the second prominent disease (19%), was more common in the lower income group; and the 60–64 years and the 75+ years age groups of the urban aged women. The remaining diseases, for example, the problems related to stomach, diabetes, headache/bodyache/fever and the diseases related to heart were prevalent in more or less the same proportion in all the three income groups and all the four age groups.

If may be noticed that the findings of both NSSO (1991) and the Ageing Survey (Rajan et al., 1993) are in agreement with each other indicating problem of bone joints and cough to be the most prominent diseases, followed by that of blood pressure. The prevalence of blood pressure problem as reported by National Sample Survey (1995–96) was 45 per cent. We can compare our results with the studies given, and conclude that possibly the problem of blood pressure is rising with time. If so, in the near future, more and more cases of the high or the low blood pressure will be reported.

In such a situation, it becomes necessary to identify the causes of the diseases prevalent among the aged women, specially the most prominent ones, and to generate awareness about the remedial and the preventive measures so as to attain 'healthy ageing'. The quantity and quality of food intake play an important role in the health status of a person. For example, epidemiological studies consistently suggest that lower blood pressure occur among the vegetarians than the non-vegetarians independent of age, weight and pulse rate (WHO, 1990). Though further research is needed to prove the conclusive role of various dietary factors in causing various diseases, yet there is substantial evidence from around the world indicating that a diet, which is low in total and saturated fats; high in plant foods (especially green and yellow vegetables) and citrus fruits; and low in alcohol, pickled, smoked and salt preserved food, is consistent with a low risk of many of the current, major diseases.

Availability of and Accessibility to Medical Facilities

Availability of timely medical aid during the sickness also plays a great role in determining the overall health status. The following description explains the availability and accessibility of medical facilities to the urban aged women of different income groups.

Frequency of Medical Consultation

The higher the income group, the higher had been the proportion of the respondents reporting 'no need' of medical consultation. The proportion of such respondents was 4 per cent, 19 per cent and 27 per cent in the lower, middle and higher income groups respectively. It also re-strengthens the earlier findings that the urban aged women of the higher income group enjoy better health status than their counterparts belonging to the comparatively lower income groups (see Table 4.12).

Table 4.12
Frequency of Medical Consultation and Income Group

Frequency of Consultation to Doctor	*Income Group*			*All*
	Lower	*Middle*	*Higher*	
Never, no need	3	14	20	37
% within income group	(4.0)	(18.7)	(26.7)	(16.4)
% out of grand total	(1.3)	(6.2)	(8.9)	(16.4)
Weekly or more frequently	12	6	4	22
% within income group	(16.0)	(8.0)	(5.3)	(9.8)
% out of grand total	(5.3)	(2.7)	(1.8)	(9.8)
Fortnightly	11	7	6	24
% within income group	(14.7)	(9.3)	(8.0)	(10.7)
% out of grand total	(4.9)	(3.1)	(2.7)	(10.7)
Monthly	20	18	31	69
% within income group	(26.7)	(24.0)	(41.3)	(30.7)
% out of grand total	(8.9)	(8.0)	(13.8)	(30.7)
Tri/bi/annually	8	22	12	42
% within income group	(10.7)	(29.3)	(16.0)	(18.7)
% out of grand total	(3.6)	(9.8)	(5.3)	(18.7)
Not regularly/rarely	21	8	2	31
% within income group	(28.0)	(10.7)	(2.7)	(13.8)
% out of grand total	(9.3)	(3.6)	(0.9)	(13.8)
All	75	75	75	225
% within income group	(100.0)	(100.0)	(100.0)	(100.0)
% out of grand total	(33.3)	(33.3)	(33.3)	(100.0)

Pearson Chi-square value = 48.479; df = 10; Asymp. sig. (2-sided) = 0.000

Among the aged women, in need of medical aid, the proportion of those obtaining weekly or even more frequent medical consultation was the highest in the lower income group, followed by the middle and the higher income group. On the other hand, those who had been seeking 'monthly' consultation, were prominent in the higher income group (41%) compared to that of 24–25 per cent in the lower and the middle income group each. These trends again reflect the poor health status and the need of more frequent medical consultation for those in the lower income group; and the better health status and the more health consciousness in the comparatively higher income groups. In other words, apathy towards health care was more in the lower income group compared to the other income groups. Statistically, a strong association between the frequency of medical consultation and 'income group' was in evidence.

Accessibility to Medical Aid

Most of the higher income group respondents who require medical aid get the aid in time. But it does not hold true for those belonging to the lower income group (see Table 4.13). A very high association was statistically also confirmed between the accessibility of medical aid in serious sickness and income group.

Table 4.13

Accessibility of Medical Aid in Serious Sickness and Income Group

Accessibility of Medical Aid in Serious Sickness	*Income Group*			*All*
	Lower	*Middle*	*Higher*	
Always	10	17	18	45
% within income group	(13.3)	(22.7)	(24.0)	(20.0)
% out of grand total	(4.4)	(7.6)	(8.0)	(20.0)
Often	15	24	24	63
% within income group	(20.0)	(32.0)	(32.0)	(28.0)
% out of grand total	(6.7)	(10.7)	(10.7)	(28.0)
Sometimes	35	13	9	57
% within income group	(46.7)	(17.3)	(12.0)	(25.3)
% out of grand total	(15.6)	(5.8)	(4.0)	(25.3)
Rarely	12	7	4	23
% within income group	(16.0)	(9.3)	(5.3)	(10.2)
% out of grand total	(5.3)	(3.1)	(1.8)	(10.2)
No need/never required	3	14	20	37
% within income group	(4.0)	(18.7)	(26.7)	(16.4)
% out of grand total	(1.3)	(6.2)	(8.9)	(16.4)
All	75	75	75	225
% within income group	(100.0)	(100.0)	(100.0)	(100.0)
% out of grand total	(33.3)	(33.3)	(33.3)	(100.0)

Pearson Chi-square value = 42.051 at df=8; Asymp. sig. (2-sided) = 0.000

Duration of Hospitalization

In this context, an attempt has been made to understand the trends of hospitalization of the urban aged women across different income and age groups. The data show that during the last five years, about one-third of the women were hospitalized. Out of them, only 5 per cent had to spend more than a month in the hospital/nursing home. The analysis and the statistical measures indicate no striking differences regarding duration of hospitalization across different income groups or age groups.

The trends, cited as above, go to show that the lower income group seems to have the poorest health status and the highest apathy towards medical consultation. And reverse were the trends highlighted by the higher income groups. Also, the urban aged women belonging to the higher income group had better access to medical aid as compared to their counterparts belonging to the comparatively lower income group.

Satisfaction from Medical Aid

The monthly expenditure on medical aid across different income groups has been described in the Chapter 3. The following is an analysis of satisfaction from medical aid in relation to different income groups.

About one-fourth respondents of the lower income group were reportedly dissatisfied with the medical facilities generally available to them. But, in the middle and higher income groups, only 3–4 per cent respondents expressed their dissatisfaction in this regard. All the dissatisfied respondents of the higher income group were unaware about the amount been spent on their medicines/medical aid. The dissatisfied respondents of the middle-income group had been spending Rs 50–500 monthly on their medical aid. And in the lower income group, this amount ranged up to Rs 1,000 (see Table 4.14).

The trends cited above show that the dissatisfaction about the medical facilities was the highest in the lower income group, and that the level of expenditure on medical facilities is positively correlated with the levels of satisfaction.

Table 4.14

Expenditure on and Satisfaction from Medical Aid by Income Groups

Monthly Expenditure on Medical Aid	*Income Group*									*ALL (I+II+III)*
	Lower			*Middle*			*Higher*			
	Satisfaction from Medical Aid			*Satisfaction from Medical Aid*			*Satisfaction from Medical Aid*			
	Satisfied	*Dis-satisfied*	*All (I)*	*Satisfied*	*Dis-satisfied*	*All (II)*	*Satisfied*	*Dis-satisfied*	*All (III)*	
Nil	14	9	23	5	—	5	3	—	3	31
% within income group	(18.7)	(12.0)	(30.7)	(6.7)		(6.7)	(4.0)		(4.0)	(13.8)
50–250	17	3	20	15	1	16	4	—	4	40
% within income group	(22.7)	(4.0)	(26.7)	(20.0)	(1.3)	(21.3)	(5.3)		(5.3)	(17.8)
251–500	14	5	19	25	1	26	9	—	9	54
% within income group	(18.7)	(6.7)	(25.3)	(33.3)	(1.3)	(34.7)	(12.0)		(12.0)	(24.0)
501–1000	3	2	5	15	—	15	11	—	11	31
% within income group	(4.0)	(2.7)	(6.7)	(20.0)		(20.0)	(14.7)		(14.7)	(13.7)
1001–7000	—	—	—	5	—	5	39	—	39	44
% within income group				(6.7)		(6.7)	(52.0)		(52.0)	(19.6)
Do not Know	8	—	8	8	—	8	6	3	9	25
% within income group	(10.7)		(10.7)	(10.7)		(10.7)	(8.0)	(4.0)	(12.0)	(11.1)
All	56	19	75	73	2	75	72	3	75	225
% within income group	(74.7)	(25.3)	(100.0)	(97.3)	(2.7)	(100.0)	(96.0)	(4.0)	(100.0)	(100.0)

The studies mention that the elderly sick lack proper familial care, and that at the same time, public health services are insufficient to meet the health needs of the elderly (Nair, 1989; Nair and Ramana, 1989; Nair, 1991 and Vijayakumar, 1991). This generates a feeling of dissatisfaction among the elderly.

To conclude, the factors influencing the health of the urban aged women may be summarized as: hard work combined with poor nutrition, inadequate, unbalanced and malnutritional diet, the non-availability and/or the poor quality of health services. And it is also the case that the health status in the lower income group of the urban sector is an index of the vicious cycle of lack of resources, hard work, less nutrition and poor health. It leads to the state of general disability and the most of the aged women of the lower income group suffer from what may be called 'deficiency illness' also. The distribution of health services and their utilization among the urban aged women is skewed in favour of the higher income groups and in the disfavour of the lower income group.

The trends such as the above also direct us to dismiss the gloomy picture of ageing by generating the hope that given the proper care, due consideration to the needs and requirements of the aged women, and a prompt health care system, the aged women can be and will be healthy, happy and satisfied. Keeping this in view, the three-pronged system, as suggested by Mehta (1987), may positively be applied to rectify the situation. It suggests: provision of curative sources, legal protection and health education to take care of medical and health problems of the aged, with special reference to the aged women, and that too, belonging to the lower income group.

Though the informal support system for the care of the aged in India; and the State Policy and Provisions have been kept outside the purview of this study, even then, it is worthwhile to mention, that these are characterized by contradictions and ambivalence. As families are growing smaller and smaller, and norms and values supporting (elder) care are getting more and more scarce, the capacity of the family to provide care and support is also weakening. Yet, efforts are being made to further encourage the family in discharging that role (Biswas, 1985; Kaldate, 1986; Bose and Gangrade, 1988; Singh, 1970 and Bali, 1995:24). Available evidences on the social support systems reveal that the dichotomy between the family and the state, as the support systems, was too sharp. Efforts should be made to develop a healthy relationship between the two.

Mobility and Interaction

In this section, an attempt is made to assess the levels of 'physical mobility', 'ability in household work' and 'social interaction' of the urban aged women. These variables are based on several related indicators. The scaling technique was used to determine the levels of urban aged women with regard to the three variables. The scale has been given and described in the earlier chapter (also see Appendix).

Physical Mobility

Physical mobility refers to the mobility involved in performing the activities of daily living (ADL): Standing up and sitting down, walking without aid, getting in and out of bed, going up and down the stairs, combing one's own hair, self-feeding, reading (proper eye-sight), ability to manage toilet and washing or bathing without help. This is also called as basic level of competence (BaCo). A composite scale was constructed for measuring the level of physical mobility. On the basis of the scale and acquired score, all the respondents were placed in any of the four categories of physical mobility: perfect, high, moderate and low.

Physical Mobility across Income Groups

The aged women belonging to the higher income group have a higher level of physical mobility as compared to those of the lower income groups. To be specific, 48 per cent respondents of the higher income group had perfect level of mobility compared to 41 per cent, and 24 per cent respondents of the middle and the lower income groups respectively. The trends cited in the table show that the higher the income group, the higher had been the level of physical mobility of the urban aged women. And statistically, the levels of income and physical mobility prove to be positively correlated (see Table 4.15).

Table 4.15
Levels of Physical Mobility and Income Groups

Levels of Physical Mobility (score value)	*Income Group*			*All*
	Lower	*Middle*	*Higher*	
Perfect (9)	18	31	36	85
% within income group	(24.0)	(41.3)	(48.0)	(37.8)
% out of grand total	(8.0)	(13.8)	(16.0)	(37.8)
High (10–12)	23	24	27	74
% within income group	(30.7)	(32.0)	(36.0)	(32.9)
% out of grand total	(10.2)	(10.7)	(12.0)	(32.9)
Moderate (13–15)	21	12	7	40
% within income group	(28.0)	(16.0)	(9.3)	(17.8)
% out of grand total	(9.3)	(5.3)	(3.1)	(17.8)
Low (16+)	13	8	5	26
% within income group	(17.3)	(10.7)	(6.7)	(11.6)
% out of grand total	(5.8)	(3.6)	(2.2)	(11.6)
All	75	75	75	225
% within income group	(100.0)	(100.0)	(100.0)	(100.0)
% out of grand total	(33.3)	(33.3)	(33.3)	(100.0)

Pearson Chi-square value = 17.765 at df=6; Asymp. sig. (2-sided) = 0.007

Physical Mobility across Age Groups

On the other hand, a negative correlation was found between the variables 'level of physical mobility' and 'age'. The analysis reveals that the levels of physical mobility and age are inversely correlated. The statistical measures indicate that this correlation is quite high (see Table 4.16).

Hence, the physical mobility is positively correlated with the levels of income. But with age, it depicts an inverse correlation. And in both the cases, this correlation is quite significant.

Ability in Household Work

The ability of urban aged women in performing household work was assessed with regard to the following activities: light household work like washing, dusting, tidying; heavy cleaning like washing floors and cleaning windows; light kitchen work like making a cup of tea; heavy kitchen work, for example, preparing a hot meal; shopping and heavy washing. A composite scale was developed to judge the ability and competence in household work

Table 4.16
Levels of Physical Mobility and Age

Level of Physical Mobility	*Age (Years)*				*All*
	60–64	*65–69*	*70–74*	*75+*	*60+*
Perfect (9)	44	24	9	8	85
% within age group	(44.4)	(38.1)	(30.0)	(24.2)	(37.8)
% out of grand total	(19.6)	(10.7)	(4.0)	(3.6)	(37.8)
High (10–12)	37	17	12	8	74
% within age group	(37.4)	(27.0)	(40.0)	(24.2)	(32.9)
% out of grand total	(16.4)	(7.6)	(5.3)	(3.6)	(32.9)
Moderate (13–15)	14	14	5	7	40
% within age group	(14.1)	(22.2)	(16.7)	(21.2)	(17.8)
% out of grand total	(6.2)	(6.2)	(2.2)	(3.1)	(17.8)
Low 16+	4	8	4	10	26
% within age group	(4.0)	(12.7)	(13.3)	(30.3)	(11.6)
% out of grand total	(1.8)	(3.6)	(1.8)	(4.4)	(11.6)
All	99	63	30	33	225
% within age group	(100.0)	(100.0)	(100.0)	(100.0)	(100.0)
% out of grand total	(44.0)	(28.0)	(13.3)	(14.7)	(100.0)

Pearson Chi-square value = 22.437 at df=9; Asymp. sig. (2-sided) = 0.008

and accordingly all the respondents were placed in either of three levels of ability: low, moderate and high.

Ability in Household Work and Income Groups

The analysis reveals that the proportion of women having the 'high' level of ability and competence in performing the household work was the highest in the higher income group, followed by that in the middle and the lower income group; and vice versa. Statistically also, it is proved that the levels of ability and income group have a strong positive correlation (see Table 4.17).

Ability in Household Work and Age

As age advances, the ability to perform the household work is gradually decreased. The analysis and the statistical measures verify this fact. In the lowest age group of the aged women (60–64), about 30 per cent aged women had the high level of ability in

Table 4.17
Levels of Ability in Household Work and Income Groups

Ability in Household Work (score value)	*Income Group*			*All*
	Lower	*Middle*	*Higher*	
High (6–9)	35	42	54	131
% within income group	(46.7)	(56.0)	(72.0)	(58.2)
Moderate (10–14)	27	25	16	68
% within income group	(36.0)	(33.3)	(21.3)	(30.2)
Low (15–18)	13	8	5	26
% within income group	(17.3)	(10.7)	(6.7)	(11.6)
All	75	75	75	225
% within income group	(100.0)	(100.0)	(100.0)	(100.0

Pearson chi-square value = 11.028 at df=4; Asymp. sig. (2-sided) = 0.026

Table 4.18
Levels of Ability in Household Work and Age

Ability in Household Work	*Age (Years)*				*All*
	60–64	*65–69*	*70–74*	*75+*	*60+*
High	66	35	19	11	131
% within age group	(66.7)	(55.6)	(63.3)	(33.3)	(58.2)
% out of grand total	(29.3)	(15.6)	(8.4)	(4.9)	(58.2)
Moderate	27	24	7	10	68
% within age group	(27.3)	(38.1)	(23.3)	(30.3)	(30.2)
% out of grand total	(12.0)	(10.7)	(3.1)	(4.4)	(30.2)
Low	6	4	4	12	26
% within age group	(6.1)	(6.3)	(13.3)	(36.4)	(11.6)
% out of grand total	(2.7)	(1.8)	(1.8)	(5.3)	(11.6)
All	99	63	30	33	225
% within age group	(100.0)	(100.0)	(100.0)	(100.0)	(100.0)
% out of grand total	(44.0)	(28.0)	(13.3)	(14.7)	(100.0)

Pearson Chi-square value = 28.706 at df = 6; Asymp. sig. (2-sided) = 0.000

performing the household work. But in the 75+ age group, the proportion of such aged women was just 5 per cent. This indicates at a very high association with a negative correlation between the 'ability in household work' and age of the urban aged women (see Table 4.18).

Clearly, the ability to perform household work is correlated positively with the income group and negatively with the age group.

Social Interaction

Social interaction is a measure of density of interactions one gets involved in with other persons. This measure is based on the five types of social interactions that occur in course of paid work, occupation or employment; shopping, playing with children and/or grandchildren; seeing or visiting relatives and seeing or visiting neighbourhood persons. Prakash (1998) has discussed more or less a similar variable called expanded level of competence (ExCo), which was a measure of the skills needed for leisure and social activities. A composite scale was constructed for measuring the level of social interaction of the urban aged women. Depending upon the scale, all the aged women were placed in any of the three categories: high, moderate and low.

Social Interaction across Income Groups

Mostly, the aged women belonging to the higher income group do not go in for paid work. They also have a tendency of avoiding too many contacts with the neighbourhood persons. Majority of them (70%) had the moderate level of social interaction and for the remaining, the level was low. Most of the middle-income group respondents were also 'not working'. But they had been more involved in their families and their household responsibilities, and hence, may be avoiding visits to neighbours or relatives. And that may be the reason why a little more than half of them had a low level of social interaction. Reverse trends were observed with the lower income group. Economic constraints push them into jobs. For reasons of living in smaller houses, with scarce resources and poor family environment, they interact more with the neighbourhood persons. And, this results in a high level of their social interaction (see Table 4.19).

Table 4.19

Levels of Social Interaction and Income Groups

Level of Social Interaction (score values)	*Income Group*			*All*
	Lower	*Middle*	*Higher*	
High (5–11)	9	4	–	13
% within income group	(12.0)	(5.3)		(5.8)
% out of grand total	(4.0)	(1.8)		(5.8)
Moderate (12–18)	46	32	53	131
% within income group	(61.3)	(42.7)	(70.7)	(58.2)
% out of grand total	(20.4)	(14.2)	(23.6)	(58.2)
Low (19–25)	20	39	22	81
% within income group	(26.7)	(52.0)	(29.3)	(36.0)
% out of grand total	(8.9)	(17.3)	(9.8)	(36.0)
All	75	75	75	225
% within income group	(100.0)	(100.0)	(100.0)	(100.0)
% out of grand total	(33.3)	(33.3)	(33.3)	(100.0)

Pearson chi-square value = 22.695 at df=4; Asymp. sig. (2-sided) = 0.000

A very high correlation between 'social interaction' and 'income group' was statistically proved. And it is concluded that the aged women of the lower income group enjoy the highest level of social interaction, followed by those belonging to the higher and the middle income group respectively. Also, the higher income group seems to be the most homogenous group in this regard, followed by the middle and the lower income group respectively. Almost all the women of the higher income group maintain a moderate or low level of social interaction.

Social Interaction across Age

The analysis reveals that the highest social interaction was enjoyed by the 65–69 years age group. This is followed by the 70–74 years age group. The age groups 60–64 and 75+ are more or less similar with regard to the pattern of social interaction. In both the age groups, the same proportion of 5–6 per cent women enjoyed the high level; 49–50 per cent had the moderate level; and 46 per cent

Table 4.20
Levels of Social Interaction and Age

Levels of Social Interaction	*Age (Years)*				*All*
	60–64	*65–69*	*70–74*	*75+*	*60+*
High (5–11)	5	4	2	2	13
% within age group.	(5.1)	(6.3)	(6.7)	(6.1)	(5.8)
% out of grand total	(2.2)	(1.8)	(0.9)	(0.9)	(5.8)
Moderate (12–18)	49	49	17	16	131
% within age group.	(49.5)	(77.8)	(56.7)	(48.5)	(58.2)
% out of grand total	(21.8)	(21.8)	(7.6)	(7.1)	(58.2)
Low (19–25)	45	10	11	15	81
% within age group.	(45.5)	(15.9)	(36.7)	(45.5)	(36.0)
% out of grand total	(20.0)	(4.4)	(4.9)	(6.7)	(36.0)
All	99	63	30	33	225
% within age group.	(100.0)	(100.0)	(100.0)	(100.0)	(100.0)
% out of grand total	(44.0)	(28.0)	(13.3)	(14.7)	(100.0)

Pearson Chi-square value = 16.525 at df = 6; Asymp sig. (2-sided) = 0.011

had the low level of social interaction (see Table 4.20). The point can be presented as:

	60–64
Level of social interaction:	< 70–74 < 65–69
in different age groups	75+

As it becomes clear, the 60–64 years age group has the lowest level of social interaction, may be due to the household responsibilities. The social interaction in the 64–69 age group shows a remarkable increase. But, it gradually comes down in the 70–74 age group. This decline continues in the 75+ age group to the extant that it is equated with that of the 60–64 age group. The health problems may be the obvious reason behind this decline.

The association of social interaction with income group and age is quite strong. The aged women of the lower income group enjoy the highest level of social interaction, followed by those belonging to the higher and the middle income group respectively.

Also, the level of social interaction increases with age but only up to 69 years and then it decreases.

Leisure Time Activities

Different scholars have defined leisure differently. It has been called as 'the best of all possessions' (Scorates) and as 'the mother of philosophy' (Hobbes). Leisure with dignity is considered as the supremely desirable object of all sane and good men (Cicero). To be able to fill leisure intelligently is the 'last product of civilization' (Russell) (Kohli and Verma, 1997). Yet no specific and satisfactory definition of leisure is available. This is partly because; needs and experiences concerning work and leisure are extremely personal and heterogeneous. Leisure is a multidimensional concept. The social milieu in which an individual resides also has an influence on the leisure time, and so have age, sex, education and ethnicity to contribute. The form of leisure is affected by factors such as health, climate, access to transportation and quality of neighbourhood.

The leisure time activities give a fairly good idea about a person's lifestyle. In our study, leisure refers to the question how do the urban aged women spend most of their time, or in which kind of activities do they involve in during whole of the day?

Routine Habits

It was thought worthwhile to examine a few of the daily routine habits also, for example, when do the aged women wake up; when do they sleep; and whether they go for a morning/evening walk or not? The following is an attempt in that regard.

Waking Time

A majority of 64 per cent aged women wake up in between 5–7 a.m. The significant number of 28 per cent wake up as early as 3–5 a.m., while about 6 per cent wake up in between 7–9 a.m. And, the remaining did not give any reply as they were suffering from sleeplessness.

The analysis across income groups reveals no remarkable trends, except that a greater proportion of the middle income group respondents (32%) had the habit of waking up before 5 a.m.

compared to 25–27 per cent respondents of the lower and the higher income group each.

Sleeping Time

The data indicated a poor association between 'sleeping time' and 'income group' of the urban aged women, yet some trends could be traced. A greater proportion of the lower income respondents had the habit of sleeping quite late (after 11 p.m.), compared to those of the higher income groups. On the other hand, a larger proportion of the higher income group respondents (40%) had been going to sleep quite early (before 9.00 p.m.) compared to that of 28 per cent of the middle, and 24 per cent of the lower income group. Also, none of the lower income group respondents was suffering from sleeplessness, whereas 3–7 per cent of the respondents from the middle and higher income groups complained of sleeplessness (see Table 4.21).

Table 4.21

Sleeping Time and Income Group

Sleeping Time (pm)	*Income Group*			*All*
	Lower	*Middle*	*Higher*	
Sleeplessness throughout night	–	5	2	7
% within income group		(6.7)	(2.7)	(3.1)
7.30–9.00-	18	21	30	69
% within income group	(24.0)	(28.0)	(40.0)	(30.7)
9.00+–11.00-	36	31	30	97
% within income group	(48.0)	(41.3)	(40.0)	(43.1)
11.00+	21	18	13	52
% within income group	(28.0)	(24.0)	(17.3)	(23.1)
All	75	75	75	225
% within income group	(100.0)	(100.0)	(100.0)	(100.0)

Pearson chi-square value = 11.344 at df = 6; Asymp. sig. (2-sided) = 0.078

Hence, it can be concluded that the higher income group respondents go to sleep earlier than their counterparts belonging to the middle and the lower income group respectively. And, the problem of sleeplessness is more a phenomenon of the higher income group than of the lower ones.

Morning or Evening Walk

These habits are an index of health consciousness. About 38 per cent of the aged women were habitual of morning or evening walk. The analysis across income groups reveals that the higher the income group, the higher is the proportion of those going for morning or evening walks; and vice versa. And, it is mainly the higher income group (59%) people who are habitual of morning or evening walk as compared to the middle and the lower income group (27–30%).

The respondents from all the age groups had been going for evening or morning walk, yet the age groups 70–74 (50%) and 60–64 (40%) showed a greater interest towards morning or evening walk.

Independent Leisure

These activities include radio listening, watching television, household work (like cooking and cleaning) and gardening. These activities have been analysed with relation to income group and age.

Independent Leisure and Income Group

Radio listening is not a popular leisure activity among the urban aged women. A majority of 76 per cent did never listen to radio or listen to it only rarely (see Table 4.22). *Watching television* was comparatively a much popular leisure time activity. Majority of 55 per cent of the aged women were regular viewers, while 9 per cent were only occasional viewers. Many aged women among the 36 per cent who did 'rarely' or 'never' watch television, reported poor eye-sight as the reason behind not watching television. The *household work* also posed almost a similar picture. About 60 per cent of aged women had been regularly involved in the household work, while only about one-fourth of them had no or 'rare' involvement in the household work. *Gardening*, as a leisure time activity, was, again, found to be more popular among the aged women of the higher income group compared to those belonging to the middle and the lower income group respectively. Lawns and gardens are supposed to be the characteristic feature of the higher income group houses. But most of the houses owned/used by the lower income group respondents do not have lawns or gardens. And this may be one of the important reasons behind the finding.

Table 4.22

Leisure Time Activities and Income Group

Leisure Time Activities	*Income Group*			*All*
	Lower	*Middle*	*Higher*	
Radio listening*				
I. Regularly	5	14	17	36
% within income group	(6.7)	(18.7)	(22.7)	(16.0)
% out of grand total	(2.2)	(6.2)	(7.6)	(16.0)
II. Occasionally	2	10	6	18
% within income group	(2.7)	(13.3)	(8.0)	(8.0)
% out of grand total	(0.9)	(4.4)	(2.7)	(8.0)
III. Rarely	46	34	47	127
% within income group	(61.3)	(45.3)	(62.7)	(56.4)
% out of grand total	(20.4)	(15.1)	(20.9)	(56.4)
IV. Never	22	17	5	44
% within income group	(29.3)	(22.7)	(6.7)	(19.6)
% out of grand total	(9.8)	(7.6)	(2.2)	(19.6)
All	75	75	75	225
% within income group	(100.0)	(100.0)	(100.0)	(100.0)
% out of grand total	(33.3)	(33.3)	(33.3)	(100.0)
Watching TV*				
I. Regularly	24	47	53	124
% within income group	(32.0)	(62.7)	(70.7)	(55.1)
% out of grand total	(10.7)	(20.9)	(23.6)	(55.1)
II. Occasionally	5	5	10	20
% within income group	(6.7)	(6.7)	(13.3)	(8.9)
% out of grand total	(2.2)	(2.2)	(4.4)	(8.9)
III. Rarely	4	—	5	9
% within income group	(5.3)	—	(6.7)	(4.0)
% out of grand total	(1.8)	—	(2.2)	(4.0)
IV. Never	42	23	7	72
% within income group	(56.0)	(30.7)	(9.3)	(32.0)
% out of grand total	(18.7)	(10.2)	(3.1)	(32.0)
All	75	75	75	225
% within income group	(100.0)	(100.0)	(100.0)	(100.0)
% out of grand total	(33.3)	(33.3)	(33.3)	(100.0)

Household work*				
I. Regularly	39	43	52	134
% within income group	(52.0)	(57.3)	(69.3)	(59.6)
% out of grand total	(17.3)	(19.1)	(23.1)	(59.6)
II. Occasionally	13	14	8	35
% within income group	(17.3)	(18.7)	(10.7)	(15.6)
% out of grand total	(5.8)	(6.2)	(3.6)	(15.6)
III. Rarely	14	13	10	37
% within income group	(18.7)	(17.3)	(13.3)	(16.4)
% out of grand total	(6.2)	(5.8)	(4.4)	(16.4)
IV. Never	9	5	5	19
% within income group	(12.0)	(6.7)	(6.7)	(8.4)
% out of grand total	(4.0)	(2.2)	(2.2)	(8.4)
All	75	75	75	225
% within income group	(100.0)	(100.0)	(100.0)	(100.0)
% out of grand total	(33.3)	(33.3)	(33.3)	(100.0)
Gardening****				
I. Regularly	6	22	42	70
% within income group	(8.0)	(29.3)	(56.0)	(31.1)
% out of grand total	(2.7)	(9.8)	(18.7)	(31.1)
II. Occasionally	6	12	14	32
% within income group	(8.0)	(16.0)	(18.7)	(14.2)
% out of grand total	(2.7)	(5.3)	(6.2)	(14.2)
III. Rarely	38	26	13	77
% within income group	(50.7)	(34.7)	(17.3)	(34.2)
% out of grand total	(16.9)	(11.6)	(5.8)	(34.2)
IV. Never	25	15	6	46
% within income group	(33.3)	(20.0)	(8.0)	(20.4)
% out of grand total	(11.1)	(6.7)	(2.7)	(20.4)
All	75	75	75	225
% within income group	(100.0)	(100.0)	(100.0)	(100.0)
% out of grand total	(33.3)	(33.3)	(33.3)	(100.0)

Note: * Pearson Chi-square value = 24.715 at df = 6; Asymp. sig. (2-sided) = 0.000
** Pearson Chi-square value = 25.67 at df = 4; Asymp. sig. (2-sided) = 0.000 (after merging 3 and 4 row)
*** Pearson Chi-square value = 06.143 at df = 6; Asymp. sig. (2-sided) = 0.407
**** Pearson Chi-square value = 55.100 at df = 6; Asymp. sig. (2-sided) = 0.000

All the trends cited above clearly indicate that the aged women belonging to the higher income group had greater involvement in all the above-mentioned leisure time activities compared to their counterparts belonging to the comparatively lower income groups. As per the earlier findings, a large number of women of the lower income group had to take up jobs out of economic compulsions. As a result, they might be left with little leisure. The women of lower income group were also found to be more prone to health problems and financial constraints. And these are the obvious factors behind why the aged women of the lower income group reported lesser involvement in all the mentioned leisure time activities. Excluding the 'involvement in the household work', all the variables described above have a strong correlation with the income group, as perceived statistically.

Independent Leisure and Age

Regarding *radio listening*, no striking differences were observed in the different age groups. All the age groups of the urban aged women had more or less same orientation towards radio listening (see Table 4.23). *Watching television*, on the other hand, was found to be slightly associated with the age. About 48–60 per cent of all the age groups was found to be quite regular in watching television. Yet, the proportion in the higher age groups (75+ and 70–74) was slightly lower. With increase in age, eyesight diminishes, and this is one of the important reasons behind the 'young' aged women enjoying television viewing more than their 'older' counterparts. On the similar pattern, involvement in *household work* was also found to be associated (though the association was not very strong) with the age. The trends cited in the table indicate that the 70–74 years age group had the maximum involvement while the 75+ age group reported the minimum involvement in the household work. Just to specify, 83, 79, 78 and 52 per cent respondents of respectively the 70–74, 60–64, 65–69 and 75+ age group had frequent (regular or occasional) involvement in the household work. As far as *gardening* was concerned, again, no striking differences were observed in the different age groups. The only point, which needs a mention is that the 75+ age group reported a little lesser involvement in gardening compared to that reported by the other age groups.

In short, of all the leisure time activities described above, only television viewing and household work were found to be associated with age. Otherwise, no remarkable differences were observed in the different age groups with regard to the leisure time activities.

Table 4.23

Involvement in Leisure Time Activities and Age

Leisure Time Activities	*Age (Years)*				*All*
	60–64	*65–69*	*70–74*	*75+*	*60+*
Listening Radio*					
I. Regularly	16	11	5	4	36
% within age group	(16.2)	(17.5)	(16.7)	(12.1)	(16.0)
% out of grand total	(7.1)	(4.9)	(2.2)	(1.8)	(16.0)
II. Occasionally	8	6	1	3	18
% within age group	(8.1)	(9.5)	(3.3)	(9.1)	(8.0)
% out of grand total	(3.6)	(2.7)	(0.4)	(1.3)	(8.0)
III. Rarely	52	35	23	17	127
% within age group	(52.5)	(55.6)	(76.7)	(51.5)	(56.4)
% out of grand total	(23.1)	(15.6)	(10.2)	(7.6)	(56.4)
IV. Never	23	11	1	9	44
% within age group	(23.2)	(17.5)	(3.3)	(27.3)	(19.6)
% out of grand total	(10.2)	(4.9)	(0.4)	(4.0)	(19.6)
All	99	63	30	33	225
% within age group	(100.0)	(100.0)	(100.0)	(100.0)	(100.0)
% out of grand total	(44.0)	(28.0)	(13.3)	(14.7)	(100.0)
Watching TV*					
I. Regularly	54	38	16	16	124
% within age group	(54.5)	(60.3)	(53.3)	(48.5)	(55.1)
% out of grand total	(24.0)	(16.9)	(7.1)	(7.1)	(55.1)
II. Occasionally	9	3	4	4	20
% within age group	(9.1)	(4.8)	(13.3)	(12.1)	(5.3)
% out of grand total	(4.0)	(1.3)	(1.8)	(1.8)	(5.3)
III. Rarely	5	2	1	1	9
% within age group	(5.1)	(3.2)	(3.3)	(3.0)	(4.0)
% out of grand total	(2.2)	(0.9)	(0.4)	(0.4)	(4.0)
IV. Never	31	20	9	12	72
% within age group	(31.3)	(31.7)	(30.0)	(36.4)	(32.0)
% out of grand total	(13.8)	(8.9)	(4.0)	(5.3)	(32.0)
All	99	63	30	33	225
% within age group	(100.0)	(100.0)	(100.0)	(100.0)	(100.0)
% out of grand total	(44.0)	(28.0)	(13.3)	(14.7)	(100.0)

Cont'd...

Cont'd...

Household work*					
I. Regularly	66	37	20	11	134
% within age group	(66.7)	(58.7)	(66.7)	(33.3)	(59.6)
% out of grand total	(29.3)	(16.4)	(8.9)	(4.9)	(59.6)
II. Occasionally	12	12	5	6	35
% within age group	(12.1)	(19.0)	(16.7)	(18.2)	(15.6)
% out of grand total	(5.3)	(5.3)	(2.2)	(2.7)	(15.6)
III. Rarely	12	11	4	10	37
% within age group	(12.1)	(17.5)	(13.3)	(30.3)	(16.4)
% out of grand total	(5.3)	(4.9)	(1.8)	(4.4)	(16.4)
IV. Never	9	3	1	6	19
% within age group	(9.1)	(4.8)	(3.3)	(18.2)	(8.4)
% out of grand total	(4.0)	(1.3)	(0.4)	(2.7)	(8.4)
All	99	63	30	33	225
% within age group	(100.0)	(100.0)	(100.0)	(100.0)	(100.0)
% out of grand total	(44.0)	(28.0)	(13.3)	(14.7)	(100.0)
Gardening**					
I. Regularly	31	21	10	8	70
% within age group	(31.3)	(33.3)	(33.3)	(24.2)	(31.1)
% out of grand total	(13.8)	(9.3)	(4.4)	(3.6)	(31.1)
II. Occasionally	17	9	4	2	32
% within age group	(17.2)	(14.3)	(13.3)	(6.1)	(14.2)
% out of grand total of 225	(7.6)	(4.0)	(1.8)	(0.9)	(14.2)
III. Rarely	29	20	12	16	77
% within age group	(29.3)	(31.3)	(40.0)	(48.5)	(34.2)
% out of grand total	(12.9)	(8.9)	(5.3)	(7.1)	(34.2)
IV. Never	22	13	4	7	46
% within age group	(22.2)	(20.6)	(13.3)	(21.2)	(20.4)
% out of grand total	(9.8)	(5.8)	(1.8)	(3.1)	(20.4)
All	99	63	30	33	225
% within age group	(100.0)	(100.0)	(100.0)	(100.0)	(100.0)
% out of grand total	(44.0)	(28.0)	(13.3)	(14.7)	(100.0)

Notes: * Pearson Chi-square value = 9.915 at df = 9; Asymp. sig. (2-sided) = 0.357
** Pearson Chi-square value = 9.915 at df = 9; Asymp. sig. (2-sided) = 0.357
*** Pearson Chi-square value = 17.217 at df = 9; Asymp. sig. (2-sided) = 0.045
**** Pearson Chi-square value = 6.793 at df = 9; Asymp. sig. (2-sided) = 0.659

A comparison of the two variables makes it clear that the leisure time activities of the urban aged women are more closely associated with their family income as compared to their age.

Involvement in Social Activities

The involvement of the urban aged women in various social activities was also analysed. These activities include: playing with grandchildren; seeing or visiting relatives; seeing or visiting neighbours; paid work; and shopping.

A very high association between the 'frequency of engagement in either of the above-mentioned activities' and the 'income group' was statistically shown (see Table 4.24). But to find out the direction or trend of this association, it is necessary to analyse each of the activities individually. An attempt in this direction is the following.

As far as *playing with the grandchildren* is concerned, the lower the income group, the higher is the proportion of those who never play with the grandchildren; and vice versa. As, about 25 per cent, 35 per cent and 52 per cent respondents of respectively the higher, middle and lower income group had never been playing with the grandchildren. From amongst the women playing with the grandchildren, and those playing daily were more in the higher income group, followed by the lower and middle income group. Hence, playing with grandchildren is the favourable leisure activity of the higher income group women followed by those of the lower and middle income group.

Almost similar patterns were observed about interaction with the relatives and interaction with the neighbours. The lower the income group, the higher is the proportion of the aged women having no interaction and vice versa. Among those who keep interacting, the lower the income group, the higher is the frequency of interaction; and vice versa. Regarding paid work, it was found that the lower the income group, the higher is the proportion of those going for *paid work*, and also, the higher is the frequency of engagement in the paid work; and vice versa.

The data highlight that 36–45 per cent respondents of all the three income groups did never go for shopping, and that the lower the income group, the higher is the proportion of the aged women who never do shopping, and vice versa. Otherwise, 17 per cent of the lower income group respondents had been 'daily' shopping, compared to 1–4 per cent of the other income groups. And those shopping just fortnightly or monthly constituted 4, 29 and 33 per cent of the lower, the middle and the higher income group respectively. It leads to the conclusion that the lower the income group,

Table 4.24

Frequency of Engagement in Various Social Interactive Activities and Income Group

Social Activity	*Playing with Grandchildren*				*Seeing or Visiting Relatives*				*Seeing or Visiting Neighbours*				*Paid Work*				*Shopping*			
Frequency of Engagement	*Income Group*			*All*	*Income Group*			*All*	*Income Group*			*All*	*Income Group*			*All*	*Income Group*			*All*
	L	*M*	*H*		*L*	*M*	*H*		*L*	*M*	*H*		*L*	*M*	*H*		*L*	*M*	*H*	
Daily	30	24	40	94	10	9	4	23	31	18	6	55	22	2	1	25	13	1	3	17
	40.0	32.0	53.3	41.8	13.3	12.0	5.3	10.2	41.3	24.0	8.0	24.4	29.3	2.7	1.3	11.1	17.3	1.3	4.0	7.6
Alternate day	1	1	3	5	12	12	13	37	21	20	40	81	11	1	—	12	16	11	4	31
	1.3	1.3	4.0	2.2	16.0	16.0	17.3	16.4	28.0	26.7	53.3	36.0	14.7	1.3		5.3	21.3	14.7	5.3	13.8
Weekly	4	8	8	20	3	15	22	40	7	19	11	37	—	—	—	—	9	10	16	35
	5.3	10.7	10.7	8.9	4.0	20.0	29.3	17.8	9.3	25.3	14.7	16.4					12.0	13.3	21.3	15.6
Fortnightly/ monthly	1	16	5	22	16	26	31	73	4	8	10	22	—	—	—	—	3	22	25	50
	1.3	21.3	6.7	9.8	21.3	34.7	41.3	32.4	5.3	10.7	13.3	9.8					4.0	29.3	33.3	22.2
Never	39	26	19	84	34	13	5	52	12	10	8	30	42	72	74	188	34	31	27	92
	52.0	34.7	25.3	37.3	45.3	17.3	6.7	23.1	16.0	13.3	10.7	13.3	56.0	96.0	98.7	83.6	45.3	41.3	36.0	40.9
All	75	75	75	225	75	75	75	225	75	75	75	225	75	75	75	225	75	75	75	225
	100.0	100.0	100.0	100.0	100.0	100.0	100.0	100.0	100.0	100.0	100.0	100.0	100.0	100.0	100.0	100.0	100.0	100.0	100.0	100.0
Pearson chi-square	Value = 31.182 df = 8 Asymp. sig. (2-sided) = .000				Value = 47.279 df = 8 Asymp. sig. (2-sided) = .000				Value = 35.861 df = 8 Asymp. sig. (2-sided) = .000				Value = 62.435 df = 4 Asymp. sig. (2-sided) = .000				Value = 41.962 df = 8 Asymp. sig. (2-sided) = .000			

L–Lower M–Middle H–Higher

the higher is the frequency with which the aged women go for shopping; and vice versa.

The frequency of engagement in either of the social activities mentioned is highly influenced by the income group of the aged women. The lower the income group, the higher is the proportion of the aged women being never involved in either of the social activities. And, for those who involve, the lower the income group, the higher is the frequency of engagement in the social activities. Hence, the lower income group either has no involvement in the activity or, if involved, involves with greater frequency/intensity as compared to the middle or the higher income group respectively. According to the intimacy of involvement of the urban aged women, the social activities can be ranked as follows:

Rank	*Activity*
1	Playing with grandchildren
2	Seeing or visiting relatives
3	Shopping
4	Interacting with neighbours
5	Paid work

Now we will examine the involvement of the urban aged women in various social organizations with relation to their income group and age.

Association with Social Organizations

About two-third of the urban aged women had no association with any of the social organizations. Among those who had been associated, religious organizations or religious sects like Bhajan-Mandali, Satsang-Groups, Swami and Jain Samaj etc. were more popular. Only 10 per cent of respondents had joined social (non-religious) organizations, for example, voluntary organizations, political parties, cooperatives and professional organizations. A few had also joined some recreational clubs and 'art of living' organization. The mode of participation in social organizations is found to be highly influenced by the income group. The analysis shows that the association with social organizations is greater in the higher income group compared to that in the middle and the lower income group. The aged women belonging to the higher income group have more opportunities and more accessibility to resources to participate in the social (non-religious) organizations as compared to those belonging to the comparatively lower income groups (see Table 4.25).

Table 4.25

Association with Social Organizations and Income Group

Association with Organizations	*Income Group*			*All*
	Lower	*Middle*	*Higher*	
N.A. (no association)	59	54	39	152
% within income group	(78.7)	(72.0)	(52.0)	(67.6)
% out of grand total	(26.2)	(24.0)	(17.3)	(67.6)
Religious organizations	16	17	18	51
% within income group	(21.3)	(22.7)	(24.0)	(22.7)
% out of grand total	(7.1)	(7.6)	(8.0)	(22.7)
Non-religious organizations		4	18	22
% within income group	—	(5.3)	(24.0)	(9.8)
% out of grand total		(1.8)	(8.0)	(9.8)
All	75	75	75	225
% within income group	(100.0)	(100.0)	(100.0)	(100.0)
% out of grand total	(100.0)	(100.0)	(100.0)	(100.0)

Pearson Chi-square value = 28.758 at df = 4, Asymp. sig .(2-sided) = 0.0

Age group analysis shows that those aged women who have no association with any social organizations were drawn from all the age groups. The maximum apathy to participation was observed in the 75+ age group with the three-fourth majority being totally non-participant, followed by the age group 60–64 with a little less proportion of those who are not participating in the social organizations. In the other age groups, the proportion of such non-participant women was 59–60 per cent. Sickness may be the obvious reasons of lower participation of the 75+ age groups. Almost all the 70+ women were associated specifically with religious organizations only. It clearly indicates that the involvement in the religious organizations increases, while that in the non-religious organizations decreases with an increase in the age (see Table 4.26).

Table 4.26

Age, Association with Various Social Organizations and Frequency of Visits

Association with Social Organizations	*AGE*																*All*
	Frequency of Visits (60–64)				*Frequency of Visits (65–69)*				*Frequency of Visits (70–74)*				*Frequency of Visits (75+)*				
	Often	*Sometime*	*Rarely*	*All*	*Often*	*Sometime*	*Rarely*	*All*	*Often*	*Sometime*	*Rarely*	*All*	*Often*	*Sometime*	*Rarely*	*All*	
N.A. (no association)	—	1 1.0[1]	71 71.7	72 72.7	—	—	37 58.7	37 58.7	—	—	18 60.0	18 60.0	—	—	25 75.8	25 75.8	152 67.6[2]
Religious organizations	8 8.1	6 6.1	1 1.0	15 15.2	10 15.9	4 6.3	3 4.8	17 27.0	9 30.0	1 3.3	1 3.3	11 36.7	4 12.1	2 6.1	2 6.1	8 24.2	51 22.7
Non-religious organizations	—	7 7.1	5 5.1	12 12.1	5 7.9	4 6.3	—	9 14.3	—	1 3.3	—	1 3.3	—	—	—	—	22 9.8
All	8 8.1	14 14.1	77 77.8	99 100.0	15 23.8	8 12.7	40 63.5	63 100.0	9 30.0	2 6.7	19 63.3	30 100.0	4 12.1	2 6.1	27 81.8	33 100.0	225 100.0
Pearson Chi-square	value = 92.527 df=4 Asymp. sig. (2-sided) = .000				value = 53.893 df=4 Asymp. sig. (2-sided) = .000				value = 39.474 df=4 Asymp. sig. (2-sided) = .000				value = 22.917 df=2 Asymp. sig. (2-sided) = .000				

Notes: 1. Percentage within age group. 2. Percentage out of grand total of 225.

Pearson Chi-square test is not very effective since at least 44.4% cells of each age group have expected count less than 5.

To conclude, the frequency of visits in social organizations increases with age but only up to 70–74 years age group. The 75+ age group shows a sudden decline in this regard. But, generally speaking, the aged women of all the age groups have more interest in the religious organizations compared to the non-religious ones. As age increases, interest in religion also increases.

Attitude Towards Life

The attitude towards life, whether optimistic or pessimistic, has a good deal of role in determining the lifestyle. Some of the aged spend life while just waiting for death. They do not involve in recreational or leisure time activities and do not take proper care of their health. But on the other hand, those who have enthusiastic or optimistic attitude spend their time positively in recreational activities. They become careful of their health and contribute more to the society.

The attitude of the aged women towards the life was analysed, and accordingly, they were categorized as enthusiastic, conditionally optimistic, neutral and pessimistic. The pessimistic women were just begging for death (stating *Bus ab to bhagwan uttha le, Hamne kuch bura kiya hoga jo abhi tak maut nahi aie).* The neutral were those who had never thought of death or life span, and had left everything to God. There were others who wished to live till they were physically active and not dependent on others; till they complete their responsibilities; or till the spouse was alive. It is obvious that their optimism was conditional. But, on the other hand, the enthusiastic women wished to live for more decades, to see their grandchildren or even marriage of their grandchildren and to just enjoy life. They do not even like to imagine anything concerning death.

Statistically, it is observed that the levels of income and prevalence of pessimism in life have a very high inverse correlation. Also, the conditionally optimistic women constituted about one-fourth of the lower income group, one-fifth of the middle income group and 17 per cent of the higher income group. So, the lower the income group, the higher is the prevalence of conditional optimism. It also indicates that this optimism can be improved by improving the facilities and environment. However, those having neutral attitude towards life were predominated in the higher income group, followed by the middle and the lower income group. But, the aged women of the middle income group are the most enthusiastic, followed by those of the higher and the lower income group respectively (see Table 4.27).

Table 4.27

Attitude towards Life and Income Group

Opinion on: If given a choice, how long would you expect to live?	*Income Group*			*Total*
	Lower	*Middle*	*Higher*	
Enthusiastic	6	20	13	39
% within income group	(8.0)	(26.7)	(17.3)	(17.3)
% out of grand total	(2.7)	(8.9)	(5.8)	(17.3)
Optimistic but conditional	18	14	13	45
% within income group	(24.0)	(18.7)	(17.3)	(20.0)
% out of grand total	(8.0)	(6.2)	(5.8)	(20.0)
Neutral	19	28	40	87
% within income group	(25.3)	(37.3)	(53.3)	(38.7)
% out of grand total	(8.4)	(12.4)	(17.8)	(38.7)
Pessimistic	32	13	9	54
% within income group	(42.7)	(17.3)	(12.0)	(24.0)
% out of grand total	(14.2)	(5.8)	(4.0)	(24.0)
Total	75	75	75	225
% within income group	(100.0)	(100.0)	(100.0)	(100.0)
% out of grand total	(33.3)	(33.3)	(33.3)	(100.0)

Pearson Chi-square value = 32.905 at df = 6; Asymp. sig. (2-sided) = 0.000

Hence, it can be stated that for the aged women, the lower the income group, the higher is the pessimism about life. And the urban aged women of the middle income group seem to be more enthusiastic, followed by those belonging to the higher and the lower income group respectively.

Compared to the higher income group, the lower income group seems to be trapped in the vicious cycle of malnutrition and addiction, poorer health, poorer health services, lesser health consciousness and lesser satisfaction. This cycle influences the other variables of life satisfaction also. 'Physical mobility' and 'ability to perform household work' are also positively correlated with the levels of income. It is obvious that the poor health negatively influences the physical mobility and the ability to perform household work. The aged women of the lower income group are compelled to work owing to economic compulsions and have smaller houses and hence interact more frequently with the neighbours. As a result, they enjoy the highest level of social interaction, followed by those belonging to the higher and the middle income group.

Compared to age, income group is found to be a more important factor influencing health and physical mobility through various direct factors like quality and quantity of food, health services etc. The aged women of the higher income group, having better health, more leisure and better access to resources, are found to be more involved in the religious and social organizations compared to the lower income groups.

We find, then, that the middle income group seems to provide more enthusiasm and satisfying environment to its aged women, followed by the higher and the lower income group.

5

Conflicts, Problems and Expectations of the Urban Aged Women

Emerging Challenges

Old age presents its unique set of challenges and these are reflected in term of conflicts, problems and expectations. In our ancient culture, old age in human life was not meant to be a stage of conflict or tension. Rather, it is looked upon as a time of unquestioned authority and respect. But the aged in the modern urban families are more likely to encounter family conflicts. The conflicts are due essentially to the rapid social changes that make the aged obsolete; there is a lack of clear definition and ceremonial recognition of the change of authority? as a person approaches ageing; and the conflicting folkways and mores govern old age behaviour. The conflict is a bundle of diverse problems and expectations.

Broadly speaking, the problems consist of failing health and loneliness caused by the death of the near and dear ones. Most problems also owe their genesis to loss of work, and reduced or no earnings. This results in loss of status, authority, recognition and social participation. 'The problems of the aged' or 'the aged with problems' become a social problem if social institutions lag behind in adapting to the needs of the older people without disturbing the fabric of society. The society basically is not prepared for the appearance of large number of the aged. From this point of view, the apathetic aspect of problem is posed for those who formulate social policy at local, state and national levels.

By analysing the problems of the aged women and the causes thereof, and identifying the factors contributing to satisfaction or dissatisfaction in the old age, the professional social workers can offer immense help to the aged (women included) in the contemporary Indian society. This chapter aims at analysing the actual conflicts, perceived problems and expectations of the aged women. It also attempts to assess the gravity of various problems confronting the aged women of the three income groups—the lower, the middle and the higher. Besides probing into their real and imaginary worries; and the factors contributing to their satisfaction and dissatisfaction, the chapter aims also at identifying the parameters of satisfaction in the old age. On the basis of the identified problems, worries and expectations of the old age, and the parameters of satisfaction in the old age, an action plan for social work intervention has been made and suggested in the next chapter.

Conflict in the Family

Conflict occurs at various levels—within a person, between members of a group and between groups. Our focus, here, is essentially on interpersonal conflict an aged woman encounters with the members of her family.

If we look at the effects of conflicts objectively, we find that at times conflict is beneficial, as it brings about social change in consequence. It also helps to maintain the stability of the family by forcing its members to air their grievances and resolve their problems. Thus, it prevents unhealthy upheavals and ill feelings within and between groups. Conflict brings out issues in the open so that public opinion helps in resolving them.

Family Conflicts across Income Groups

The analysis reveals that the lower the income group, the higher had been the frequency of conflicts faced by the respondents; and vice versa. Frequency of conflict increases with a decrease in the level of the income group (see Table 5.1). It will be seen that the aged women of the lower income group are more prone to family conflicts and tensions compared to those belonging to the comparatively higher income groups.

Table 5.1

Frequency of Conflicts in the Family, Family Pattern and Income Group

Conflict in the Family	*Income Group*												*All (LT+M T+ HT)*
	Lower				*Middle*				*Higher*				
	Family Pattern				*Family Pattern*				*Family Pattern*				
	Joint	*Nuclear*	*Living Alone*	*All (LT)*	*Joint*	*Nuclear*	*Living Alone*	*All (MT)*	*Joint*	*Nuclear*	*Living Alone*	*All (HT)*	
Never	2	7	—	9	6	21	2	29	23	24	2	49	87
	(22.7)*	(11.5)	—	(12.0)	(28.6)	(41.2)	(66.7)	(38.7)	(71.9)	(60.0)	(66.7)	(65.3)	(38.7)***
	(2.7)**	(9.3)		(12.0)	(8.0)	(28.0)	(2.7)	(38.7)	(30.7)	(32.0)	(2.7)	(65.3)	
Rarely	3	16	1	20	9	12	1	22	2	5	1	8	50
	(33.3)	(26.2)	(20.0)	(26.7)	(42.9)	(23.5)	(33.3)	(29.3)	(6.3)	(12.5)	(33.3)	(10.7)	(22.2)
	(4.0)	(21.3)	(1.3)	(26.7)	(12.0)	(16.0)	(1.3)	(29.3)	(2.7)	(6.7)	(1.3)	(10.7)	
Occasionally	4	20	1	25	5	12		17	4	8		12	54
	(44.4)	(32.8)	(20.0)	(33.3)	(23.8)	(23.5)	—	(22.7)	(12.5)	(20.0)	—	(16.0)	(24.0)
	(5.3)	(26.7)	(1.3)	(33.3)	(6.7)	(16.0)		(22.7)	(5.3)	(10.7)		(16.0)	
Often	—	18	3	21	1	6		7	3	3		6	34
		(29.5)	(60.0)	(28.0)	(4.8)	(11.8)	—	(9.3)	(9.4)	(7.5)	—	(8.0)	(15.1)
		(24.0)	(4.0)	(28.0)	(1.3)	(8.0)		(9.3)	(4.0)	(4.0)		(8.0)	
All	9	61	5	75	21	51	3	75	32	40	3	75	225
	(100.0)	(100.0)	(100.0)	(100.0)	(100.0)	(100.0)	(100.0)	(100.0)	(100.0)	(100.0)	(100.0)	(100.0)	(100.0)
	(12.0)	(81.3)	(6.7)	(100.0)	(28.0)	(68.0)	(4.0)	(100.0)	(42.7)	(53.3)	(4.0)	(100.0)	
Pearson Chi-Square at df=6	Value=6.639 Asymp. Sig. (2 Sided)=.356; N.S.***				Value=4.938 Asymp. Sig. (2 Sided)=.552; N.S.				Value=.3994 Asymp. Sig. (2 Sided)=.677; N.S				

Note: *Percentage within family pattern category, ** Percentage within income group, ***Percentage out of grand total of 225, **** Not-significant.

Family Conflicts and Family Patterns

It is generally presumed that the aged enjoy better status in a joint family compared to a nuclear one, and that the aged will feel more satisfied in the kind of family where they have less conflict with the other members.

It is thought that the joint family system has the considerable implication on the emergence of conflicts. But, the majority of the aged women belonging to the joint families observe family peace in all the three income groups. Yet, it varied across the different income groups as more than half, i.e., 56 per cent were experiencing the rare occasions of conflicts among the lower income group, while their proportion was more than three-fourth as 72 and 78 per cent among the middle and higher income groups respectively. In other words, they were enjoying the peaceful environment in their respective families. Compared to this, the situation in the nuclear families is found to be poorer. Among the aged women belonging to the nuclear families of the lower income groups, the majority, i.e., 62 per cent was facing conflicts frequently. But, in the middle and higher income groups, such women constituted approximately one-third (i.e., 35%) and one-fourth (i.e., 28%) respectively. It is inferred that the aged women belonging to the nuclear families are more exposed to family conflicts as compared to those belonging to the joint families. And this is true for all the three income groups (see Table 5.1).

The aged women of the middle and higher income groups who were living all alone reported rare instances of conflict with the members of their families. But amongst such aged women of the lower income group, most (i.e., 80%) complained of frequent conflicts with the members of their families (see Table 5.1), the urban aged women belonging to the lower income group in general and amongst those living all alone in particular, are more prone to family conflicts compared to their counterparts of the middle and the higher income groups respectively.

Factors affecting Conflict

The major factor of conflict was related to health and related problems (18%), followed by financial matters (16%), isolation

(12%) and disrespect by members of the family (7%) (see Table 5.2).

Table 5.2

Main Issues of Conflict in the Family and Income Group

Reason/Issue of Conflict ↓	*Income Group*			*All*	*Chi square At df=2*
No. of Respondents →	*Lower* 75 (100.0) (33.3)	*Middle* 75 (100.0) (33.3)	*Higher* 75 (100.0) (33.3)	225 (100.0) (100.0)	
Financial	25 (33.3) (11.1)	6 (8.0) (2.7)	6 (8.0) (2.7)	37 (16.4) (16.4)	23.354 <.000
Isolation	6 (8.0) (2.7)	11 (14.7) (4.9)	9 (12.0) (4.0)	26 (11.6) (11.6)	1.652 N.S.*
Disrespect by members of the family	9 (12.0) (4.0)	5 (6.7) (2.2)	1 (1.3) (0.4)	15 (6.7) (6.7)	6.857 < .032
Health and related problems	14 (18.7) (6.2)	15 (20.0) (6.7)	11 (14.7) (4.9)	40 (17.8) (17.8)	0.678 N.S.*

Note: *Not significant.

The analysis reveals that financial crisis is the major factor causing conflicts among the aged women belonging to the lower income group. Health problem, for the lower income group, was the second prominent factor of conflict, while for the middle and the higher income group it was the most prominent factor affecting conflict. Disrespectful behaviour of members of the family caused conflict more in the lower income group (12%) compared to that in the middle (7%) and the higher income group (1%). The lower income group is characterized by lesser access to resources, low education level and more children/members to share whatever may be the available resources. Hence, there remain more chances of clash of interests in the lower income group. The interplay of the above-mentioned factors may be the obvious reasons behind the disrespectful behaviour of members of the families. Almost similarly, Shah (1993) concludes that the elderly, having no substantial assets or fairly good income and who are economically dependent, find the attitude and behaviour of the family members as unsatisfactory. The younger generation treats the older people as a burden and their presence in the family irks most of the family members, as per Kaur and Kaur (1987).

'Isolation' was quoted as the least important factor of conflict by the lower income group respondents (9%) while it was the second most important factor of conflict quoted by the middle (15%) and the higher (12%) income group respondents. Due to small houses, more members in their families and their preoccupation with various other problems, only a few aged women of the lower income group must be feeling lonely as compared to their counterparts belonging to the higher and the middle income groups.

The following are the specific responses about the factors/reasons of conflict, as mentioned by the urban aged women:

Specific Responses about the Factors/Reasons of Conflict

Monetary

- Son is unemployed. There is no regular source of earning.
- Distribution of property: Children want us to sell off our property and distribute the money amount among them. We do not want to sell the property.
- So many responsibilities are to be taken care of like marriage of the daughter/s, education of the children and treatment of spouse. From where would the money will come?
- Daughter-in-law objects to giving gifts to daughters.

Problem of Accommodation

- I have to stay by turn with my four sons. But I find it very difficult to shift here and there after the (informal) contract period is over. *Mujhe kanhi bhi apnatv nahi milta* (I do not get affection anywhere). It is very painful for me. I want to get settled at one place and spend the rest of my life there.
- There are four rooms in our house. We (the aged woman and her spouse) have four sons. Each son has occupied one room. We do not have a room to live in. We have to live in the corridor.

Behaviour Pattern

- Children are careless and self-centred.

Cont'd...

Cont'd...

- Family members have very aggressive attitudes. I don't dare to say anything to them.
- Children do not obey us. They do not pay us respect and recognition. I do not react. I try to make adjustments and keep my temperament/emotions under control. But there is a limit. Sometimes I loose my temper.

When family members do not come up to my (the aged woman's) expectations, I have to react:

- I do not allow the daughter-in-law to scold my grandchildren.
- If the children don't obey me, don't respect me and don't work properly or on time, I loose my temper.
- Son-in-law avoids taking gifts.
- I disapprove the dressing and/or living style of the daughter-in-law.
- Daughter-in-law is infertile. She wants to adopt a child. I want my son to go for a second marriage.
- Children want inter-caste/love marriage. I don't like all this.

When I (the aged woman) cannot come up to the expectations of members of the family, they become angry:

- I have no physical stamina. I have to work under compulsion.
- Husband is very aggressive. If I cannot complete the work on time, he starts using abusive language. He even beats me. He is an alcoholic.
- If work is not done on time, the daughter-in-law gets irritated.
- Husband asks me not to work and to take rest. But I can't sit idle. If I fall sick, he gets irritated.
- I have joined *bhajan mandli* and I want to go on a pilgrimage (*tirath yatra*). Husband does not like my involvement in this kind of activities.

Sickness/Health Problems

- Husband is paralytic. I, myself, also remain sick. I don't have any stamina. May he get well or better he dies! I can't take care of him.
- I am sick; I can't do anything. Children are good. They do a lot for us. But, very often, they loose their temper. But, it is none of their fault. It is really difficult to manage.
- When somebody falls sick, conflict arises regarding the responsibilities of the household work.

Nothing specific or serious

- Misunderstanding, difference of opinion

The responses as above describe how and why the various factors—financial, behavioural, health-related, etc., become the bases of conflict/s. And, the following is an account of problems, worries and expectations of the aged women, as perceived by them and identified as such in our study.

Problems in the Old Age

The state of health was the most prominent problem (63%) followed by loneliness, social isolation and excess of spare time (37%), neglect by family members (33%) and financial problems (32%). The conflict in the family (19%), the responsibilities about children's education, marriage and job, etc. (7%), and the dependency—financial, physical and social (4%) were the other main problems reported by the aged women (see Table 5.3). It is surprising that though most of the aged women had been dependent, economically, physically, socially or emotionally, on their families, yet they did not consider their dependency to be problematic. In fact, in India, most of the aged women relish this kind of dependency, unless and until family members are readily taking care of them. It is only when the families express unwillingness or refusal to take care of them, they realize their dependency to be problematic. And, it may be the reason why, amongst various problems reported by the aged women, the dependency was the least mentioned. However, it may also be due to the traditional family bonds.

Gravity of the Problems across Income Groups

The analysis reveals that the state of health was quoted as the most severe problem among all the income groups. However, the aged women belonging to the middle income group seem to face lesser problems of health as compared to their counterparts belonging to the lower and the higher income groups. In fact, the gravity of the problem was the highest in the lower income group (weightage (wt) = 136) followed by that in the higher (wt = 116) and the middle (wt = 91) income groups respectively (see Table 5.4).

On the other hand, the responsibility of the family and the dependency were considered to be the least problematic, occupying 7th or 8th ranks, in all the three income groups.

The gravity of financial problems was found to be increasing with the lowering in the level of the income group. In the lower

Table 5.3

Self-Rating of Priority-wise Three Main Problems faced by the Aged Women Against their Income Groups

Main Problems Faced by Aged Women	*Income Group*												*All 225 (LT +MT +HT)*
	Lower				*Middle*				*Higher*				
	75				*75*				*75*				
	Prio-rity (I)	*Prio-rity (II)*	*Prio-rity (III)*	*All (LT)*	*Prio-rity (I)*	*Prio-rity (II)*	*Prio-rity (III)*	*All (MT)*	*Prio-rity (I)*	*Prio-rity (II)*	*Prio-rity (III)*	*All (HT)*	
Financial problem	15	22	11	48	5	7	2	14	5	3	1	9	71
(% out of 225)	(6.7)	(9.8)	(4.9)	(21.3)	(2.2)	(3.1)	(0.9)	(6.2)	(2.2)	(1.3)	(0.4)	(4.0)	(31.6)
weight	45	44	11	100	15	14	2	31	15	6	1	22	153
Health problem	36	11	6	53	26	4	5	35	22	19	12	53	141
(% out of 225)	(16.0)	(4.9)	(2.7)	(23.6)	(11.6)	(1.8)	(2.2)	(15.6)	(9.8)	(8.4)	(5.4)	(23.6)	(62.7)
weight	108	22	6	136	78	8	5	91	66	38	12	116	343
Children's responsibility	4	3	3	10	1	—	—	1	1	2	2	5	16
(% out of 225)	(1.8)	(1.3)	(1.3)	(4.4)	(0.4)	—	—	(0.4)	(0.4)	(0.9)	(0.9)	(2.2)	(7.1)
weight	12	6	3	21	3			3	3	4	4	9	33
Family conflict	6	7	4	17	4	3	3	10	5	8	3	16	43
(% out of 225)	(2.7)	(3.1)	(1.8)	(7.6)	(1.8)	(1.3)	(1.3)	(4.4)	(2.2)	(3.6)	(1.3)	(7.1)	(19.1)
weight	18	14	4	36	12	6	3	21	15	16	3	34	91

Cont'd...

Cont'd...

Neglect by family members	3	6	3	12	5	11	6	22	7	18	16	41	75
(% out of 225)	(1.3)	(2.7)	(1.3)	(5.3)	(2.2)	(4.9)	(2.7)	(9.8)	(3.1)	(8.0)	(7.1)	(18.2)	(33.3)
weight	9	12	3	24	15	22	6	43	21	36	16	73	140
Disrespect in the family	3	5	12	20	3	6	4	13	3	9	7	19	52
(% out of 225)	(1.3)	(2.2)	(5.3)	(8.9)	(1.3)	(2.7)	(1.8)	(5.8)	(1.3)	(4.0)	(3.1)	(8.4)	(23.1)
weight	9	10	12	31	9	12	4	25	9	18	7	34	90
Loneliness/isolation	3	6	5	14	7	8	6	21	28	9	10	47	82
(% out of 225)	(1.3)	(2.7)	(2.2)	(6.2)	(3.1)	(3.6)	(2.7)	(9.3)	(12.4)	(4.0)	(4.4)	(20.9)	(36.4)
weight	9	12	5	26	21	16	6	43	84	18	10	112	181
Dependency (all kinds)	—	1	3	4	1	1	—	2	—	1	3	4	10
(% out of 225)	—	(0.4)	(1.3)	(1.8)	(0.4)	(0.4)	—	(0.9)	—	(0.4)	(1.3)	(1.8)	(4.4)
weight	—	2	3	5	3	2	—	5	—	2	3	5	15
No response	5	14	28	—	23	35	50	—	4	6	19	—	—
(% out of 225)	(2.2)	(6.2)	(12.4)		(10.2)	(15.6)	(22.2)		(1.8)	(2.7)	(8.4)		
weight	—	—	—		—	—	—		—	—	—		
All	75	75	75	—	75	75	75	—	75	75	75	—	—
	(100.0)	(100.0)	(100.0)		(100.0)	(100.0)	(100.0)		(100.0)	(100.0)	(100.0)		

income group, it was considered to be the second most severe problem just followed by the problem of health, while in the middle and the higher income groups it occupied 4th and 6th rank respectively.

Gravity of Problems in Old Age

The respondents were asked to mention the three most severe problems faced by them. The self-rating of the problems faced by the aged women is presented against their income groups by way of the Table 5.3. The table shows frequency and percentage distribution of the respondents and weight assigned to the problems mentioned. The weight was decided on the basis of the priority given by the respondents to a problem as follows:

Weight Assigned to a Problem

Priority (given by the respondent)	*Weight*
Most severe problem	3
2nd most severe problem	2
3rd most severe problem	1

Thus, for each response (problem), the weight was allotted accordingly. The total weight assigned to a problem was an indicative of the gravity of that problem. And the problem with the maximum total weight was considered as the most severe problem of the concerned income group and vice versa. The weight and the rankings (gravity-wise) of the problems have been presented against the income groups in the Table 5.4. Table 5.4 is basically a summarized version of the Table 5.3.

Loneliness is a feeling of being left alone. This feeling has its basis in interpersonal dissatisfaction or breakdown. Loneliness can also be based on distortion about relationships, i.e., one does not get what one expects out of a relationship. Loneliness in the elderly is generally characterized by emptiness, isolation and alienation. The causes of loneliness are numerous, of which a few, according to Kanwar and Chadha (1988) are widowhood, housing dissatisfaction, decreased income, having fewer close friends and contacts. Weeks (1994) has reviewed the concepts of loneliness with particular reference to old age and suggested that successful treatment of loneliness in life reduces the risk of more serious complications, such as feeling of meaninglessness, decrease in social contacts, self-esteem and trust. Rokach (1996) has shown

Table 5.4
Weight and Rank Order of Main Problems faced by Urban Aged Women of the Three Income Groups

Main Problems Faced	*Income Group*			*All*
	Lower	*Middle*	*Higher*	
Health problems	136* (1)**	91 (1)	116 (1)	343 (1)
Loneliness/Social isolation	26 (5)	43 (2.5)	112 (2)	181 (2)
Financial problems	100 (2)	31 (4)	22 (6)	153 (3)
Neglect by members of the family	24 (6)	43 (2.5)	73 (3)	140 (4)
Conflict in the family	36 (3)	21 (6)	34 (4.5)	91 (5)
Disrespect by members of the family	31 (4)	25 (5)	34 (4.5)	90 (6)
Responsibilities of children (their education, marriage, service and family, etc.)	21 (7)	3 (8)	9 (7)	33 (7)
Dependency—physical, financial, emotional or of all kinds	5 (8)	5 (7)	5 (8)	15 (8)

* *Weight* ** *Rank*

that loneliness at any age level could be reduced by acceptance and reflection, social interaction and increased activity. Similarly, Patel and Broota (2000) found that greater perceived responsibility and control were associated with less loneliness.

Perhaps, the higher the income group, the greater are the expectations from the members of the family, and hence, more intense is the feeling of loneliness. However, it is clear from the above details that loneliness is a personal and social problem, experienced more by the aged women of the higher income group (wt=112) followed by those belonging to the middle (wt=43) and the lower income group (wt=26) respectively.

Feeling of neglect generally results in loneliness and isolation. Feeling of neglect of the urban aged women may have its genesis in two factors: First, the younger generation has become too busy in its own life. Their studies, peer groups, jobs, channels of communication like television, and now, also computers, e-mail and the Internet consume most of their time. They neither have the need nor the interest to go to their elderly. More the competition they face, the more they become involved in their own business. In the changing scenario, needless to say, the aged women will lose, and actually already have lost, considerable powers in the wake of their contact with the industrial world.

In many patriarchal societies like those prevailing in most of the regions of India, women join husbands at marriage, the young daughters-in-law of the household not only relieve mothers-in-law of more burdensome tasks, but also work under their close scrutiny. They are expected to be submissive, showing respect and submitting to the will and whims of their mothers-in-law. The changes that give women of the young generation the opportunities to choose their spouses weaken the elder women's control over marriage arrangements, daughters-in-law and grandchildren. Also, new or expanded wage earning opportunities for young women, for example, often reduce aged women's authority. The young women now have economic resources of their own, and are less likely to work under aged women's supervision. All this results in the feeling of neglect among the urban aged women

Secondly, the aged women find it difficult to adapt to the changes. They are still very demanding, having great expectations from the members of their families. They compare themselves with the other aged women who luckily still enjoy the authority over their daughters-in-law or children. They may not openly admit, but this comparison makes them more demanding. And when their expectations are not met, they feel neglected. It results in their loneliness. And, many a time, it becomes the basis of conflict in the family.

It is inferred from the above facts and the available data that higher the income group, more prone the urban aged women will be to the feeling of neglect (see Table 5.4).

Regarding maladjustment in the family, the aged women of the middle income group were better off. Family conflict was reported to be more a phenomenon of the lower income group (wt=36), followed by the higher (wt=34) and the middle income group (wt=21). And the disrespect in the family was reported more by the aged women of the higher income group (wt=34), followed by the lower (wt=31) and the middle (wt=25) income group.

Cultural traditions often die-hard and age norms are no exception. The middle income group and to some extent, the higher income group also are considered as the reservoir of cultural traditions. But these traditions are found to be very weak in the lower income group. Therefore, the domestic authority of the aged women may be the cause of conflict in the middle or the higher income groups. Foner (1989) has argued that older women have a strong interest in maintaining the subordinate position of the young women in the family. For healthy and active women in many non-western cultures, the later years are a time when they come into their own. Old age offers them the chance to achieve greater freedom, influence and prestige within and beyond the family group. While women's opportunities often expand with age, young women are, for the moment, left behind. They may not voice their frustrations openly, but tensions may lie beneath the surface. And whenever the young women get the chance, they also exploit their old mothers-in-law. Wherever serious imbalances of privilege, power and opportunities for autonomy exist between older and young women, tensions and resentments are likely to surface.

But, in the lower income group, the aged women have already lost the authority. Generally, they suffer from health problems and have lesser control over children. The conflict is mostly over resources. The children frequently show disrespect or even abuse their elders. There had been cases where the son tried to kill his mother to get the room occupied by her vacated; or four sons of an aged couple living with them just to get free accommodation, but not offering any kind of support to the parents; not even emotional support (do not even ask about their health), what to talk about financial support. The poor woman in such cases has to raise her voice to live and to get some resources for her survival. Alcoholism and health problems are also reported to cause family conflicts and tensions.

It can be now stated that the health problem is the most severe problem, whereas the 'familial responsibilities' and the 'dependency—physical, social or emotional' are reported to be the least problematic for the aged women of all the three income groups. Also, the lower the income group, the graver are the financial problems. And the elderly women of the higher income group are more prone to the feelings of social isolation, loneliness and neglect by members of the family. The disrespect in the family is also felt more by the aged women of the higher income group, followed by the lower and the middle income group respectively. Regarding health problems, family conflicts and family responsibilities, the old women of the lower income group seem to be the main sufferers, followed by those of the higher and the middle income group respectively.

Worries in Old Age

Worries are inherent part of human personality. To a limited extent, everybody feels worried. But worrying too much is harmful. Worries and happiness are generally found to be negatively correlated. The happy aged have lesser worries. The intensity and the types of worries may, thus, be considered as the parameters of happy ageing. To make ageing a happy phenomenon, some workable strategies need to be developed so as to keep the worries away from the aged persons.

Types of Worries

An account of the types of worries faced by the aged women of the three income groups show that the familial worries (54%) predominated among the urban aged women, followed by the personal (51%) and the financial worries (39%). Also, the lower the income group, the more had been the worries, and vice versa. This was true for all types of worries—personal, familial and financial (see Table 5.5).

Real Worries and Imaginary Fears

The worries may be real, generated out of the present problems faced by a person, or, they may be imaginary. An attempt to describe the real and imaginary worries of the urban aged women follows.

Real Worries

A little more than half of the urban aged women had been worried about their own failing health. About one-third of them was worried due to lack of any source of earning, uncertain future of the children and illness of the spouse or other members of the

Table 5.5

Type of Worries and Income Groups of Urban Aged Women

Type of Worries	*Income Group*			*All 225 (100.0)*
	Lower 75 (100.0)	*Middle 75 (100.0)*	*Higher 75 (100.0)*	
Personal	63	35	16	114
% within income group	(84.0)*	(46.7)	(21.3)	(50.7)
Familial	51	45	26	122
% within income group	(68.0)*	(60.0)	(34.7)	(54.2)
Financial	46	26	15	87
% within income group	(61.3)*	(34.7)	(20.0)	(38.7)

Note: * These percentages may not add up to 100 because of multiple worries reported by most of the respondents.

Table 5.6

Perceived Real Worries and Income Groups

Real Worries (Pearson chi-square value at df=2)	*Income Group*			*All 225 (100.0)*
	Lower 75 (33.3)	*Middle 75 (33.3)*	*Higher 75 (33.3)*	
Failing health (own)	62	38	22	122
(χ^2=43.546; Asymp.sig.=.000)	(27.6)*	(16.9)	(9.8)	(54.2)
Illness of spouse/family members	34	24	10	68
(χ^2=18.378; Asymp. sig.=.000)	(15.1)*	(10.7)	(4.4)	(30.2)
Lack of source of earning	51	14	5	70
(χ^2=73.949; Asymp. sig.=.000)	(22.7)*	(6.2)	(2.2)	(31.1)
Children's uncertain future	30	22	18	70
(χ^2=4.645; Asymp. sig.=.098)	(13.3)*	(9.8)	(8.0)	(31.1)
Problem of social isolation	30	19	13	62
(χ^2=9.930; Asymp. sig.=.007)	(13.3)*	(8.4)	(5.8)	(27.5)
Indifferent/Self-centred family member/s	33	13	10	56
(χ^2=22.300; Asymp. sig.=.000)	(14.7)*	(5.8)	(4.4)	(24.9)
Death of spouse/family member/s	23	8	9	40
(χ^2=12.831; Asymp. sig.=.002)	(10.2)*	(3.6)	(4.0)	(17.8)
Misbehaviour by family members, about property, etc.	7	2	4	13
(χ^2=3.102; Asymp. sig.=.212)	(3.1)*	(0.9)	(1.8)	(5.8)

Note: * Percentage within income group. These percentages may not add up to 100 because of multiple worries reported by a few of the respondents.

Table 5.7

Perceived Imaginary Fears and Income Groups

Imaginary Fears (Pearson chi-square value at df=2 and level of significance)	*Income Group*			*All 225 (100.0)*
	Lower 75 (33.3)	*Middle 75 (33.3)*	*Higher 75 (33.3)*	
Fear of being dependent ($\chi2$=8.393; Asymp.sig.= 0.015)	12 (5.3)*	3 (1.3)	4 (1.8)	19 (8.4)
Fear about children's future ($\chi2$=2.529; Asymp. sig.= 0.282)	13 (5.8)*	8 (3.6)	7 (3.1)	28 (12.4)
Fear of being isolated ($\chi2$=8.001; Asymp. sig.= 0.018)	9 (4.0)*	2 (0.9)	2 (0.9)	13 (5.8)
Fear about spouse's health/death ($\chi2$=4.976; Asymp. sig. = 0.083)	14 (6.2)*	9 (4.0)	5 (2.2)	28 (12.4)
Fear of financial insecurity ($\chi2$=6.250; Asymp. sig. = 0.044)	6 (2.7)*	3 (1.3)	—	9 (4.0)
Fear of murder/theft/accident ($\chi2$=.295; Asymp. sig. = 0.863)	2 (0.9)*	2 (0.9)	3 (1.3)	7 (3.1)

Note: * Percentage out of 225. These percentages may not add up to 100 because of multiple worries reported by a few of the respondents.

family. Social isolation and indifference or self-centred attitude of members of the family were the factors over which about one-fourth of the aged women had been worried. The proportion of the aged women suffering from these worries was higher in the lower income group compared to the middle and the higher income group respectively (see Table 5.6).

The death (18%) and misbehaviour (6%) of member/s of the family were the other causes of worry as reported by the aged women. These worries were more prominent in the lower income group followed by the higher and the middle income group.

Imaginary Fears

As compared to the real worries, the perceived imaginary fears were less prevalent. Yet, a significant proportion (12%) of the aged women had been suffering from various imaginary fears. Fear about spouse's failing health or death (12%), fear of some mishappening with the children (12%) and fear of loss of income

(4%) were reported more by the aged women of the lower income group, followed by those belonging to the middle and the higher income groups. The fears of being physically dependent on others (8%) and being isolated (6%) were also reported more by the aged women of the lower income group. But, the proportion of such respondents was more or less similar (1–2%) in the middle and higher income groups. About 3 per cent respondents, belonging almost in equal proportion to the three income groups, had also been afraid of murder, theft or accident (see Table 5.7).

Perception about Real Worries and Imaginary Fears

The following is an account of perceptions of the urban aged women about their real worries and imaginary fears

Perception about Real Worries:

About Loneliness

— During the interview, a number of the aged women said that they had been feeling lonely. Since, nobody was there with whom they could share their feelings, sorrows and problems or who could take care of them at the time of their serious sickness. Prasad (1987) had rightly described the situation as "a new type of destitution—there are too many relatives but there is none to bear any responsibility".

Fear of Being Isolated

— The currently married respondents thought that they and their spouses wouldn't die together. They were at a loss as to imagine how one would pass life after the death of the other. A few of the aged women who were socially and financially dependent on their unmarried daughters were worried that nobody would be there to take care of them after their marriage. Otherwise also, many of the aged women were found to be afraid that they might become lonely after the marriage of their children.

About Health

— An aged woman was suffering from breast cancer. She needed immediate operation. She was afraid of the surgery and was tense to imagine of her body with the removed breast.

— Most of the currently married respondents were worried about the failing health of their spouses. The husbands of two of the aged women were paralytic and bed ridden for the last few years. The aged women themselves were also weak and in poor health. Still, they had to take care of their spouses. One of the women was so fed up of the situation that she wished "Better he (her paralytic spouse) dies!"

About Children and Grandchildren

- A significantly high proportion of the aged women did not know how to secure future of their children. The children were unmarried/unemployed/ divorcee/widowed/ mentally disturbed or non-serious/irresponsible.
- Daughters of a few of the aged women were barren. The aged women were afraid that their sons-in-law might abandon their daughters and remarry. The aged women who had no grandchildren were worried about their sons. They said that if anything happened to the sons, nobody would be there to bear their responsibilities. In old age, one needs help and assistance. The aged women were worried that how their sons would pass their life in old age; and that, when they (the sons) would die, who would perform their last rites. The respondents were afraid that in such a situation their sons wouldn't get *moksha* after the death.

About Income, Money and Property

- Some of the respondents were totally dependent on the house rent for their survival. They were afraid that the tenants might vacate the house. They had no other source of income. On the other hand, the aged women living all alone were at their wit's end since nobody was there to take care of or inherit their property. The thought, "what would happen to the property after our death", disturbed them a lot.

Degrading Values

- The aged women were disturbed due to degenerate fashion prevalent especially among women and were worried about the degrading values of the society.

Perception about Imaginary Worries:

- Most of the aged women were afraid of being physically dependent on others. They wished "Better to die rather than becoming physically dependent on others."
- Some of the higher and middle income group respondents had the fear that somebody might kill them for their property and money.

Perception behind No Worries:

- There were aged women who had no worries. They reportedly had all the facilities and could do all their work of their own. They were not dependent on anybody.
- The others were of the opinion that everything was left on God. Whatever be the circumstances, they were ready to face. A few of the aged women used to believe in present and did not bother about the future.

Expectations in Old Age

The following is an account of expectations of the urban aged women from the families, the neighbours and they themselves.

Opinion about Role of Family in Helping the Aged

About half (55%) of the sampled aged women opined that the family groups could do a lot to help their aged. A few (8%) did not consider family groups to be responsible, or capable of helping their aged. And, the remaining did not express a clear opinion.

A strong association between the 'opinion' and the 'income group' was statistically noticed. And it clearly seems as if the aged women of the lower income group expect more help from the family as compared to their counterparts belonging to the middle and the higher income group respectively.

Expectations from Members of the Family

The one-third of the aged women, irrespective of their income group, expected emotional support, love, care and respect from the families. They (4%) also wanted the basic facilities like food, medicine, clothing, etc., to be arranged properly for them. Respectful behaviour of members of the family was expected mainly by the higher income group respondents (4%) followed by the middle and the lower income group respectively. The aged women, mainly belonging to the lower income group (6%) followed by the higher (1%) and the middle income group (2%) respectively, also suggested the families to extend some financial assistance to their aged. The 3 per cent respondents, with majority belonging to the middle income group followed by the higher and the lower income group wanted that the family members should obey their aged. Also, a few (3%) of the aged women were such that they had no other expectation from the members of their families except that they (the family members) become independent and self-reliant.

The elderly women of the lower income group, as per the earlier findings, had more health problems. The deteriorating health may be the reason why 4 per cent respondents from this group and only negligible number of respondents from the middle and higher income group wanted the families to understand their needs and to help them in routine activities.

In a nutshell, the aged women expect emotional support, love, care and respect from the families. They also want the basic facilities like food, medicine, clothing, etc., to be taken care of properly for them. Help in the day-to-day activities, financial assistance, respectful behaviour and zeal to be self-reliant and independent were some of the other expectations of the aged women from the members of the family.

Perception about Role of Neighbours in Helping the Aged

A little more than one-fourth of the aged women felt that the neighbours had no role in helping the aged. Approximately 42 per cent of the women were undecided in this regard. And the remaining felt that the neighbours could do a lot to help the aged. The analysis reveals that the aged women of the lower income group (40%) had greater expectations from the neighbours compared to those of the middle (27%) and higher (24%) income group respectively. Given below is an account of these expectations from the neighbours:

Expectations (as expressed by the respondents) from the Neighbours:	
1.	They should keep contacts with the aged and should timely enquire about their health. This is thought to be more than what could be expected from them.
2.	They should maintain good behaviour and co-operative attitude.
3.	They should give company and emotional support to their aged friends.
4.	In case the family does not/cannot take care of the elderly, the neighbours should come forward to help them. They may provide food, medical aid, shelter and emotional support to the needy aged.
5.	In case of conflict situation, they should intervene and should play a positive role in resolving the conflict.

But some of the aged women were of the opinion that the aged were the responsibilities of only the families. The neighbours, being generally self-centred and selfish, did not keep any contacts. In a situation, when even the families were not responsible enough, it was thought impractical to expect anything from the neighbours.

Opinion about the Aged Women

About 40 per cent of the aged women opined that they themselves could do much to improve their situation. In this regard, the aged women of the higher income group (45%) appeared to be more optimistic about their role as compared to those belonging to the middle (38%) and the lower income group (38%). The remaining respondents either considered the aged women helpless—owing to poor health, powerlessness or lack of knowledge; or gave no clear opinion in this regard.

Expectations from the Aged Women

Those, who thought that the aged women could play a role in improving their own situation, came up with some suggestions. A change in the attitude, ideology and thinking of the aged women was suggested (by 16% respondents, belonging in almost equal proportion, to the three income groups) so as to improve their situation. The specific strategies mentioned in this regard were: Be optimistic. Be caring and supportive to the family members. Have faith in God and spend some time in worship. Try to remain physically fit by morning/evening walk, proper diet and light exercises. Remain busy. And try to avoid all kinds of dependency, physical, economic or emotional.

The other suggestion (by 6%, 5% and 4% respondents belonging to the lower, middle and higher income group respectively) was that the aged women should play a positive and constructive role in familial adjustment. The strategies suggested in this regard were: Avoid unnecessary intervention in all family matters. Try to be changed rather than changing the others. Cooperate in work and household responsibilities. And play a positive role in maintaining peace. Avoid tension, speak politely and control behaviour/ temperament.

About one-tenth of the aged women (majority being from the lower income group followed by the middle and the higher income group respectively) suggested that the aged women should try to be economically independent and should also try to gain control over financial matters.

A few of the higher (5%) and middle income group respondents (1%) were of the opinion that the aged women should make self-help groups so as to help the other aged women. But not even a single respondent of the lower income group was found to be thinking on this line.

All the suggestions given by the respondents have practical utility and are worth implementing.

Parameters and Correlates of Satisfaction in Old Age

To identify the parameters of satisfaction in old age, the respondents were asked to express their satisfaction level at a three point scale: satisfactory, neither satisfactory nor dissatisfactory (so-so) and dissatisfactory. The following is an attempt to analyse the satisfaction level with relation to the level of physical mobility, the level of competence in the household work, the level of social interaction and the income group (The three levels, i.e., the measures obtained after scaling, have been described in the Appendix). A probe into the factors contributing to satisfaction and dis-satisfaction in the old age is presented below.

Level of Physical Mobility

The level of physical mobility, a measure of capability of performing activities of daily living (ADL), has been analysed with relation to the satisfaction level (see Table 5.8). Amongst those having the perfect level of mobility, 45 per cent of aged women felt satisfied. The satisfied aged women constituted 33 per cent and 29 per cent of those having the moderate and the low level of mobility respectively. This indicates that the higher the level of physical mobility, the higher will be the level of satisfaction in old age. However, the chi-square value indicates only a poor association between the two variables.

Table 5.8

Levels of Physical Mobility and Satisfaction in Old Age

Level of Physical Mobility (score values)	*Opinion about Old Age*			*All*
	Satisfactory	*So-so*	*Dissatisfactory*	
Perfect (9)	38	33	14	85
% within level of physical mobility	(44.7)	(38.8)	(16.5)	(100.0)
% out of grand total	(16.9)	(14.7)	(6.2)	(37.8)
Moderate (10–14)	34	47	21	102
% within level of physical mobility	(33.3)	(46.1)	(20.6)	(100.0)
% out of grand total	(15.1)	(20.9)	(9.3)	(45.3)
Low (15+)	11	14	13	38
% within level of physical mobility	(28.9)	(36.8)	(34.2)	(100.0)
% out of grand total	(4.9)	(6.2)	(5.8)	(16.9)
All	83	94	48	225
% within level of physical mobility	(36.9)	(41.8)	(21.3)	(100.0)
% out of grand total	(36.9)	(41.8)	(21.3)	(100.0)

Pearson chi-square value = 7.180 at df=4; Asymp. sig. (2-sided) = 0.127

Level of Competence in Household Work

The level of competence, a measure developed to judge the capability of performing household work, has been analysed with relation to the expressed satisfaction level (see Table 5.9). The trends indicate a negative association between the 'level of competence in the household work' and the 'opinion about satisfaction' in old age. In other words, it can be stated that *the lower the competence in the household work, the higher is the level of satisfaction in old age* and vice versa.

Table 5.9

Levels of Competence in Household Work and Satisfaction in Old Age

Competence in Household Work (score values)	*Old Age*			*All*
	Satisfactory	*So-so/ Can't say*	*Dis-satisfactory*	
Low (6–9)	55	51	25	131
% within satisfaction level	(66.3)	(54.3)	(52.1)	(58.2)
% out of grand total	(24.4)	(22.7)	(11.1)	(58.2)
Moderate (10–14)	23	33	12	68
% within satisfaction level	(27.7)	(35.1)	(25.0)	(30.2)
% out of grand total	(10.2)	(14.7)	(5.3)	(30.2)
High (15–18)	5	10	11	26
% within satisfaction level	(6.0)	(10.6)	(22.9)	(1 1.6)
% out of grand total	(2.2)	(4.4)	(4.9)	(11.6)
All	83	94	48	225
% within satisfaction level	(100.0)	(100.0)	(100.0)	(100.0)
% out of grand total	(36.9)	(41.8)	(21.3)	(100.0)

Pearson chi-square value = 10.463 at df=4; Asymp. sig. (2-sided) = 0.033

The chi-square value indicates that the above-described association is significant, though not remarkably high.

Level of Social Interaction

The level of social interaction is a measure of frequency of interactions with other individuals. It has been analysed with relation to the expressed satisfaction level about old age. Amongst the satisfied aged women, about 70 per cent had a moderate level of social interaction, while those with a high and a low level of interaction constituted 27 per cent and 4 per cent respectively. On the other extreme, out of the dissatisfied respondents, 46 per cent had a moderate level of interaction, 44 per cent had a high level of interaction while the level of interaction of the remaining 10 per cent was low (see Table 5.10).

Table 5.10

Level of Social Interaction and Satisfaction in Old Age

Social Interaction (score values)	*Old Age*			*All*
	Satisfactory	*So-so/ Can't say*	*Dis-satisfacto ry*	
Low (5–11)	3	5	5	13
% within satisfaction level	(3.6)	(5.3)	(10.4)	(5.8)
% out of grand total	(1.3)	(2.2)	(2.2)	(5.8)
Moderate (12–18)	58	51	22	131
% within satisfaction level	(69.9)	(54.3)	(45.8)	(58.2)
% out of grand total	(25.8)	(22.7)	(9.8)	(58.2)
High (19–25)	22	38	21	81
% within satisfaction level	(26.5)	(40.4)	(43.8)	(36.0)
% out of grand total	(9.8)	(16.9)	(9.3)	(36.0)
All	83	94	48	225
% within satisfaction level	(100.0)	(100.0)	(100.0)	(100.0)
% out of grand total	(36.9)	(41.8)	(21.3)	(100.0)

Pearson chi-square value = 9.341 at df=4; Asymp. sig. (2-sided) = 0.053

These trends support that the aged women with a moderate level of social interaction consider their old age to be more satisfactory compared to those having a high and a low level of interaction respectively (χ^2 = 9.341 at df=4; Asymp. sig. = .053). The chi-square value indicates that this association is strong.

Income Group

The proportion of the dissatisfied respondents decreases while that of satisfied respondents increases with an increase in the level of income. To be specific, 12 per cent, 33 per cent and 66 per cent aged women of the lower, middle and higher income groups respectively expressed satisfaction about their old age (see

Table 5.11). This clearly shows that 'the lower the income group, the more will be the dissatisfaction about the old age' and vice versa. And, this association is remarkably high.

Table 5.11

Income Group and Satisfaction in Old Age

Income Group	*Old Age*			*All*
	Satis-factory	*Neither satisfactory nor dis-satisfactory*	*Dis-satisfactory*	
Lower	9	39	27	75
% within income group	(12.0)	(52.0)	(36.0)	(100.0)
% out of grand total	(4.0)	(17.3)	(12.0)	(33.3)
Middle	25	39	11	75
% within income group	(33.3)	(52.0)	(14.7)	(100.0)
% out of grand total	(11.1)	(17.3)	(4.9)	(33.3)
Higher	49	16	10	75
% within income group	(65.3)	(21.3)	(13.3)	(100.0)
% out of grand total	(21.8)	(7.1)	(4.4)	(33.3)
All	83	94	48	225
% within income group	(36.9)	(41.8)	(21.3)	(100.0)
% out of grand total	(36.9)	(41.8)	(21.3)	(100.0)

Pearson chi-square value = 51.932 at df=4; Asymp. sig. (2-sided) = 0.000

In sum, the higher the level of physical mobility; the lower the level of competence in the household work; and the higher the income group, the higher will be the level of satisfaction in old age; and vice versa. These findings indicate that, to be satisfied in old age, one is required to be in good health so as to be capable of independently performing, at least, the activities of daily living (ADL). The finding about the competence in the household work indicates that the aged women, perhaps, want disengagement from the household work to feel satisfied. Also, the higher income group respondents are in better health and position to enjoy a choice in this regard and otherwise also, and hence feel more satisfied than their counterparts belonging to the middle and the lower income groups respectively.

As far as the level of social interaction is concerned, those having a moderate level enjoy the higher level of satisfaction, followed by those with a high and a low level of social interaction.

In other words, those who maintain a balance between engagement and disengagement, feel more satisfied than those with a high level (reflecting engagement) and a low level (showing disengagement) of social interaction.

In other words, to be satisfied in old age, women need to maintain good health so as to be physically active, enjoy choice/freedom as far as household responsibilities are concerned, and maintain a moderate level of social interaction. These findings also indicate that neither the disengagement theory nor the activity theory is entirely applicable. Rather the aged women, who maintain a balance between activity and disengagement, are found to be more satisfied in their old age.

Factors Contributing to Satisfaction/Dissatisfaction

Following is an attempt to identify the factors which contribute to satisfaction and dissatisfaction in old age:

Factors Contributing to Satisfaction in Old Age

More leisure time (48%), increase in amenities (38%), less family worries (38%) and improved health (19%) are the main factors contributing to satisfaction in the old age. And regarding all these

Table 5.12

Factors Contributing to Satisfaction in Old Age and Income Group

Factors Contributing to Satisfaction in Old Age (Pearson chi-square value at df=2)	*Income Group*			*All* 225 *(100.0)*
	Lower 75 *(33.3)**	*Middle* 75 *(33.3)*	*Higher* 75 *(33.3)*	
Increase in amenities and facilities (χ^2=42.613; Asymp. sig.= 0.000)	12 (5.3)	24 (10.7)	50 (22.2)	86 (38.2)
More time (χ^2=24.593; Asymp. sig= 0.000)	20 (8.9)	39 (17.3)	50 (22.2)	109 (48.4)
Less family worries (χ^2=19.324; Asymp. Sig. = 0.000)	18 (8.0)	24 (10.7)	43 (19.1)	85 (37.8)
Improved health (χ^2=10.408; Asymp. Sig. = 0.005)	8 (3.6)	12 (5.3)	23 (10.2)	43 (19.1)

Note: * Percentage out of grand total of 225.

factors, the higher income group is better off, followed by the middle and the lower income group (see Table 5.12).

Factors Contributing to Dissatisfaction in Old Age

As compared to the factors of satisfaction in old age, these factors are more in number. Deterioration in health (44%) is the most prominent factor of dissatisfaction in old age, followed by the feeling of lack of friends (42%), more household worries (32%), lack of income (30%), lack of amenities (27%) and excess of leisure time (25%). Morbid anxiety (18%), isolation (16%) and little respect in family (12%) were also reported as contributing significantly to the dissatisfaction in old age (see Table 5.13).

Table 5.13

Factors Contributing to Dissatisfaction in Old Age and Income Group

Factors Contributing to Dissatisfaction in Old Age (Pearson chi-square value at df=2)	*Income Group*			*All 225 (100.0)*
	*Lower 75 (33.3)**	*Middle 75 (33.3)*	*Higher 75 (33.3)*	
Less amenities (χ^2=89.379; Asymp. sig. = .000)	50 (22.2)	7 (3.1)	4 (1.8)	61 (27.1)
Less income (χ^2=99.939; Asymp. sig. = .000)	55 (24.4)	9 (4.0)	4 (1.8)	68 (30.2)
More household worries (χ^2=43.353; Asymp. sig. = .000)	45 (20.0)	20 (8.9)	8 (3.6)	73 (32.4)
Deterioration in health (χ^2=63.324; Asymp. sig. = .000)	61 (27.1)	23 (10.2)	16 (7.1)	100 (44.4)
Less friends (χ^2=49.227; Asymp. sig. = .000)	56 (24.9)	22 (9.8)	17 (7.6)	95 (42.2)
Little respect in family (χ^2=14.766; Asymp. sig. = .001)	18 (8.0)	3 (1.3)	7 (3.1)	28 (12.4)
More leisure time (χ^2=32.284; Asymp.sig. = .000)	36 (16.0)	14 (6.2)	7 (3.1)	57 (25.3)
Fear of death (of self or spouse) (χ^2=7.397; Asymp. sig. = .025)	21 (9.3)	11 (4.9)	9 (4.0)	41 (18.2)
Isolation (χ^2=15.496; Asymp. sig. = .000)	19 (8.4)	14 (6.2)	2 (0.9)	35 (15.6)
Miscellaneous	4 (1.8)	3 (1.3)	2 (0.9)	9 (4.0)

Note: * Percentage out of grand total of 225.

Little respect in the family was felt more by the aged women of the lower income group, followed by those belonging to the higher income group. The middle income group women were better off in this regard. Regarding all the other factors described above, the lower income group women were the main sufferers followed by the middle and the higher income group. Statistically also, these variables were found to be associated closely with the 'income group'.

To be noticed, excess of leisure contributes to the satisfaction of 48 per cent of the aged women. And the same (excess of leisure time) proves dissatisfactory for 25 per cent respondents. Obviously, it is the attitude of the respondents, which makes the difference.

The above is an account of the problems, worries, fears and expectations of the urban aged women; and the parameters and correlates of satisfaction in old age. On the basis of this account, a *plan of action* for social work intervention has been drawn and suggested in the following chapter.

6
Social Work Intervention in Ageing

By analysing the problems of the aged women and the causes thereof, and identifying the factors contributing to satisfaction or dissatisfaction in the old age, the professional social workers can offer valued help to the aged (women included) in the contemporary Indian society. Enabling the aged in reality perception and adjustment by providing required information (role of an enabler); bringing out necessary changes in the attitude and behaviour patterns through required guidance and counselling (role as a guide); getting the desired changes in public policy and social legislation introduced (role of an advocate and change agent); contacting different departments/organizations/agencies providing servi -ces for the aged and acting as a link between them and the aged (role of a liaison person); ensuring availability of different types of services in an integrated manner (role of a coordinator); mobilizing community resources to meet out the needs of the aged (role of a community organizer); protesting and lobbying against the unjust practices of various government and non government organizations, for example, not properly utilizing the funds meant for the aged, corruption or carelessness in the distribution of the old age pension, employing non-professionals where social workers need to be employed (role of a social activist), and a host of similar strategies may be adopted by the social workers to resolve the problems faced by the aged.

On the basis of the problems faced by urban aged women and the parameters of satisfaction, a course of action is being suggested with a view to make old age a satisfied and happy phenomenon. To begin with, some of the international and national efforts to tackle the challenges of 'ageing populations' may be noted.

An attempt will also be made to analyse the role of professional social work in this regard. The course of action is suggested with particular reference to the concerned area. It is developed keeping in view the latent goodwill, the resource persons residing and the NGOs functioning in the area, besides the social workers and government organizations/departments.

International and National Efforts

In 1982, the United Nations (UN) convened the historic World Assembly on Ageing to promote awareness of the developmental and humanitarian implications of ageing. In the Assembly, there was consensus on adoption of the International Plan of Action on Ageing. The objectives of the plan include: advance understanding of the economic, social, cultural and humanitarian implications of the ageing population; stimulating action-oriented policies and programmes for social security and enhancing their participation in and benefit from development; developing appropriate education, training and research; and fostering an international exchange of skills and knowledge in the field of ageing. The international seminar was held from September 9–20, 1985 at the October Palace of Culture at Kiev, the Ukrainian Soviet Socialist Republic with the aim of promoting and implementing the International Plan of Action for ageing at various levels (UN, 1986).

The last two decades of the previous century have witnessed considerable discussions and debates on the impact of demographic transition and of changes in society and economy on the situation of older persons. The UN Principles for Older Persons adopted by the UN General Assembly in 1991, the Proclamation on Ageing and the Global Targets on Ageing for the year 2001 adopted by the General Assembly in 1992, and various other resolutions adopted from time to time, were intended to encourage governments to design their own policies and programmes in this regard (Government of India, 1987).

The representatives of the governments meeting at the Second World Assembly on Ageing at Madrid decided to adopt an International Plan of Action on Ageing, 2002. The plan calls for changes in attitudes, policies and practices at all levels in all sections so that enormous potential of ageing population in the twenty-first century may be fulfilled. The plan intended to be a practical tool to assist policy-makers to focus on the key priorities associated with individual and population ageing. The priorities were: older persons and development; advancing health and well-being in old age; and ensuring enabling and supportive environments. A number of central themes running through the plan included:

1. The full realization of all human rights and fundamental freedom of all older persons.
2. The achievement of secure ageing and eradicating poverty in old age.
3. Empowerment of older persons to fully and effectively participate in the economic, political and social lives of their societies.
4. Provision of opportunities for individual development, self-fulfilment and well-being throughout one's life.
5. Ensuring the full enjoyment of economic, social and cultural rights, and civil and political rights of persons and eliminating all forms of violence and discrimination against older persons.
6. Commitment of gender equality among older persons through, inter alia, elimination of gender-based discrimination.

The Plan further reaffirmed the principles and recommendations for action endorsed by the UN General Assembly of 1982 and UN Principles of Older Persons, adopted by the General Assembly in 1991, which provided guidance in areas of independence, participation, care, self-fulfilment and dignity.

The international efforts, as mentioned above, became instrumental in making India realize various challenges posed due to the ageing of the population. The various international, regional and national level bodies have recommended various Plans of Action. Enactment of a concrete and effective National Policy on Older Persons (NPOP) had always been an inherent part of these recommendations. Well-being of older persons has also been mandated in the Constitution of India. The Article 41, a Directive Principle of State Policy, has directed that the state shall, within the limits of its economic capacity and development, make effective provisions for securing the right to public assistance in cases of old age.

As a result of the above-mentioned factors, in August 1998, the Ministry of Social Justice and Empowerment, of the Government of India announced the National Policy on Older Persons. This policy again draws a plan of action with some specific recommendations for the governmental and non-governmental institutions. (The critical appraisal of the policy is given in the second chapter.)

The Government of India has been slow to recognize its responsibilities towards the aged, particularly the aged women. To our politicians, ageing seems to be the issue, which may easily be shifted to the last priority. In such a situation, NPOP, 1999 is definitely a landmark. Keeping in view our limited resources and the apathetic attitude of the society, it is yet doubtful whether there will be any desired change in the status of the aged, particularly the aged women, since whatever policies and programmes we have, are not free from gender bias. And they do not give due consideration to the special needs of the aged women. Hence, recognizing the special needs of the aged women, we should carefully review the options for dealing with their special needs.

Social Work Profession's Concern for Gerontology: An Analysis

Though, the aged and their problems have received national and international attention, but they are not the sole concern of only the states. The whole society bears some responsibility towards its aged. Hence, the non-government and educational institutions have a big deal in rectifying the situation. The social work profession also has a prime role to play in this regard. But in India, the social work institutions have not shown the satisfactory concern. However, an attempt towards developing gerontological social work was undertaken by different national, regional and international platforms. The National Seminar on Globalization and Ageing: Implications for Gerontological Social Work

(Mumbai), organized on December 22–24, 1997 (IJSW, 1998), needs a special mention in this regard. The seminar recommended:

Adoption of Guiding Principles for Older Persons by the State

On the basis of the United Nations Principles for Older Persons (organized in five clusters: independence, participation, care, self-fulfilment and dignity), the government may develop the following principles to guide the national policy for the well-being of older persons: positive perception of older persons; need for outreach to vulnerable older persons; rights of older persons; family and community as natural support systems; sensitivity to the background of older persons; barrier-free environment; and participatory approach. These guiding principles for work with older persons need to be integrated in the legislation, old age pension schemes and grant-in-aid schemes of the Ministry of Welfare, and policies and programmes of the other ministries. Services, when made available, should also be accessible to those who need them and people should be made aware of their availability. The state needs to coordinate and collaborate with the voluntary organizations, academic institutions and international organizations to promote the principles for the well-being of older persons.

Developmental Work by the Voluntary Organizations

The voluntary organizations should plan and implement the following activities guided by the above-stated principles: developmental programmes for preparing for and coping with old age in the areas of health and nutrition, work and financial security, property and housing, recreation and mobility, changes in roles and interactions with family and community; developmental programmes for preparation for death and bereavement, including spiritual and religious education; and family and community awareness programmes about ageing and death.

Curriculum Planning for 'Social Work with Ageing'

Course curricula of schools of social work all over the country vary, but according to the University Grants Commission's Second Review Committee Report, subjects of bachelor's and master's levels may be grouped under the following heads: foundation courses, method courses, social work administration and policy courses and social research courses. The contents of gerontological social work should be integrated appropriately into these various courses as well as in their fieldwork, so as to have a multifaceted emphasis on old age in the context of the life span model. Distribution of the components between the bachelor's and the master's level courses, may be done by the respective schools, in the context of their total programme. Wherever the pattern of electives exists, gerontological social work could be offered as an elective.

But, perhaps, this Seminar did not gather momentum and lacked a follow-up. That may be the reason why, even after realizing the gravity of the problems posed due to graying of the population, only one social work Institute (Department of Social Work, Andhra University, Vishakhapatanam, A.P.) has so far started specialization in gerontological social work. Out of those institutes where the pattern of electives exist, only a few offer gerontological social work as elective, for example, Delhi School of Social Work (DSW, 1999–2000). UGC model course curriculum also suggests gerontological social work to be just an optional paper (UGC, 2001). Others like the Indore School of Social Work, the Karve Institute of Social Sciences (Pune) and the Udaipur School of Social Work deal with the problems of the aged in the courses on fields of social work, psychology for social workers or social welfare administration. But, the Tata Institute of Social Sciences has only some mention of ageing in the basic course human growth and behaviour (mention of *ageing* besides other phases of life like infancy, childhood, etc.) and the optional course social work in industry (mention of problems of the older employees). Except this, there is absolutely no mention of aged or gerontological social work in either of its basic courses, optional courses or specialization courses (TISS, 2000–2002).

In 2006, there were 178 educational institutes of social work all over India (TISS, February 3, 2006). Rajasthan has only two institutes. The Udaipur School of Social Work is one of the ten oldest institutes of social work in the country. The other one, started just during the last decade, is situated at Ladnoon. Most of the institutes provide master's (117 institutes), bachelor's (65 institutes) and Ph.D. (36 institutes) degrees in social work. And 21 of them are also offering M. Phil degree or certificate courses (4 institutes) in social work.

There is no uniformity about the pattern of courses. Some of the institutes provide generic courses, the others do offer specialization courses. The specializations include: family and child welfare, labour welfare and personnel management, rural development, medical and psychiatric social work, criminology, etc. These specializations were started keeping in view the requirements of the society and the available job prospects for the professional social workers. Now to start specialization in gerontological social work is really a need of time. The social work profession has dual challenge: first, to prepare gerontological social workers by offering the concerned specialization; and secondly, generating job avenues for these social workers in various social organizations. Presently, the social organizations and institutions for the aged are far from satisfactory—both quantity-wise and quality-wise. There is a need to intervene at the policy level also. By doing this, at least the social work institutes may fulfil their responsibilities towards the ageing population. No matter, it will just be a small step to rectify the situation. If like social work profession, the other social institutions (including religious, political and social) simultaneously show some sensitivity and responsibility towards the aged, the situation will improve a great deal.

Future Course of Action

Based on the findings of this study, the following is an attempt to redefine the agenda of social work profession by deriving a course of action for the social workers. The findings and the course of action may not be universally applicable. Hence, it is suggested to conduct similar studies in different regions and different populations of 'Ageing India'; draw the plans of action based on the respective findings and implement the plans with the help of available resources, may be governmental, non-governmental and community resources.

Basic Strategies

Identifying the Latent Goodwill from amongst the Aged Women

First, let us see what and how the social work profession can offer in concrete terms to the aged women (the population) of the present study. The social work philosophy believes in helping the clients to help themselves. It makes clear that without active involvement of the aged women, their problems cannot be resolved. So, the first step towards framing the plan of action is to identify the latent goodwill and resources from amongst the aged women belonging to the three income groups—the lower, the middle and the higher. For this, the aged women were asked that if given a choice, would you like to participate in any social work activity. The data show that out of the total of 225, a majority of 70 per cent aged women expressed their unwillingness to participate in any of the activities. The analysis reveals a striking trend. To be specific, 92 per cent of the aged women of the lower income group expressed their unwillingness to participate compared to 65 per cent and 52 per cent of the aged women of the middle and the higher income group respectively.

However, those willing to participate expressed their interests in: care for infants of working mothers (8%), health care for the other old and sick persons (8%) and sewing classes for young girls (7%). To be noticed, the lower income group respondents were less educated than those belonging to the higher income groups. That may be the reason why some of the respondents from only the middle and the higher income group expressed their willingness to participate in adult education drive (6%) and employment guidance to youth (3%). A few of the aged women were also willing to participate in tree plantation drive (2%), cultural programmes (0.5%) and taking vocal music classes (0.5%).

To be noticed, 21 per cent of the aged women of the higher income group and 4 per cent women of the middle income group were enthusiastic enough to take part in all of the above mentioned activities. But not even a single respondent of the lower income group showed that enthusiasm. It is clear from the data that the apathy towards participation was more prominent in the lower income group compared to the comparatively higher income group. Obviously, the efforts to promote participation are required to be in proportion to the apathy prevailing in the respective income groups.

Formation of Self-Help Groups (SHGs)

Obviously, some of the aged women of the higher and middle income groups had desired to form SHGs. The SHGs of women and micro-credit systems are doing a good business in some of the states like Maharashtra and Kerala, though those SHGs are different from the aged groups. In some localities of Delhi, the 'self-help groups' of the aged are also doing a remarkable job (Khan, 1997). But, in Rajasthan, particularly the urban areas of Udaipur district, the SHG movement has attained little momentum. In such a situation, the desire to form SHGs by the aged women themselves is really a welcome feature. The social workers and the social work students placed in different agency settings may act as a catalytic agent in organizing SHGs of the aged women. For this, they can start only with those aged women who want to form SHGs or who want to participate in various social work activities. Later on, the other aged women including those of the lower income group may also be involved in the SHGs.

Involvement of Resource Persons from within the Community

Besides, in almost all the urban communities including those of our study area, there are a number of aged women who are retired professionals like doctors, nurses, advocates, IAS and IPS officers, bank employees, management personnel, judges, lecturers and teachers. A few of them may also be feeling a vacuum or loneliness.

Such aged women are, in fact, very good resource persons. The social workers can motivate them to render their part-time services to the SHGs. Thus, an umbrella service for the aged can be developed in the community through the interconnectivity and inter-control. A few non-government organizations active in the concerned areas may also be involved in this umbrella service for the aged, as shown in the Diagram 6.1.

Diagram 6.1
Umbrella Service for the Aged

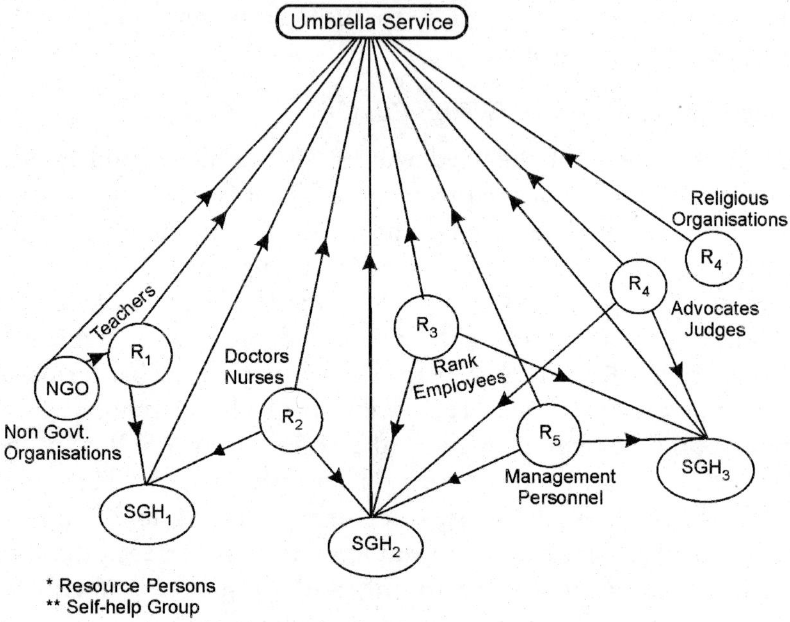

Expanding Childline Service to Include the Aged also in its Ambit

Some of the states like Maharashtra and Kerala are providing childline services for helping the children. At present, the service is available in 35 cities across India with ongoing preparatory work in 15 other cities. The Ministry of Justice and Empowerment is the policy-making, funding and controlling agency for the childline services. The Ministry has launched the childline service in the Udaipur city of Rajasthan also.

Any child feeling lonely, disturbed, depressed or tortured may phone at 1098 for help. According to the need, counselling, health care, police protection, etc., are provided to the children. The childline service requires extensive fieldwork so as to deliver the services wherever required. Such services should be extended to include the aged also into their ambit. It would not require any additional infrastructure. Rather, the voluntary services of the elderly may help the state to bring the expenditure of these services down.

Umbrella service for the aged	→ ←	Helpline service for the aged (Childline ↔ Senior Line)

Diagram 6.11

Senior Line

Where the childline services are not in operation, independent senior line services should be provided by the government, NGOs or in collaboration of both. However, the Helpage India has launched a senior line, which is a one-window service for the senior citizens who are lonely, ailing or facing physical and psychological fatigue or abuse (Ramesh, 1998).

Through the helpline services, umbrella services and SHGs, most of the problems of the aged women can be resolved without involving too much of the government aid or assistance, as described below.

Secondary Strategies for Social Workers to the Aid of the Aged Women Regarding Health Problems

Out of the various problems quoted by the aged women, the health problems are reported to be the most severe for all the three income groups. But, the gravity of the health problems is, however, more in the lower income group followed by the higher and the middle income group respectively. Malnutrition may be the reason of poor health status of the lower income group. Lethargic lifestyle, lack of exercise, and inadequate food cause health problems to the aged women in general, and those belonging to the higher income groups in particular. Stresses and strains, are reportedly more a phenomena of the lower income group, and have positive correlation with the health problems. Social nutrition[1] is also found to be lacking in the lower income group, compared to that in the higher and middle income groups respectively.

Health promotion strategy for the aged women must give due consideration to the following:

Cost of Health Care Services

In India, only recently, most of the governmental health care services were free of cost, particularly for the lower income groups. Even then, the aged women of the lower income group used to avoid taking medical consultation, might be, due to their inbuilt habits, apathetic attitude or financial constraints (to avoid expenses on conveyance to a doctor or a hospital). [The earlier findings also show that the aged women of the lower income group least frequently get medical consultation (see Chapter 4).] With changes in the government policies, the health services even in the government hospitals have become a paid service. One has to give some amount for getting the entry card made, for all the tests to be conducted and even for each diet. Though a nominal fee may avoid unnecessary dependency of a few on the hospitals, but it will also create obstacles to the poor aged to avail themselves of medical services, whenever required.

To overcome the negative repercussions of the above-mentioned changes, special, more frequent and affordable mobile health care services should be provided particularly in the lower income group localities.

Health Insurance

There is every possibility that in an era of economic liberalization and privatization, the poor will no doubt become victims of privatization of medicare. They, still, have to spend a disproportionate amount of their meagre income in overcoming medical episodes like malaria, viral fever, TB, etc. The solution lies in introducing a comprehensive health insurance suitable for the Indian situations. The government should be pressurized to start such insurance schemes keeping in view the lower income group also. Once started, people should be made aware of and be motivated to get their health insured.

Health Care System by Volunteers

Old age and sickness are closely related. Women have been the traditional caregivers of the aged in the families. With more and more women in the paid labour force, informal caregivers are not so readily available for long term care of the aged. Formal care system is not yet fully developed in India. But it is required to be developed. The social workers can play an important role in developing this kind of system. As far as our sample is concerned, 8 per cent aged women (comprised of 1%, 7% and 15% aged women of the lower, middle and higher income groups respectively) have expressed their willingness to render health care to the other old and sick persons. The social workers may organize these and such other women into voluntary organizations, which should be ready to render health care to the needy aged, if and when the family is unable to give health care to them.

Awareness regarding Proper Diet

There is a need of an awareness campaign for not only the aged women but also for the younger generation, regarding balanced, rich, regular and timely diet. There are some food items that are cheap as well as nutritive. Even, the lower income group may have an access to these items. From time to time, information about such items should be spread. Again and again, the aged women should be reminded that as age increases, one needs to be very cautious about the diet. Intake of liquid or light diet with more of vegetables and fruits should be preferred. Spicy and oily food, alcohol and smoking should deliberately be avoided. As far as possible, the aged should take food in pleasant family environment, with other members of the family.

Awareness about Suitable Eating Habits

Dietary control can bring tremendous improvements in the health status of the elderly. Efforts should be made to check the tendency of the aged women of not giving importance to the diet adequate for them; to sacrifice their share for other members of the family; to avoid expensive food; to take food in the last, and to satisfy themselves from what is left.

It is basically the eating habits of the young age that result in poor or good health in the old age. It is in the young age itself, healthy food habits should be inculcated.

Since, with age, faith of the aged women in religion is found to be increasing, the various religious platforms can effectively be used in the awareness generation campaigns for the aged ones. To make younger generation aware about good dietary habits, street plays, skits, competitions, etc., should be organized besides imparting physical education. Mass media like television and newspaper can also play an important role in this regard.

Indigenous Methods of Treatment

Many of the aged women avoid taking allopathic medicine. "Neither we go to a doctor nor take any allopathic medicine" is a common phrase, one may hear from these elderly women. Our indigenous methods of treatment may prove to be very effective. These measures may be publicized at adequate platforms. Besides, yoga and meditation sessions may be arranged. The aged women should be motivated to join these sessions. This may help them in overcoming depression or stress arising out of circumstances of life.

Training in Gerontology

There is evidence that many of the old age diseases and problems are preventable and treatable. Training in gerontology is needed to prepare people to grow old gracefully without illness and disability; and to educate families to provide for the changing needs of senior members (see Prakash, 2007).

Overcoming Financial Problems

Financial constraint is reportedly the second most prominent problem of the women of lower income group. But, for the middle and higher income groups, it is found to be respectively the 4th and 6th ranked problem. To help the aged women overcoming the financial constraints, following measures can be adopted:

Old Age Pension

On August 15, 1995, the Government of India announced the National Old Age Pension Scheme for the poor. The scheme covers those aged 65+ who are landless, destitute and/or have no regular means of subsistence. The assistance was initially Rs 75 per month and was later revised to Rs 150. A few of the states have just revised the amount of pension to be Rs 275 in Gujarat, Rs 300 in Delhi, Rs 400 in West Bengal, and Rs 500 in Goa. In Rajasthan, the amount of pension is Rs 100 for females aged 55+ and males aged 58+, Rs 200 for those aged 65+ and Rs 300 for destitute couple (Helpage India, 2002).

The scheme is implemented in the states and union territories through panchayats and municipalities. Both panchayats and municipalities are encouraged to involve voluntary agencies as much as possible in benefiting the elderly destitute.

The needy, many a time, do not get old age pension even after being entitled for it. While others who have earning member/s in their families and other kind of facilities get pension just because of their links. There is a need to identify the defaulters (the aged who enjoy the pension though not eligible for it) as well as the needy, who could not get the pension.

Even those entitled for old age pension do not get pension for months together.

Generally, the pension is paid through the post office. But, in order to fill up the form, for periodic verification or completing other formalities, the aged (women included) have to go to the government offices/social welfare departments. This is a cumbersome process and sometimes leads to harassment. These days, the conveyance has become too expensive. Hence, nobody wants to frequently visit government offices for a meagre amount of the pension. Hence, the 'pension service at the doorstep' should be started, particularly for the infirm aged. The amount of the pension should also be raised. The amount of pension should be justifiably uniform in all the states. Now a days, it varies from Rs 60 in Assam to Rs 500 in Goa.

If the government really intends to maintain the sanctity of the old age pension, it will have to reframe the mechanism for the old age pension. The social workers, however, may also act as a link between the government schemes and the needy aged by creating awareness about the scheme, by helping them in completing the formalities and by trying to simplify the procedures. Also, regular monitoring, evaluation and research need to be undertaken by the government, NGOs and social workers.

Pre-retirement Counselling

Pre-retirement counselling programmes have become the need of the day. Often, the aged (women included) spend all the money they get at the time of their retirement on financially risky assignments/business, marriage of the children or gifts to the children. And later on, they become economically dependent on others. Intelligent pre-retirement counselling can positively turn the life of many of the aged. This requires qualified counsellors who not only know about good investment schemes, job opportunities, vocational trainings and placements, but are also competent to deal with the feelings, concerns, anxieties and grievances of the aged.

Small Income Generation Projects

In order to instil dignity and independence in the lives of the aged people, particularly those who have no source of income, income generation projects need to be started. For example, envelop-making, paper-folding, book-binding, cutting of frills, etc. Many aged women of the lower income group are already involved in the above-mentioned and similar activities. But, there are the others who want to work, but do not get the opportunities. Wherever required, efforts should be made to introduce such projects. In running these projects, the main problems relate to coordination and transportation required in arranging for the raw material and marketing of the products. The aged women can just involve in the main activity, say, paper-folding or envelope-making, because of lack of business skills and difficulty in travelling. The SHGs, the NGOs and the social workers should take the initiatives to launch the projects. The unemployed youth of the locality may be motivated to be involved in these projects.

Micro-credit System

In some states, the micro-credit schemes have proved very beneficial for the lower income group. Here, again, social workers may become instrumental in starting the micro-credit system. To motivate people, video films, in which women of different states are shown running the micro-credit system successfully and confidently, should be exhibited. And, the relevant literature in the form of pamphlets, leaflets, charts, etc., should also be circulated. Person-to-person contacts and in-group discussions are also required. In the initial phase, the resource persons of the area may play an important role in keeping funds, records, etc., in contacting the bank employees and in completing the necessary formalities. Gradually, the interested aged women may also acquire the required skills to deal with the system.

'Adopt a Dependent Aged Woman of the Area' Scheme

The micro-credit systems are beneficial for those who maintain a minimum level of physical mobility and social interaction. But there may be poor aged women who are very sick and have very little financial backing as such. However, the number of such dependent aged women is expected to be very small. For them, a scheme may be started which encourages an aged woman of the higher income group to indirectly and informally adopt a needy dependent aged woman of the lower income group. In India, religious sentiments, particularly in old age, become stronger. Indian aged women, unlike those belonging to the developed countries who generally are self-centred, want to devote some of their resources in philanthropy. Hence, the rich aged women can well be motivated to adopt a poor woman of the community to render some assistance in terms of not directly money but goods, medicines or expenses of medical care. It is not at all an easy task to introduce the scheme and keep it going. Dedicated and honest social workers will again be required to win the faith of the community and to train the people to ultimately take over the responsibility.

Regarding Adjustment Problems

Day Care Centres

In most of the states, government runs community centres. These may be used as the day care centres for the aged. These centres are required to run various programmes for the aged, for example, community awareness for enriched interactions; health check up camps; information, awareness and referral services for prevention of problems and treatment; counselling and legal aid; meditation and yoga, naturopathy classes, acupressure therapy, etc.

Day care centres for children may be integrated with those for the older persons so that day care needs of both the groups can be met in an integrated manner.

Outreach Units

The outreach units may run various home/family-based services for older persons confined to home such as mobile meals, clinics and libraries; volunteer's visits for help in home-making and running external errands; and information and referral services.

Sensitizing Younger Generation

There is a need to sensitize the younger generation about their responsibilities towards the aged (women included) and to make them understand the problems of the younger generation and to adapt to the changes taking place in the society.

The human and spiritual values of mutual affection, respect, kindness, sympathy, compassion, understanding, humility and of course non-violence, and considering each person in each phase of his/her life as equal and worthy human being and divine soul are fast declining (Kapoor, 1997). Inculcation of human and spiritual values among the younger and older generations is absolutely imperative. The aged in the joint families used to be important institutions to inculcate such values among the children. With the breaking of joint families into smaller units has resulted in loss of such institutions for the children. But, the vacuum needs to be filled in a planned way. Through various other social and religious institutions, such values are required to be developed among the younger generation. '*Shaktiman*'—a television serial popular among children—needs a special mention here. Heroic stories and books should be wildly circulated in the schools. Parents should also note that their children go through such literature and audio-visual text.

School Education Programme

Thus is a need to start a strong nationwide school education programme which focuses bringing children closer to their elders. The Helpage India claims to run such a programme (*Helpage India Manual: Adding Life to Years*). But, there is a need to make it more popular and widespread. Street plays, essay competitions and role model strategies may also be adopted for the purpose.

Coordination of Schools with Old Age Homes

There is a need to coordinate schools with the old age homes. Through the National Social Service Scheme or Senior Citizens Help Scheme, students should be motivated to regularly visit old age homes, spend time with the aged and as far as possible, resolve their problems.

Use of Mass Media

Mass media also has a positive role to play in this regard. It can glorify those values, which advocate paying respect to our elderly. For example, an advertisement on television channel shows an old person finding it difficult to pull his tractor out of a gutter. A young man comes out of his car to help the aged. And, in the background, it is said that we still respect our values.

The government has already entrusted some responsibility of creating social awareness to the Doordarshan channel. Small clippings on balanced diet, hygiene/cleanliness, impact of alcohol, Think a Little (*Zara Sochiye*), etc., have been telecast on it. But perhaps, the private channels have little statutory obligation of creating social awareness. And, nowadays, people have more access to and interest in these private channels. There is a need of lobbying to compel policy makers so that devoting a minimum time in creating social awareness becomes mandatory for these channels too.

Community Check System (Civil Society)

Young parents should be motivated and urged to give proper treatment to their aged parents, not for the sake of the elderly but for their own better future. Since, unconsciously, they become the role models for their own children.

The aged, by tradition and nature, do not favour isolated life. The old age homes do not offer any solution to their problems. There is a need to strengthen, through the above-described mechanisms, traditional kinship and family bonds. But even then if some cases are identified where the children do not take care the responsibility of their aged, community check systems should be used to rectify the situation. The NGOs, social workers, and other responsible citizens of the locality should come together to generate pressure on such children. The media also has a responsibility. The names of the children who abuse or abandon their aged parents should be publicized in the local newspaper or cable. It may seem to be an ineffective strategy to some. But, many a time, it is more effective than any other persuasive or power strategy to influence those who do not fulfil their responsibilities towards their aged.

Peer Counselling

To change the negative attitude of the aged women as well as the members of their families, peer counselling should be provided through the SHGs. In peer counselling, persons who have experienced the problems themselves offer help and solutions.

Strategies to Deal with Death Anxiety

Besides, the aged women should be provided with counselling to overcome morbid anxiety, a factor, which reportedly contributes to the dissatisfaction of the aged women. The two realities of certainty of death and uncertainty of its time have to be conveyed to the aged in order to help them deal with the anxieties related to their own and their spouses' death. Spiritual/religious education for understanding death may be useful as Asgarali Patel and Broota (2000) also found that the religious elderly experience significantly less loneliness and morbid anxiety than the non religious elderly.

Regarding Destitution and Loneliness

Planning for Quality Ageing

In India, people have been relying on families to provide all the physical and emotional requirements in old age. The changing trends indicate a high probability of their being disappointed. The aged should be prepared to face the hard realities of life.

Most people, when they plan for old age, think in terms of economic security and hardly ever think beyond finances. They need to learn to plan for quality ageing which is relatively new (see Prakash, 2007). To facilitate this learning, there is a need to develop modules for training in several areas such as managing finance, legal and emotional issues, handling issues of death and dealing with community and government (Prakash, 2006 has developed some of such modules).

Old Age Homes

Although non-institutional services should be given priority over institutional ones, yet, for the destitute and infirm aged or the unmarried and childless aged, particularly the women, there is a need to start old age homes, as also recommended in the NPOP.

Many institutionalized aged complain that employees in old age homes and day care centres are incompetent and insensitive (Singh, 1999). Most of the old age homes do not employ professional social workers. Every old age home should necessarily employ social workers so as to take care of emotional and environmental needs of the aged.

Future Action

Institutions Involved in the Subject to Address the Problem

All the institutions of the society should join hands to solve the problems of the ageing population. Political, administrative and welfare institutions should not only be prompt but also sensitive to the needs, problems and risks to which the aged population is exposed to.

Research

Aged women have gender specific needs like shelter, economic security, etc., which need to be identified and analysed by research. Also, there is a need to evolve ways of caring for the aged women. Research to regularly monitor and evaluate the existing schemes and programmes is also a need of time.

Social Action

Social action, as a method of social work, has always been given a secondary status, as is also reflected from the UGC Model Course Curriculum, 2001. That may be the reason why social workers could not make a place of their own at the micro level. They have been involved in such micro-level changes, as helping the client by counselling, etc. But, there is a need to use pressure tactics, lobbying, advocacy, demonstration, *dharna*, etc. to build new institutions for the aged or to discipline the old ones. There is a need to change the policies so as to make the induction and services of professional social workers mandatory in all the old age homes, day care centres and government departments dealing with the old age pension, childline services, senior line services and school education programme for the aged. The social workers should necessarily be nominated in all the government committees and bodies being appointed to discuss or decide the issues related to the aged (women included).

Social workers should undertake concerted, organized and continuous efforts to sensitize social work profession towards the needs and problem of the aged. Bringing relevant changes in the course curriculum and training being imparted can achieve this end. The social workers are required in true sense, to be, professionals who would have strong knowledge base and expertise in offering counselling services.

The Association of Schools of Social Work in India (ASSWI) and various other forums for the social workers, which are functional at the international, national, state and local levels, may play an important role in creating opportunities for mutual development and promotion of 'social work education and practice' for the benefit of the greater society.

Let us grow together, together we can, together we must.

Let not the above plan lie dormant in this book. The functionaries and workers have to be stimulated, energized, motivated, oriented and made responsible to prove their credibility in assuring its full implementation. If the element of accountability be kept before the eyes and there be devotion to the cause, we will achieve the targets as proclaimed by the suggested course of Action.

Note

1. 'Social nutrition is considered to be a science wherein besides the quality and quantity of the food, the other major determinant of the body's nutrition status is the environment and family support given during meal consumption. Here, 'family support and environment' refers to the food service, eating alone or with other members of the family and eating habits moulded in accordance with the family conditions. Eating together, family conditions and food service have a greater bearing on the 'quality' nutrition, hence the term 'social nutrition' (Vijayalakshmi, Shobha and Reddy, 2000: 17).

Appendix

Scales to Measure Levels of Physical Mobility, Ability in Household Work and Social Interaction

Physical Mobility

Physical mobility refers to the mobility involved in performing the activities of daily living (ADL): (1) standing up and sitting down, (2) walking without aid, (3) getting in and out of bed, (4) going up and down the stairs, (5) combing one's own hair, (6) self-feeding, (7) reading (proper eyesight) (8) attending to one's own toilet, and (9) washing or bathing without help. Prakash (1989: 27), however, called it basic level of competence (BaCo).

A composite scale was constructed for measuring the level of physical mobility. The urban aged women were asked nine questions which concerned the activities mentioned above. (The general question put up was: Do you have difficulty in the activity?) Each response was analysed. Accordingly, numeric value 'one' was assigned to a 'no difficulty' response, 'two' to a response 'difficulty but can do of my own' and three to a 'difficulty, cannot do of my own' response.

Thus total score acquired by a respondent ranged from 9–27. On the basis of the acquired score, all the respondents were placed in either of the four levels as shown in Table 1.

Table 1
Levels of Physical Mobility

Level	*Score Value*
Perfect	9
High	10–12
Moderate	13–15
Low	16–27

Ability in Household Work

Ability and competence of urban aged women in performing household work was assessed with regard to the following activities: (1) light household work like washing, dusting, tidying; (2) heavy cleaning like washing floors and cleaning windows; (3) light kitchen work like making a cup of tea; (4) heavy kitchen work, for example, preparing a hot meal; (5) shopping and (6) heavy washing. A composite scale was developed to judge the competence in household work and accordingly all the respondents were placed in either of three categories of competence: low, moderate and high.

The respondents were asked "Here are some activities which you may or may not do for yourself, but could you do without difficulty?" The responses regarding each of the six activities mentioned above were obtained from every respondent on a three point scale: 'no difficulty', 'difficulty but can do', and 'difficulty, can not do'. Accordingly, the numerical values 'one', 'two' and 'three' were allotted respectively to the three responses. Thus, the total score acquired by a respondent ranged from 6–18. On the basis of the acquired scores, all the respondents were placed in either of the three levels as mentioned in the Table 2.

Table 2
Levels of Ability in Household Work

Level	*Scores*
Low	6–9
Moderate	10–14
High	15–18

Social Interaction

Social Interaction is a measure of density of interactions one gets involved in with other human beings. This measure has been based on five types of social interactions: that occur during the course of (1) paid work/occupation/employment, (2) shopping, (3) playing with children/grandchildren, (4) seeing or visiting relatives and (5) seeing or visiting neighbours. Prakash has (1998: 27) discussed more or less a similar variable called expanded level of competence (ExCo), which was a measure of the skills needed for leisure and social activities.

The urban aged women were asked questions about the frequency of their involvement in each of the above-mentioned activities. And the responses for each of the questions were collected on a five-point scale: (1) daily, (2) often, (3) sometimes, (4) rarely and (5) never. The numerical value 'one' was allotted to a 'daily' response, two to an 'often' response, three to a 'sometimes' response, four to a 'rarely' response and five to a 'never' response. Thus, the total score value acquired by an aged woman ranged from 5–25. On the basis of the acquired score, all the aged women were placed in either of the three levels mentioned in the Table 3.

Table 3
Levels of Social Interaction

Level	*Score Value*
High	5–11
Moderate	12–18
Low	19–25

Scaling technique, thus, was used to judge the levels of physical mobility, competence in household work and Social Interaction of the urban aged women.

Bibliography

Achamba, B., (1987): "Social and Emotional Problems of Men and Women, Joint and Nuclear Families", K. Subba Rao and V. Prabhakar (eds.), *Aging: A Mulifactorial Dimension,* Association of Gerontology, University of Hyderabad, 97–102.

—, (1991): "Time Judgements in Younger and Older Persons", I.J. Prakash (ed.), *Quality Ageing: Collected Papers,* Varanasi (India): Association of Gerontology, 124–28.

Adelmann, Pamela K., (1994): "Multiple Role and Physical Health among Older Adults: Gender and Ethnic Comparisions", *Research on Ageing,* Vol. 16 (2), 142–166.

Allen, Kautherine R. and Pickett, Robert S., (1984): "Historical Perspectives on the Life Course of Elderly Women Born in 1910", *Journal of Applied Gerontology*, 3(2), December, 61–170.

Anantharam, R.N., (1990): "Certain Associates of Physical Health in Old Age", *Journal of Psychological Researches*, 34, 88–92.

Anderson, John E., (1960): "Research in Ageing" in E.W. Burgess (ed.), *Ageing in Western Societies,* Chicago: University of Chicago Press, 354–375.

Anuradha, B.R. and Prakash I.J., (1991): "Life Satisfaction in Relation to Social Interaction and Loneliness among the Elderly", I.J. Prakash (ed.), *Quality Aging: Collected Papers*, Varanasi, (India): Association of Gerontology, 151–157.

Ardelt, Monika, (1997): "Wisdom and Life Satisfaction in Old Age", *Journal of Gerontology-Psychological Sciences*, 52B (1), 15–27.

Aries, Philippe, (1962): *Centuries of Childhood* translated by Hobert Baldick, New York: Alfred A. Knopf.

Arora, P.N. and Shalini Saxena, (1997): "A Study of Pattern of Adjustment of Retired Working and Non-Working Women", M.G. Husain (ed.), *Changing Indian Society and Status of Aged*, New Delhi: Manak Publications Pvt. Ltd., 171–177.

Asgarali, J.M. and Aruna Broota, (2000): "Loneliness and Death Anxiety among the Elderly: The Role of Family Set Up and Religious Belief", *Research and Development Journal*, Vol. 6(3), June-September, 28–35.

Asha, C.B. and K.A. Subramanian, (1990): "Problems of Elderly Women", *Indian Journal of Community Guidance,* 7(3), 64–67.

Audiarayana, N., (1999): Living Arrangements of the Widowed and Currently Married Elderly Women in Tamil Nadu State, India, Women's Health and the Nation's Gain: An International Conference with a Special Focus on Women in Asia, Singapore: TSAO Foundation.

Auslander, Gail K. and Howard Litwin, (1998): "Religious Life Style and Service Utilization among Elderly Jews of Jerusalem", United States: *Journal of Aging and Judaism*, 3, 1–2, Fall-winter, 29–40.

Bagchi, Kalyan, (1997): "Concern for Aged Women", K. Bagchi (ed.), *Elderly Females in India: Their Status and Sufferings*, New Delhi: Society for Gerontological Research and Help Age India.

—, (ed.), (1997): *Elderly Females in India: Their Status and Sufferings,* New Delhi: Society for Gerontological Research and Help Age India.

Bagga, Amrita, (1994): "Health Status of Women of Old Age Homes", *Ageing and Society: The Indian Journal of Gerontology*, 4(3 and 4), 11–21.

—, (1997): "A Study of Women in Old Age Homes of Pune", Indrani Chakravarty (ed.), *Life in Twilight Years*, Calcutta: Kwality Book Company.

Bali, Arun P., (1995): "Status of Gerontology and Geriatric Research in India: An Overview and Guidance for Further Research", *Research and Development Journal*, Vol. 1, No. 2, February Issue.

—, (1996): "Role of the Family in the Care of the Elderly: Changing Caregiving Situation", Vinod Kumar (ed.), *Indian Perspective and Global Scenario*, New Delhi: AIIMS, 157–163.

—, (1997): "Elderly Females: An Ignored Silent Majority", Kalyan Bagchi (ed.), *Elderly Females in India: Their Status and Suffering*, New Delhi: Society for Gerontological Research and Helpage India, 23–44.

Bambawale, Usha, (1991): "Changing Roles in the Lives of Older Women: With Special Reference to Authority", Indira Jai Prakash (ed.), *Quality Aging: Collected Papers*, Varanasi: Association of Gerontology, 246–256.

—, (1993): "Ageing and the Economic Factor in Later Life", *Ageing and Society: The Indian Journal of Gerontology*, 3(1), 1–19.

—, (1995): "Aged Women and Television Vieweing", S. Vijay Kumar (ed.), *Challenges Before the Elderly: An Indian Scenario*, New Delhi: M.D. Publications, 167–178.

—, (1996): "Abuse of the Aged", Vinod Kumar (ed.), *Ageing: Indian Perspective and Global Scenario*, New Delhi: AIIMS.

—, (1997): "Ageing Women and Media Habits", *Ageing and Society: The Indian Journal of Gerontology*, 7(3 and 4), 1–5.

—, (2004): "Abuse of Elderly: A Myth or Reality", P.V. Ramamurti and D. Jamuna (eds.), *Handbook of Indian Gerontology*, New Delhi: Serials Publications, 243–267.

Bandyopadhyay, D., (2000): "Gender and Governance in India", *Economic and Political Weekly*, Vol. XXXV, No. 31, (July 29-August 4), 2696–2700.

Bansal, Rahul, (2000): "Health Promotion for the Elderly", *Research and Development Journal*, Vol. 6, No. 2, February-May.

Banthia, Jayant K., (2001): *Censes* of *India Series–1, Provisional Population Totals,* (Paper–1), India: Registrar General and Censes Commissioner.

Barai, D.C., (1991): "Population Characteristics of the Elderly in the Major Cities of South India", I.J. Prakash (ed.), *Quality Ageing: Collected Papers*, Varanasi: Association of Gerontology, 76–86.

Bavadam, Lyla, (1999): "A Silent Syndrome", *General Issues*, 119–120.

Becker, Carl L., (1959): "What are Historical Facts", in Hans Meyerhoff, Ed., *The Philosophy of History in Our Time. Garden City*, N.Y.: Doubleday, Anchor Books, 132–33.

Bengston, V.L., (1973): *The Social Psychology of Ageing*, Indianapolis: Baggs-Morril.

Bhatia, H.S., (1983): *Ageing and Society: A Sociological Study of Retired Public Servants*, Udaipur (India): The Arya's Book Centre Publishers.

Bhatia, V.J., (1995): "Ageing in India", *Ageing and Society: The Indian Journal of Gerontology*, 5(1and 2), 79–85.

Bhatla, P.C. (ed.), (1998): *Aged Women: Coping with Life,* New Delhi: National Institute of Primary Health Care.

Binstock, R. and E. Shanas (eds.), (1985): *Handbook of Ageing and Social Sciences,* (2nd ed.), New York: Van Nostrand Reinhold.

Binstock, Robert H. and Linda K. George, (2006): *Handbook of Ageing and Social Sciences,* (6th ed.), USA: Academic Press, Elsevier.

Biswas, S.K., (1985): "Dependency and Family Care of the Aged in a Village of India: A Case Study", *Journal of the Indian Anthropological Society*, 20(3), 283–257.

Blau, P.M., (1964): *Exchange and Power in Social Life*, New York: John Wiley.

Bond, John and Peter Coleman (eds.), (1990): *Ageing in Society: An Introduction to Social Gerontology*, New Delhi: Sage Publications.

Booth, T., (1985): *Home Truths: Old People's Homes and the Outcome of Care,* Aldershot: Gower.

Bose, A.B., (1988): "Policies and Programmes for the Aging in India", A.B. Bose and K.D. Gangrade (eds.), *The Ageing in India*, New Delhi: Abhinav Publications.

Bose, A. and K.D. Gangrade, (1988): *The Ageing in India: Problems and Potentialities,* New Delhi: Abhinav Publications.

Bound, J., G.I. Duncan, D.S. Laren and L.C. Oleinick, (1991): "Poverty Dynamics in Widowhood", *Journal of Gerontology*, 46(3), 115–124.

Branigan, Karen P. and Sandra O'Brien Cousins, (1995): "Older Women and Beliefs about Exercise Risk: What has Motherhood Got to Do With It?", United States: *Journal of Women and Ageing*, 7(4), 47–66.

Brien, Mary, (1991): "Never Married Older Women: The Life Experience", *Social Indicators Research*, 24(3), May, 301–315.

Burgess, E.W., (1960): *Ageing in Western Societies*, Chicago: The University of Chicago Press, 20.

Bury, Michael and Anthea Holme, (1991): *Life after Ninety,* London: Routledge.

Calleja, James, (ed.) (1997): *Eliminating Poverty in Old Age,* Malta: United Nations International Institute on Ageing.

Carlton Laney, Iris, (1992): "Elderly Black Farm Women: A Population Risk", *Social Work*, 37(6), November, 517–523.

Carolina, A., M. Kulak and J.P. Bilezikian, (1998): Osteoporosis: Preventive Strategies, *International Journal of Fertility*, 56–64.

Chadha, N.K. et al., (1991): "Leisure Time Activities Among the Aged: A Comparative Study", *Social Science International,* 7(2), 12–24.

Chadha, N.K., (1989): Impact of Institutionalization on the Psychological Well Being and Depression among the Aged, National Symposium on Stress, Anxiety and Depression in Modern Life, November, 3–4, Patiala: Punjabi University.

—, (1991): "Self-Concept and Life Satisfaction Among Aged", *Indian Journal of Gerontology*, 5(1–2), 47–54.

—, (1994): "Psychological Well Being and Depression among Institutionalized Aged", *Disabilities and Impairments,* 8(2), 71–79.

Chadha, N.K., D. Chao, P. Majumdar and R. Sharma, (2006): "Marital Status and Leisure Activities among the Elderly", *Research and Development Journal*, Vol. 12(3), October, 8–13.

Chakrabarti, Prafulla, (1997) "Who Cares for the Elderly? A Study of Health, Management and Care", N.K. Chadha (ed.), *Ageing and the Aged*, Delhi: Friends Publications, 115–140.

Chakraborti, Rajagopal Dhar (2004): *The Greying of India: Population Ageing in the Context of Asia*, New Delhi: Sage Publications.

Chakrapani, C., (1995): "The Elderly in Search of Work", S. Vijay Kumar (ed.), *Challenges Before the Elderly*, New Delhi: M.D. Publications, 117–24.

Chakravarty, Indrani, (1994): "Defence for the Aged", *Ageing and Society: The Indian Journal of Gerontology*, 4(3 and 4), 22–25.

Chaudhary, Aabha (ed.): *Active Ageing in the New Millennium: An Indian Scenario*, India: Anugraha.

Chetna, (2001): Action Research to Assess, Understand and Improve the Status of Ageing Women, Project Report, Gujarat: Chetna.

Chouhan, T.S., (1996): *Encyclopaedia of Rajasthan*, Jodhpur: Vigyan Prakash.

Christopher, A.J., (1992): "Give them their Due", *Social Welfare*, 39(7 and 8), October-November, 6–8.

Cockerham, W.C., (1991): *This Ageing Society*, USA: Prentice Hall, Inc.

Coleman, Peter, (1990): "Adjustment in Later Life" in Bond, John and Coleman Peter (eds.): *Ageing in Society: An Introduction to Social Gerontology*, New Delhi: Sage Publications, 89–122.

Collado, Anna, (1989): "Undesirable Effects of the Process of Ageing in Spanish Society", Spain: *Journal Revista-Espanola-de-Investigaciones-S ocialogicas*, 48, October, 199–209.

Comfort, A., (1957): "The Biological Approach in the Comparative Study of Ageing", G.E.W. Wolstenholme and C.M.O. Connor (eds.) *Methodology of the Study of Ageing*, London: J. and A. Churchill.

Cottrell, L., (1942): "The Adjustment of the Individual to his Age and Sex Roles", *American Sociological Review*, 7, 617–20.

Cowgill, D.O. and L.D. Holmes, (1972): *Ageing and Modernization*, New York: Appleton Century-Crofts.

Cowgill, Donald O., (1986): *Ageing Around the World*, Belmont, CA: Wadsworth.

D'Souza, V.S., (1989): "Changing Social Scene and its Implication for the Aged", K.G. Desai (ed.), *Aging in India*, New Delhi: Ashish Publishing House.

Dandekar, Kumudini, (1993): "The Aged, their Problems and Social Intervention in Maharashtra", *Economic and Political Weekly*, 28(23), 5 January, 1188–94.

—, (1996): *The Aged in India*, New Delhi: Sage Publications.

Daniels, Jean E., (2004): "Biographical Sketches of Elderly African-American Women in Later Life", *Journal of Women & Aging*, Vol. 16(3/4), 169–178.

Darshan, Shailesh, M.L. Sharma and S.P. Singh, (1987): "Health Needs of Senior Citizens" in M.L. Sharma and T.M. Dak (eds.), *Ageing in India Challenge for the Society*, Delhi: Ajanta Publications, 207–230.

Dass, A., (1998): "Special Medical Problems in Aged Women: An Overview", P.C. Bhatla (ed.), *Aged Women: Coping with Life,* New Delhi: NIPHC, 8–10.

DAV Indore, 2000 and onwards: M.A. (Social Work), General Rules, Scheme of Examination and Courses of Studies etc., Faculty of Social Sciences, Devi Ahilya Vishwavidhyalaya, Indore (M.P.): The Registrar.

DCHB, (1991): District Census Hand Book (DCHB) Series 21, Part XII A and B, District Udaipur, Rajasthan: Directorate of Census Operation, Government of Rajasthan Publications.

De Alvarez, J.T., (1991): "Special Problems Facing Elderly Women in Developing Countries", *Bold*, 2(1), 2–4.

De Souza, Alfred, (1982): "The Social Organization of Ageing among the Urban Poor", De Souza A. and W. Fernandes (eds.), *Ageing in South Asia*, New Delhi: Indian Social Institute.

Deptt. of HDFS and Faculty of Home Science, (1997): Proceedings of the National Seminar on Ageing: Directions for Programmes and Policies organised on November 13–15 by Department of Human Development and Family Studies (Under the Auspices–UGC/DSA) and Facility of Home Science, M.S. University of Baroda, Vadodara.

Desai, K.D. and R.D. Naik, (1972): Problems of Retired People in Greater Bombay, Unpublished Research Report, Mumbai: Tata Institute of Social Sciences, Series No. 27.

Desai, Murli, (1999): "Ageing of Women in Post-Menopausal Stage: Need for Intervention", *Economic and Political Weekly,* XXXIV (44), October 30, WS.57-WS.62.

Desai, Murli, Raju Siva and V. Rosamma, (1997): *A Classified Bibliography on Social Gerontology in India,* Mumbai: Tata Institute of Social Sciences.

Devasahayyam, M., (1988): "Aged Females: The Most Deprived among the Deprived", *The Indian Journal of Social Work*, 49(3), 261–270.

Devi, D. Radha, S. Santhosh, A. Asharaf and T.K. Roy, (1999): Aged in a Changing Society: A Case Study of Kerala, (Unpublished Project Report), International Institute for Population Studies, Deonar, Mumbai.

Devi, Dayabati and Amrita Bagga, (1997): "Health Status of Older Women of Manipur", *Ageing and Society: The Indian Journal of Gerontology*, 7(1 and 2), 27–42.

Dhillon, P.K., (1992): *Psycho-Social Aspects of Ageing in India*, New Delhi: Concept Publishing Company.

Dissenbacher, H. (1989): "Neglect Abuse and the Taking of Life in Old People's Homes", *Ageing and Society*, 9(1), 61–71.

Dixon, A.L. Sinikka, (1997): "Gender Differences in Religiosity, Health, Self-Esteem, Life-Style and Life-Satisfaction", Canadian Union University Coll. College Heights Alberta.

Dowd, J., (1980): *Stratification Amongst the Aged*, Monterey, Brooks/Cole.

DSSW, (1970–74): A Study of the Aged in Delhi, Unpublished Research Project, New Delhi: Department of Social Work, Delhi School of Social Work, University of Delhi.

Duraisamy, M. and P. Duraisamy, (1999): "Women in the Professional and Technical Labour Market in India: Gender Discrimination in Education, Employment and Earnings", *The Indian Journal of Labour Economics*, 42(4), 599–612.

Easwaramoorthy, S. Supatil and Godawari Patil, (1991): "A Study on Adjustment in Relation to Marital Status Among the Rural Aged", Indira Jai Prakash (ed.), *Quality Ageing*, Varanasi, (India): Association of Gerontology, 129–134.

Ellickson, J., (1988): "Never the Twain Shall Meet: Ageing Men and Women in Bangladesh", *Journal of Cross-Cultural Gerontology*, 3, 57–70.

Erickson, E.H., (1982): *The Life Cycle Completed: A Review*, New York: Norton.

Fairhurst, E., (1976): "Sociology and Ageing: An Alternative View", *Concord*, 6, 43–54.

Feinson, M.C., (1987): "Mental Health and Ageing: Are There Gender Differences?", *The Gerentologist*, Vol. 27, 301–311.

Fisher, D.H., (1978): *Growing Old in America*, New York: Oxford University Press.

Fisk, M.J., (1986): *Independence and the Elderly*, London: Croom Helm.

Foner, Nancy, (1989): "Older Women in Non-Industrial Cultures: Consequences of Power and Privilege", *Women in Later Years*, New York: The Haworth Press, 227–237.

Fontana, Andrea, (1977): *The Last Frontier: The Social Meaning of Growing Old*, Beverly Hills, C.A.: Sage Publication, 176.

Ford, J. and R. Sinclair, (1987): *Sixty Years On: Women Talk About Old Age*, London: The Women's Press.

Franklin, W.J., (1991): "Health Care Trends for Older People", *Bio Feedback and Self-Regulation*, 16, 337–47.

Ganesh, Kamala, (1997): "Common Gynaecological Morbidity Pattern in Elderly Females", Kalyan Bagchi (ed.), *Elderly Females in India*, New Delhi: Society has Gerontological Research and Helpage India, 65–78.

Gangrade, K.D., (1996): "Family and Care of Aged in India", Vinod Kumar (ed.), *Indian Perspective and Global Scenario*, 164–170.

Ganguli, L. and S.I. Rajan, (1999): "The Added Years: Elderly in India and Kerala", *Economic and Political Weekly*, XXXIV (44), October 30, WS.46-WS.51.

Ganguli, L., (1992): "Dimensions of Female Ageing and Widowhood: Insights from Kerala Experience", *Economic and Political Weekly*, October 24–31, WS.93-WS.98.

Gibson, D., (1996): "Broken Down by Age and Gender: The Problem of Old Women Redefined", *Gender and Society*, 10(4), 433–48.

Gokhale, S.D., N. Pandit and R. Raj (1994): *Economic Potential of the Elderly and Local Level Policy Development in Conferences of Ageing in India*, New York: United Nations (Asian Population Studies Series).

Goode, W.J. and P.K. Hatt (1952): *Methods in Social Research*, New York, Toronto, London: Mc Graw-Hill Book Company, Inc.

Gopinath, Vrinda, (2000): "Road to Pension is Long, Crooks Wait by Wayside", Malini Karkar (ed.), *Elderly in India: An Annotated Bibliography*, Vol. 2, Mumbai: TISS.

Government of India, (1987): National Policy on Older Persons: A Draft, Ministry of Social Justice and Empowerment.

—, (1991): Census of India.

—, (1991): Village Prakriya Census Abstracts (Rajasthan State).

—, (1998): National Policy on Older Persons (NPOP) Draft, New Delhi: Government of India.

—, (1999): National Policy on Older Persons (NPOP), New Delhi: Government of India, Ministry of Social Justice and Empowerment, Shastri Bhawan.

—, (1999): Guidelines, National Social Assistance Programme, New Delhi: Ministry of Rural Development, October.

—, (2001): Census of India.

—, (2002): *India*, New Delhi: Director, Publications Division, Ministry of Information and Broadcasting, GoI, Patiala House.

—, (2002): Statement by India at the Second World Assembly on Ageing; Madrid, Union Minister for Social Justice and Empowerment,

Government of India at the Second World Assembly on Ageing at Madrid, Spain 8th to 12th April, 2002.

Goyal, R.S., (1997): "Implications for the Elderly of the Demographic Transition: An Illustration from India", *Bold*, 7(2), 2–10.

Gray, J.A.M. and G. Wilcock, (1981): *Our Elders*, Oxford: Oxford University Press.

Gray, R.M. and D.O. Mobery, (1962): *The Church and the Older Person*, Michigan: William B.E. Publishing Co.

Guha Roy, S., (1989): "Perspectives on Population Aging in India", S.N. Singh, M.K. Premi, P.S. Bhatia and A. Bose (eds.), *Population Transition in India*, Vol. 1, New Delhi: B.R. Publishing House.

Guhan, S., (1993): "Ageing in Kerala: A Review Article", *Economic and Political Weekly,* 28(35), 28 August 1802.

Gupta, A.C. (ed.), (1998): *Sujas Varshiki,* Jaipur: Directorate of Information and Public Relations, Rajasthan.

Gupta, K.B. and Anita Pal, (1998): "Genital Neoplasm in the Elderly Women of Himachal Pradesh: 6 Years Study", *Journal of Indian Medical Association*, 96(5), May, 141–42.

Gurudass, S. and T.R. Laxminarayan, (1989): "A Study of Life Satisfaction in Relation to Marital Status among the Aged", *Indian Journal of Social Work,* Vol. 50, No. 2, April, 236–238.

Gurumurthy, K.G., (1998): *The Aged in India*, New Delhi: Reliance Publishing House.

Hagestad, G. and B. Naugarten, (1985): "Age and the Life Course", R.H. Binstock and E. Shanas (eds.), *Handbook of Ageing and Social Sciences*, (2nd Edition), New York: Van Nostrand Reinhold.

Handler, P., (1960): "Radiation and Ageing", N.W. Shock (ed.), *Ageing,* Washington: D.C. American Association for the Advancement of Science.

Harell, G.T., (1969): "Training for Practice of Clinical Gerontology: The Training Programme and Setting", *Interdisciplinary Topics in Gerontology*, Vol. 5, Karger Barel, 62–67.

Hashimoto (Akiko), (1996): *Gift of Generations: Japanese and American Perspectives on Aging and the Social Contract,* Cambridge: Cambridge University Press.

Havighurst, R.J., (1968): "Personality and Patterns of Ageing", *The Gerontologist*, 8, 20–23.

Havighurst, R.J., Munnichs, J.M.A., Neugarten, B.L. and Thomae, H., (1969): *Adjustment to Retirement*, The Netherlands: Van Goreum and Comp., N.V.

Havighurst, Robert, (1963): "Successful Ageing", R.H. Williams, C. Tibbitts and W. Donahoe (eds.) *Process of Ageing*, Vol. I, New York: The University of Chicago Press, Chicago, 311–315.

Hazan, Haim, (1994): *Old Age Constructions and Deconstructions*, Cambridge: Cambridge University Press.

Helpage India (1998): A Study to Assess the Kind of Support Required by the Aged Living in Families, Final Unpublished Report by Help Age India, Sponsored by Ministry of Welfare, Government of India.

—, (2002): Senior Citizens Guide (Revised Edition), New Delhi: Research and Development Division, Helpage India.

Hendricks, J., (1995): "Older Women in Social and Economic Development", *Ageing International*, 22(2), 55–8.

Herbert, Blumer, (1969): *Symbolic Interaction*, Englewood Cliffs NJ: Prentice-Hall.

Hess, B.B. and Markson, E.W., (1980): *Ageing and Old Age: An Introduction to Social Gerontology*, New York: Macmillan Publishing Co.

—, (1980): *Old Age Constructions and Deconstructions*, New York: Cambridge University Press.

Heycox, K., (1997): "Older Women: Issues of Gender", A. Borowski, S. Encel and E. Ozanne (eds.), *Ageing and Social Policy in Australia*, Cambridge: Cambridge University Press, 94–118.

Homans, G., (1961): *Social Behaviour: Its Elementary Forms*, New York, Harcourt, Brace and World.

Hooman, N.R. and Kiyan, H.A., (1988): *Social Gerontology: A Multidisciplinary Perspective*, USA (University of Washington): Allyn and Bacon, Inc.

Hoskins, I., (1992): "Gender, Ageing and Development: Emerging Issues and Policy Recommendation", *Ageing International*, 19(1), 12.

—, (1996): *Combining Work and Elder Care: A Challenge for Now and the Future*, Geneva: ILO.

Hosmath, R.S., Gaonkar, V. and Khadi, P.B. (1993): "Life Satisfaction during Later Years", *Man in India*, 73(3), 229–231.

Human Development Report (HDR), (1991, 1999, 2000) Published for the United Nations Development Programme, USA: Oxford University Press, Inc.

ICSSR, (1972): An Empirical Investigation of Roles and Problems of Middle Aged and Older People, Unpublished Research Project, New Delhi: Indian Council of Social Science Research.

Iecovich, Esther, (2005): "Elder Abuse and Neglect in Israel: A Comparison Between the General Elderly Population and Elderly New Immigrants", *Family Relations,* Vol. 54(Issue 3), July, 436–447.

IJG, (1988): "Depression in Old Age", *Indian Journal of Gerontology*, 12(1 and 2), 40–42.

IJSW, (1998): An Attempt to Develop Gerontological Social Work in India, (Report of National Seminar on Globalisation and Ageing: Implication for Gerontological Social Work, Organized by TISS and Family Welfare Agency on December 22–24, 1997), *Indian Journal of Social Work*, Vol. 59(2), April, 674–95.

Iyer, Ananth, (1998): "Study on Acceptance of HRT", *Medivision*, Vol. 1(40), November, 12.

Jamuna, D. and Ramamurti, P.V., (1988): "Adjustment Patterns of Middle Aged and Older Widows and Non-widows", *Indian Journal of Applied Psychology*, 25(2), 48–50.

—, (1997–99): Correlates of Quality of Life among Indian Elderly Man and Women, ICHMR, Project Report, New Delhi.

—, (1999): Correlates of Long Lived Individuals, Project Report, New Delhi: UGC.

Jamuna, D. and Reddy, L.K., (1991): "Impact of Age and Length of Widowhood on the Self-concept of Elderly Widows", *Indian Journal of Gerontology*, 7(3 and 4), 91–95.

Jamuna, D., (1985): "Self Concept among Middle Aged and Older Women", *Journal of Indian Academy of Applied Psychology*, 11(2), 16–18.

—, (1985): A Study of Some Factors Related to Adjustment of Middle Aged and Older Women, Doctoral Dissertation (Unpublished), S.V. University, Tirupati.

—, (1987): "Adjustment Patterns among Pre and Post Menopausal Rural Women", *Journal of Psychological Researches*, 31(2), 88–92.

—, (1987): "Self and Care Givers' Perception of Needs and Problems of Elderly Women", *Indian Journal of Community Guidance Services*, Vol. 4(3), 25–31.

—, (1987): "Sensation Seeking Behaviour and Adjustment in Old Age", K. Suba Rao and V. Prabhakar (eds.), *Ageing: A Multi-Factorial Analysis*, Varanasi: Association of Gerontology.

—, (1988): "Role-Activity and General Adjustment of Middle Aged and Older Women", *Journal of Psychological Researches*, 32(1 and 2), 37–40.

—, (1989): "Psychological Problems and Perspectives of Aged Women", R.N. Pati and B. Jena (eds.), *Aged in India: Socio-Demographic Dimensions*, New Delhi: Ashish Publishing House.

—, (1990): "A Comparison of Need Hierarchy among Middle Aged and Elderly Women of the Social Classes and their Relationship to Happiness and Life Satisfaction", Rameshwar Singh and G.S. Singhal (eds.), *Perspectives in Ageing Research: Biological, Medical and Social,* New Delhi: Today and Tomorrow Printers and Publications.

—, (1990): "Caring for the Elderly Women: Perspectives at the Turn of the Century", *Journal of Indian Academy of Applied Psychology*, 16, 17–23.

—, (1992): Status, Needs and Determinants of Problems of Older Women of Forward and Scheduled Caste Groups, Unpublished Project Report, New Delhi: UGC.

—, (1994): "Caring for Elderly Women: Perspectives on the Turn of the Century", C.R. Rama Chandran and Bela Shah (eds.), *Public Health Implications of Ageing in India* (Compendium of papers presented in the Indo-UK Workshop held under the auspices of the Indian Council of Medical Research), New Delhi: ICMR, 106–113.

—, (1994): "The Psychological and Social Correlates of Successful Ageing among Elderly Indian Women", *Indian Journal of Gerontology*, 8(1 and 2), 18–23.

—, (1995): "Ageing Women in India: A Profile", *Help Age India Research and Development Journal*, 1(3), 3–12.

—, (2000): "Ageing in India: Some Key Issues", *Ageing International*, Vol. 25, Number 4/March 1, 16–31.

—, (2001): An Investigation of Psychological Factors including Quality of Life of Very Senior Citizens from Rural and Urban Areas of Andhra Pradesh, New Delhi: ICSSR.

Jamuna, D., Ramamurti, P.V. and Sudharani, N.N., (1995): Psychological Aspects of Elderly Widows, Proceedings of International Symposium and Conference, New Delhi: AGI.

—, (1996): "Psychological Aspects of Elder Widows", Vinod Kumar (ed.), *Aging: Indian Perspectives and Global Scenario*, New Delhi: AIIMS, 303–306.

Jamuna, D., L.K. Reddy and P.V. Ramamurti, (1991): "The Widowed Rural Elderly: Status of Mental Health and Adjustment", *The Creative Psychologist*, 3, 45–50.

Jatan, A. et al., (1991): "Some Experiences with a Rapid Test of Mental Function in the Elderly", I.J. Prakash (ed.), *Quality Ageing: Collected Papers*, Varanasi (India): Association of Gerontology, 179–185.

Jerrome, D., (1981): "The Significance of Friendship for Women in Later Life", *Ageing and Society*, 1(2), July 175–197.

—, (1983): "Lonely Women in a Friendship Club", *British Journal of Guidance and Counselling*, 11(1), 10–20.

Jesser, Clinton Joyce, (1975): *Social Theory Revisited*, USA: The Dryden Press, Hinsdate, Illinois.

Johoda, M., Deutsch, M. and Cook, S.W. (1995): *Research Methods in Social Relations*, USA: Holt, Rinehart and Winston, Inc.

Joseph, James, (1991): *Aged in India, Problems and Personality*, Allahabad: Chugh Publications.

Kabir, Zarina Nahar, (1999): Traditional Norms versus Reality: The Case of Elderly Men and Women in Bangladesh, Women's Health and the Nation's Gain: An International Conference with a Special Focus on Women in Asia, Singapore: TSAO Foundation.,

Kaladate, S.V., (1986): Socio-familial Stresses Faced after Retirement: A Study of Retired Persons in Aurangabad, paper presented at XI World Congress of the International Sociological Association, August 19–22, New Delhi.

Kalche, A. and Kickbusch, I., (1998): "A Global Strategy for Healthy Ageing", *Swasth Hind* (Special Issue: 50 Years of Health and Family Welfare), New Delhi: Central Health Education Bureau, Directorate General of Health Services, Ministry of Health and Family Welfare, January, 127–28.

Kanwar, Priya and Chahda, N.K., (1988): "Psycho-Social Determinants of Institutionalized Elderly: An Empirical Study", *Indian Journal of Gerontology*, Vol. 12, Nos. 1 and 2, 27–39.

Kapoor, Promilla, (1997): "Elderly Abuse: Some Counselling Tips", *Helpage India Research and Development Journal*, Vol. 3(3), 13–23.

Karkar, Malini, (1999): "Ageing and Women in India", *Economic and Political Weekly*, XXXIV (44), October 30, WS 54–56.

—, (1999): *Elderly in India: An Annotated Bibliography*, Vol. 1, Mumbai: TISS.

—, (1999–2000): "Let Us Care for Our Older Women", *HelpAge India: Research and Development Journal*, 6(1), October-January, 19–21.

—, (2000a): "Ageing and Women in India", *Ageing and Society: The Indian Journal of Gerontology*, 10 (3 and 4), 1–14.

—, (2000b): *Elderly in India: An Annotated Bibliography*, Vol. 2, Mumbai: TISS.

—, (2000c): "Grappling with the Problem of Kerala's Very Old Women", *The Indian Express*, Kochi, January 13.

Kart, C.S., (1981): *The Realities of Ageing*, Boston: Allyn & Bacon, Inc.

Kasthoori, R., (1996): *The Problems of the Aged: A Sociological Study*, New Delhi: Uppal Publishing House.

Kathy, V.M. and Carson, B.R., (1992): "Health Locus of Control and Self-Efficacy Beliefs in a Healthy Elderly Sample", *American Journal of Health Promotion*, 6, 302–09.

Kaur, Satnam and Kaur, Malik, (1987): "Psychosocial Problems of the Aged", M.L. Sharma and T.M. Dak (eds.), *Ageing in India: Challenge for the Society*, Delhi: Ajanta Publications.

Khan, M.Z. and Kaushik, Archana, (1999): "Where do the Elderly Stand in the Changing Economic Scenario", *Social Welfare*, 46(1), April, 35–39.

Khan, M.Z., (1989): Voluntary Welfare Services for the Aged, Unpublished Study, Department of Social Work, New Delhi: Jamia Milia Islamia.

—, (1994): The Aged: Their Problems, Social Intervention and Future Outlook, Unpublished Study, Department of Social Work, New Delhi: Jamia Milia Islamia.

—, (1997): *Elderly in Metropolis*, New Delhi: Inter India Publications.

Khan, M.Z., Agrawal, B.B. and Mishra, S.K., (1997): "A Study of Anxiety and Pessimism-Optimism among the Aged in Delhi", M.G. Husain (ed.), *Changing Indian Society and Status of Aged,* New Delhi: Manak Publications Pvt. Ltd., 82–98.

Khetarpal, Kamla, (1998): "Endocrinological Problems of Aged Women", P.C. Bhatla (ed.), *Aged Women: Coping with Life*, New Delhi: NIPHC, 14–15.

KKWS Hospital and TSAD Foundation, (1999): Women's Health—Nations Gain: An International Conference with a Special Focus on Older Women in Asia, Organized by K.K. Women's and Children's Hospital and TSAD Foundation on 5–7 July, Singapore: KKWS Hospital and TSAH Foundation.

Kleban, Morton H., Elaine M. Brody, Claire, B. Schoonover, and Christine Hoffman, (1989): "Family Help to the Elderly: Perceptions of Sons-in-Law regarding Parent Care", *Journal of Marriage and Family*, 51(2), 303–312.

Knapp, M., (1977): "The Activity Theory of Ageing: An Examination in the English Context", *Gerontologist*, 17(5), 553–55.

Kohli, A.S., (1996): *Social Situation of the Aged in India,* New Delhi: Anmol Publishing Pvt. Ltd.

Kohli, Adarsh and Verma, S.K., (1997): "Old Age and Leisure Time", *Research and Development Journal*, Vol. 3, No. 3, June.

Kulkarni, A.T., (1999): "Proactive Approach to Geriatric Care", *Social Welfare*, 46(7), Oct., 8–10.

Kumar, Narender, (1999): "Gender Perspectives in Eco-management", *Social Welfare,* January Issue.

Kumar, S., (1991): "Ageing of Population: An Investigation in Indian Context", I.J. Prakash (ed.), *Quality Ageing—Collected Papers*, Varanasi: Association of Gerontology, 55–75.

Kumar, S. Vijay (ed.), (1995): *Challenges Before the Elderly: An Indian Scenario*, New Delhi: M.D. Publication Pvt. Ltd.

Kumar, S. Vijay, (1991): *Family Life and Socio-Economic Problems of the Aged*, Delhi: Ashish Publishing House.

—, (1997): "Family and Health of the Aged", Indrani Chakravarty (ed.), *Life in Twilight Years*, Kwality Book Company, 153–154.

—, (1999): "Population Ageing in India", *Helpage India Research and Development Journal*, 5(2), 3–16.

—, (1999): Quality of Life and Social Security of the Rural Elderly, (Unpublished Study Sponsored by ICSSR), Hyderabad (India): C.D. Deshmukh Impart Centre, Council for Social Development, Southern Regional Office.

Kumar, Sanjay, (1991): "Aging of Population: An Investigation in Indian Context?", Indira Jai Prakash (ed.), *Quality Aging*, Varanasi: (India) Association of Gerontology, 55–75.

Kumar, Vinod (ed.), (1996): *Ageing: Indian Perspectives and Global Scenario*, New Delhi: Vinod Kumar, AIIMS.

Kundal, A., (1994): "Urbanisation and Ageing in India", *Economic Development Record,* 1(1), 17–22.

Kurup, A.M., (1996): "The Challenges of Ageing in India", Vinod Kumar (ed.), *Ageing: Indian Perspectives and Global Scenario*, New Delhi: AIIMS, 23–25.

Kuypers, J.A. and Bengtson, V.L., (1973): "Competence and Social Break down", *Human Development*, 16(2), 37–49.

Lalitha, L., (1996): "Women's Empowerment through Cooperatives", *Social Welfare*, September, 1996.

Lawton, M.P., (1975): "The Philadelphia Geriatric Center Morale Scale: A Revision", *Journal of Gerontology,* 30, 85–89.

Lebra, J., Paulson, J. and Everett, J. (1984): *Women and Work in India*, New Delhi: Promilla & Co. Publishers.

Lemon, B.W., Bengtson, V.L., and Peterson, J.A., (1972): "Activity Types and Life Satisfaction in a Retirement Community", *Journal of Gerontology*, 27(4), 511–23.

Lewis, M., (1985): "Older Women and Health: An Overview", *Women and Health*, 10, 1–16.

Lewis, S., (1987): "Drug-Induced Dementia", *Women and Ageing: A Clinical Social Work Perspective,* www.informaworld.com.

Linton, R., (1942): "Age and Sex Categories", *American Sociological Review*, Vol. 7, 589–603.

Longino, C.F. and Kart, C.S., (1982): "Explicating Activity Theory: A Formal Replication", *Journal of Gerontology*, 37, 713–722.

Lopata, H.Z., (1979): "Women as Widows: Support Systems", N.Y. Elsevier as mentioned in I.J. Prakash, *Gender Ageing: Psycho-social Issues*, (1994), op. cit.

Lowy, L., (1985): *Social Work with the Ageing*, New York: Longman Inc.

Luthra, P.N., (1991): "Do not Segregate the Aged from the Mainstream: Aging and Welfare of the Elderly in India", *Social Welfare*, 38(3), June, 33–36.

MacDonald, B. and Rich, C., (1984): *Look Me in the Eye Old Women: Ageing and Ageism*, London: The Women's Press.

Maclean, U., (1984): "Women and Health in Europe: The Scope and Limits of Epidemiology", *International Journal of Health Services*, 15, 665–76.

Maddox, G., (1968): "Persistence of Lifestyle among the Elderly: A Longitudinal Study of Patterns of Social Activity in Reaction to Life Satisfaction". In B.L. Neugarten (ed.), *Middle Age and Aging*. Chicago: University of Chicago Press, 181–83.

Maddox, G.L. (1970): "Themes and Issues in Sociological Theories of Human Ageing", *Human Development*, 17–27.

Maddox, G.L. (1976): "Scope, Concepts and Methods in the Study of Aging", In R.H. Binstock and E. Shanas (eds.) *Handbook of Ageing and Social Sciences*, New York: Van Nostrand Reinhold Co.

Mahajan, A., (1987): *Problems of Aged in Unorganised Sector*, Delhi: Mittal Publications.

Manandhar, Mary, (1999): Undernutrition and Poor Function amongst Older Women in Indian Slums, Women's Health and the Nation's Gain: An International Conference with a Special Focus on Women in Asia, Singapore: TSAO Foundation.

Mansharamani, G.C. and Chakravarty, M., (1998): "Mortality and Morbidity in Elderly Women", P.C. Bhatla (ed.), *Aged Women: Coping with Life*, National Institute of Primary Health Care.

Marshall, Victor W., (1981): *Aging in Canada: Social Perspectives*, Ontario: Fitzhenry and Whiteside Ltd.

Marulasiddaih, H.M., (1968): *The Older People of Makunta*, Dharwar: Karnataka University Press.

Mauss, M., (1954): *The Gift*, New York: Free Press, Glencoe.

McCallum, John, (1992): "Asia Pacific Retirement: Models for Australia, Fiji, Malaysia, Philippines and Republic of Korea", *Journal of Cross-Cultural Gerontology*, 7(1), January, 25–43.

Mead, G.C. (ed.), (1934): *Mind, Self and Society*, Chicago: The University of Chicago Press.

Mehta, A. Kapoor, (1996): "Recasting Indices for Developing Countries: A Gender Empowerment Measure", *Economic and Political Weekly*, October 26, WS–83.

Mehta, S.R., (1987): "A Strategy for Health and Medical Care of the Aged", M.L. Sharma and T.M. Dak (eds.), *Ageing in India: Challenges her Society*, New Delhi: Ajanta Publications, 222–27.

Minkler, M. and Estes, C., (1984): *Reading in Political Economy of Ageing*, New York: Farmingdale, Baywood.

Minkler, M. and Stone, R., (1985): "The Feminization of Poverty and Older Women", *Gerontologist*, 25, 351–357.

Mishra, Sarswati, (1989): *Problems and Social Adjustment in Old Age: A Sociological Analysis*, New Delhi: Gyan Publications.

Mishra, U. Shankar, (2000): "Old Age and Health", *Rajasthan Patrika* (Hindi Daily), May 7, 5.

Mohanpuria, K.L., (1996): "Constitutional and Legal Aspects for Elderly Welfare", Vinod Kumar (ed.), *Indian Perspectives and Global Scenario*, New Delhi: AIIMS, 97–98.

Moneer, Alam, 2006: *Ageing in India: Socio-economic and Health Dimensions*, Delhi: Institute of Economic Growth.

Muthayya, B.C., (1995): "The Rural Elderly: A Study of their Existing Conditions and Problems", Vijay Kumar (ed.), *Challenges Before the Elderly: An Indian Scenario*, New Delhi: M.D. Publications Pvt. Ltd., 3–14.

Nag, N.G., (1987) "Welfare Services for the Aged", *Encyclopaedia of Social Work*, Vol. III, New Delhi: Director, Publication Division, Ministry of Information and Broadcasting, Government of India, 344–53.

Nagesh, H.V., (1992): "The Problems and the Care of the Aged in India", Shanker Jogan (ed.), *Social Problems and Welfare in India*, 277–85.

Nagla, B.K., (1987): "Ageing and Health: A Sociological Analysis", M.L. Sharma and T.K. Dak (eds.), *Ageing in India: Challenges for the Society*, New Delhi: Ajanta Publications, 193–206.

Nagpal, Nishi and Chadha, N.K., (1991): "Institutionalized and Non-Institutionalized Elderly: Problems and their Solutions", *Journal of Psychological Researches*, Dec. Issue.

Nair, P.S., (1989): "The Aged in Rural India: A Study of the Socio-Economic Health Profile", S.N. Singh et al. (eds.), *Population Transition in India*, Vol. 2, Delhi: B.R. Publishing, 63–70.

Nair, T.N. and Ramana, K.V. (eds.), (1989): *Ageing and Welfare of Elderly in India*, Madras Institute of Ageing.

Nair, T.N., (1991): Community Care for the Elderly? A Study of Family and Community Based Services for the Elderly in Madras, Ph.D. Thesis, Andhra University.

Nalini, B., (1997): "Institutional Care for the Aged: The Issues and Implications", Indrani Chakravarty (ed.), *Life in Twilight Years*, Calcutta: Kwality Book Company, 63–79.

Nanda, A.R., (1992): Final Population Totals: Brief Analysis of Primary Census Abstracts, Census of Indian (Series-I) Paper II, 218–315.

Nandan, D.S., Khatri, R.S. and Kadian, R.S., (1987): "Ageing Problems in the Structural Context", M.L. Sharma and T.M. Dak (eds.), *Ageing in India*, New Delhi: Ajanta Publications, 106–16.

Natarajan, C.N., (2000): "Approach to the Aged", M.A. Sudhir (ed.) *Ageing in Rural India: Perspectives and Prospects*, Delhi: Indian Publishers Distributors.

National Sample Survey Organisation, (1991): "Socio-Economic Profile of the Aged Persons", NSS 42nd Round, July 1986-June1987, *Sarvekshana*, Vol. 15, No. 2.

Neugarten, B., (1974): "Age Groups in American Society", *Annals of the American Academy of Political and Social Science*, 415, 187–198.

NIPHC/HCPT, (1996): Services for the Aged: A National Commitment. Proceedings of National Institute of Primary Health Care: An activity of Health Care Promotion Trust Seminar held on October 1, New Delhi: NIPHC/HCPT.

NSSO, (1991): "Socio-Economic Profile of the Aged Persons", NSS 42nd Round July 1986-June1987, *Sarvekshana*, Vol. 15(2), New Delhi.

NSSO, (1995–96): The Aged in India: A Socio-economic Profile, NNS 52nd Round, July 1995–June 1996, National Sample Survey Organisation (NSSO), Department of Statistics, Ministry of Planning and Programme Implementation, Government of India, Calcutta, 1998.

Nyanguru, A., (1987): "Residential Care for the Destitute Elderly", *Journal of Cross-Cultural Gerontology*, 2(4), 345–7.

Observer, (26, November 1989): "Old People's Homes Go to Multinationals: Charities Fear Big Business Granny Farms".

Palmore, E. (ed.), (1974): *Normal Ageing II: Report from the Duke Longitudinal Study*, Durham, N.C.: Duke University Press.

Palmore, E., (1968): "The Effects of Ageing on Activities and Attitudes", *The Gerontologist*, 8, 259–63.

Palmore, E.B. and Luikart, C., (1972): "Health and Social Factors related to Life-satisfaction", *Journal of Health and Social Behaviour*, 13(1), 68–80.

Panda, Archana Kaushik, (2005): "Life-satisfaction among Elderly Females in Delhi", *Help Age India: Research and Development Journal,* 11(1), January, 21–29.

Parthasarathy, N.R., (1980): "On Some Aspects of Aging in India", *Indian Journal of Social Work*, Vol. XL, No. 4, January, 381–388.

Patel, A.A., (1998): "Loneliness among the Elderly: The Role Perceived Responsibility and Control", *Recent Researches in Education and Psychology*, Vol. 3, Nos. I-II, 21–25.

Patel, J.M. Asgarali and Broota, Aruna, (2000): "Loneliness and Death Anxiety among the Elderly: The Role of Family Set-up and Religious Beliefs", *Helpage India-Research and Development Journal*, Vol. 6, No. 3, June-September.

Patil, Godavari, M. Patil and D.S. Kumar, (1991): "Impact of Ageing on Life Satisfaction of Elderly Women", I.J. Prakash (ed.), *Quality Aging: Collected Papers,* Varanasi (India): Association of Gerontology, 141–150.

Peplau, L.A., Bikson, T.K., Rook, K.S. and Goodchilds, J.D., (1982): "Being Old and Living Alone", L.A. Peplau and L.D. Perlman (eds.), *Loneliness: Source Book of Current Theory, Research and Therapy*, New York: John Wiley.

Perls, Thomos T., (1995): "The Influence of Demographic Selection upon the Oldest Old", *Journal of Geriatric Psychiatry,* 28(1), 35–56.

Pinto, A.S. and I.J. Prakash, (1991): "Life Quality of the Aged: Elderly Care at Home and Institute", I.J. Prakash (ed.), *Quality Ageing: Collected Papers,* Varansai (India): Associations of Gerontology, 162–168.

Poon, L.W., (1992): *The Georgian Centenarian Study*, New York: Baywook Pub. Co.

Prabha, Girimaji, (1991): "Protection of the Legal Rights of Elderly Women", Indira Jai Prakash (ed.), *Quality Aging: Collected Papers,* Varanasi (India): Association of Gerontology, 230–233.

Prakash, Chandra, (1998): "Renal Diseases in Aged Women", P.C. Bhatla (ed.), *Aged Women: Coping with Life*, New Delhi: NIPHC, 34–37.

Prakash, I.J. and Anuradha, B.R., (1988): "Physical and Mental Health of Rural Women", I.J. Prakash (ed.), *Indian Women, Issues and Perspectives*, Bangalore: Bangalore University.

Prakash, I.J., (1987): "Social Ageing and Perception of Age Appropriate Behaviour", Subba Rao and V. Prabhakar (eds.), *Ageing: A Multifactorial Analysis,* Association of Gerontology, Varanasi, 91–96.

—, (1988): Widowhood and the Ageing Indian Women, Trivandrum: Proceedings of the ICSSR Workshop on Problems of the Aged in Contemporary Society.

—, (1989): Life Cycle Changes in Ageing Indian Women, Career Award Project Report Submitted to UGC New Delhi.

—, (1991): "Psychological Profile of Ageing Indian Women", I.J. Prakash (ed.), *Quality Ageing: Collected Papers,* Varanasi (India): Associations of Gerontology, 234–245.

—, (1993): "Gender Ageing: Psycho-social Issues", *Indian Journal of Gerontology,* 7 (1 and 2), 24–29.

—, (1994): "Gender Ageing", C.R. Ramachandran and Bela Shah (eds.), *Public Health Implications of Ageing in India,* New Delhi: Indian Council of Medical Research, 99–105.

—, (1994): "Ageing Indian Women", C.R. Ramachandran and Bela Shah (eds.), *Public Health Implications of Ageing in India,* New Delhi: ICMR, 187–191.

—, (1994): "Gender Ageing: Psycho-social Issues", C.R. Ramachandran and Bela Shah (eds.), ibid., 99–105.

—, (1995): "Psycho-social Situation of Older Women Lives in India and Potentials for Empowerment", Saviour Formosa (ed.), *Age Vault: An Anthology from International Institute of Ageing,* Malta: United Nations, 69–86.

—, (1996): "Ageing Women: A Liability or an Asset?", *Help Age India Research and Development Journal,* 2(2), 28–32.

—, (1997): "Women and Ageing", *Indian Journal of Medical Research,* 106, 396–408.

—, (1997a): "Hindu World View and Well Being of Ageing Women", *Helpage India Research and Development Journal,* 3(2), 43–49.

—, (1997b): "The Status and Conditions of Elderly Widows in India", Kalyan Bagchi (ed.), *Elderly Females in India: Their Status and Sufferings,* New Delhi: Society for Gerontological Research and Help Age India, 45–64.

—, (1997c): "Ageing Indian Women", C.R. Ramachandran and Bela Shah (eds.), *Public Health Implications of Ageing in India,* New Delhi: Indian Council of Medical Research, 187–91.

—, (1998): "Living Arrangements of the Elderly in India: Implications for Care Giving", *Ageing and Society,* Vol. 9, (3 and 4), 1–10.

—, (1998): "Maintenance of Competence in Daily Living and Well Being of Elderly", *Helpage India Research and Development Journal*, 4(2 and 3), 26–34.

—, (1999): "Senior Women's Perception of Leisure in India", *Tourism Recreation Research*, 24(1), 82–85.

—, (2004): "Mental Health of Older People in India", P.V. Ramamurti and D. Jamuna (eds.), *Handbook of Indian Gerontology*, New Delhi: Serials Publications, 176–207.

—, (2006): *Training Modules in Gerontology*, Bangalore: Bangalore University.

—, (2007): "Training in Gerontology: Do We Need to "Train" to Grow Old?", *Helpage India Research and Development Journal*, 13(1), 6–9.

—, (ed.), (2003): *Ageing: Emerging Issues*, Bangalore: Bangalore University.

—, (ed.), (2005): *Ageing in India: Retrospect and Prospect*, Bangalore: Bangalore University.

Prasad, Rajeshwar, (1987): "Problems of the Aged in India: Some Reflections", M.L. Sharma and T.M. Dak (eds.), *Ageing in India: Challenge for the Society,* Delhi: Ajanta Publications, 33–39.

Punia, Deep and Sharma, M.L. (1987): "Family Life of Rural Aged Women", M.L. Sharma and T.M. Dak (eds.), *Ageing in India: Challenges for the Society*, New Delhi: Ajanta Publications.

Ragbai, (1960): *Notes and Queries*, London: Routledge and Kegan Paul Ltd.

Rajagopal, L.S. and Royce, Saramma (1995): "Socio-Cultural Status of Elderly Women in Urban Settings", *Research Highlights,* 5(4), October, 165–170.

Rajan, S. Irudaya and U.S. Mishra, (1995): "Defining Old Age: An Indian Assessment", *Bold* (Journal of United Nations Institute on Aging, Malta), Vol. 5(4), 31–35.

Rajan, S. Irudaya, (1989): "Ageing in Kerala: One More Population Problem?", *Asia Pacific Population Journal*, Vol. 4(2), 19–48.

Rajan, S. Irudaya, (2002): "Social Security for the Unorganized Sector in South Asia", *International Social Security Review*, Vol. 55(4), 143–156.

Rajan, S. Irudaya, U.S. Mishra and Mala Ramanathan, (1993): "Population Aging in Kerala, India", *Social Development Issues*, Vol. 13, Spring, No. 3, 90–99.

—, (1993): "Two Child Family in India: Is it Realistic?", *International Family Planning Perspectives*, Vol. 19, No. 4, 125–28 and 154.

Rajan, S. Irudaya and K.S. James (2000): "The Interdependence of Vital Events: Twentieth-Century Indian Kerala?", *Journal of Interdisciplinary History*, Vol. 31(1), 21–41.

Rajan, S. Irudaya, U.S. Mishra and P.S. Sharma, (1993): India: National Ageing Trends..., *Economic and Political Weekly*, 27(23), 5 June, 1188–94.

—, (1995): "Living Arrangements among the Indian Elderly", *Hongkong Journal of Gerontology*, Vol. 9, No. 2, 20–28.

—, (1995): "An Agenda for National Policies on Ageing in India", *Helpage India Research and Development Journal,* 1(2), 38–53.

—, (1995): "The Elderly Speak", S. Vijay Kumar (ed.), *Challenges Before the Elderly: An Indian Scenario*, New Delhi: M.D. Publications, 179–213.

—, (1996): "Living Arrangement among the Indian Elderly: An Analysis from the National Ageing Survey", Vinod Kumar (ed.), *Ageing: Indian Perspective and Global Scenario,* New Delhi: AIIMS, 282–287.

—, (1999): *India's Elderly: Burden or Challenges*, New Delhi: Sage Publications.

—, (2000): "Ageing in India: Retrospect and Prospect", *Indian Social Science Review*, New Delhi: Sage Publications, 2(1), 1–47.

—, (2001): "Health Concerns among the India's Elderly", *International Journal of Aging and Human Development*, Vol. 53(3), 191–204.

Rajan, S. Irudaya, Sudha, S. and Mohanachandran, P., (2000): "Fertility Decline and Worsening Gender Bias in India: Is Kerala No Longer an Exception?", *Development and Change*, Vol. 31(4), 1085–92.

Rajkumar, S., (1995): "The Tragedy of Alzheimer's Disease", *Helpage India Research and Development Journal,* 1(3), 32–38.

Ramachandra, C.R. and Bela Shah (eds.), (1994): *Public Health Implications of Ageing in India,* New Delhi: The Indian Council of Medical Research.

Ramamurti, P.V. and Jamuna, D., (1992): Markers of Successful Ageing among a Sample of Indian Elderly, Project Report, Basle: Sandoz International Foundation.

—, (1993): "Psychological Dimensions of Ageing in India", *Indian Journal of Social Sciences*, 6(4), 309–331.

—, (1995): "Perspectives of Gero-psychology in India: A Review", *Indian Psychological Abstracts and Reviews*, 2(2), 207–267.

—, (1999): "Frontiers of Ageing Research in India", S.D. Gokhale et al., (eds.), *Ageing in India*, Mumbai: Somaiya Publishers Pvt. Ltd.

—, (2004): *Handbook of Indian Gerontology*, New Delhi: Serials Publications.

Ramamurti, P.V., (1970): "Life Satisfaction in the Older Years", *Indian Journal of Gerontology,* Vol. 2(3–4), 68–70.

—, (1989): The Status, Psychological Adjustment and Mental Health of Middle Aged and Older Widows, Centre for Research on Ageing,

Department of Psychology, S.V. University, Tirupati, Research Report. Mimeographed.

—, (1989a): The Status, Psychological Adjustment and Mental Health of Middle Aged and Older Widows, Project Report, New Delhi: ICSSR.

—, (1989b): Old Age as a Stress: Strategies for its Management, Abstracts of the Workshop in Awareness, Welfare and Productive Utilisation of Elder Components of Human Population, Rewa: Chinmaya Seva Trust.

—, (1990): "Correlates of Successful Ageing among Elderly Men", Rameshwar Singh and G.N. Singhal (eds.), *Perspectives in Ageing Research*, New Delhi: Today and Tomorrow Publications, 237–239.

—, (1994): "Concept of Ageing: Contribution of Culture and Public Attitude", C.R. Ramachandran and Bela Shah (eds.), *Public Health Implications of Ageing in India*, New Delhi: Indian Council of Medical Research, 12–14.

—, (1997): "The Psychological Scenario of the Elderly: Problems, Priorities and Perspectives", M.G. Husain (ed.), *Changing Indian Society and Status of Aged*, New Delhi: Manak Publications.

—, (1999): Knowledge and Attitude towards Health as a Factor of Well Being in Old Age, Women's Health and the Nation's Gain: An International Conference with a Special Focus on Women in Asia, Singapore: TSAO Foundation.

Ramesh, R., (1998): "Help for the Aged is Just a Phone Call Away", *The Times of India,* September 28.

Ramnath, Rajlaxmi, (1989): "Problems of Aged", R.N. Pati and B. Jena (eds.), *Aged in India*, New Delhi: Ashish Publishing House.

Randhawa, M.S., (1991): *The Rural and Urban Aged*, New Delhi: National Book Organization.

Rao, Radha Krishan (1999): "Growing Population of Elder Population", *Social Welfare*, Vol. 45, No. 10, January.

Rao, Venkoba, (1990): *Psychiatry of Old Age in India*, Ahmedabad: Torrent Laboratories, 1989. Berkeley and Los Angeles: University of California Press.

—, (1990): Health Care of the Rural Aged, ICMR Task Force Research Project Report, New Delhi.

Rao, V., (1991): Mental Health and Ageing, ICMR Bulletin, 21(5), 49–54.

Rao, Venkoba, (1991): *Health Care of the Rural Aged*, New Delhi: ICMR Task Force Project Report.

Razzaque, M.A. and Satter, M.A, (1994): "Urbanization and Ageing in Bangladesh", *Journal of Family Welfare*, 40(1), 44–48.

Reddy, L.K., Jamuna, D. and Ramamurti, P.V., (1992): "Widowhood Customs and Practices: Perceptions of Widows and Non-Widows of Different Caste and Age Groups", *Journal of Social Change*, 22, 52–56.

Reddy, M.N.S., Ramamohan, Vijayalakshimi and Sobha, I. (NN): "How do the Aged Live?", *Ageing and Society: The Indian Journal of Gerontology*, Vol. 10 (1 and 2), 1–13.

Reddy, N. Vani and Padmini, N.C., (1989): "A Study of Problems of Institutionalized and Non-Institutionalized Elderly Men and Women", *Journal of Psychological Researches*, 33(2), May, 7–9.

Reznikov, Semen Gersnevich and Rozhkov, A.G., (1991): *Boarders in Boarding Houses for Old Persons (A Sociological Portrait)*, Republic of Russia: Sotsiologichesakie—Issledovaniya, 18(2), 71–73.

Riley, M., Johnson, M. and Foner, A., (1972): *Ageing and Society*, Vol. 3, *Sociology of Age Stratification*, New York: Russell Sage.

Riley, M.W., (1971): "Age Strata in Social Systems", R. Binstock and E. Shanas (eds.), *Handbook of Ageing and Social Sciences*, New York: Van Nostrand Reinhold, 189–217.

—, (1985): "Age Strata in Social Systems", R. Binstock and E. Shanas (eds.), *Handbook of Ageing and Social Sciences*, New York: Van Nostrand Reinhold, 369–414.

Rix, S.E., (1992): "Older Women: Making a Difference in Development", *Ageing International*, 19(1), 1–11.

Roberto, Karen A., (1993): "Osteoporosis and Older Women: Productive Life Style Strategies", *Journal of Women and Ageing*, 5(3–4), 43–59.

Rokach, A., (1996): "The Subjectivity of Loneliness and Coping with it", *Psychological Reports*, Vol. 79(2), 475–81.

Rose, A.M. and Peterson, W.H., (1965): *Old People and their Social World*, Philadelphia: F.A. Davis.

Rosow, I., (1985): "Status and Role Change through the Life-Cycle", R. Binstock and E. Shanas (eds.), *Handbook of Ageing and Social Sciences*, New York: Van Nostrand Reinhold, 62–93.

Rossell, C., (1981): *The Ageing Experience*, Sydney: George Allen and Unwin.

Rundd, Zudith, German, Tony, and Deborah, (1999): *The Ageing and Development Report: Poverty, Independence and the World's Older People*, London (UK): Earthscan Publications Ltd., 42.

Ruprail, Nirmal, (2002): *Silver Generation in India: A Bibliographical Study (1889–2000)*, New Delhi: ICSSR and Anamika Publishers and Distributors (P) Ltd.

Russell, C., (1987): "Aging as a Feminist Issue", *Women's Studies International Forum*, 10, 125–132.

Sahi, Santosh, (1998): "Medical and Health Problems in Post-Menopausal and Elderly Women", P.C. Bhatla (ed.), *Aged Women: Coping with Life*, New Delhi: NIPHC, 11–15.

Saraceno, Chiara, (1992): "Growing Old between Biography and Society", Italy: *Socialogia*, 26, 2–3, 417–430, Sociological Abstract.

Sati, P.N., (1988): *Retired and Ageing People*, Delhi: Mittal Publications.

—, (1996): *Needs and Problems of Aged*, Udaipur, Delhi: Himanshu Publications.

Sawhney, M. et al., (1998): *Directory of Old Age Homes in India*, New Delhi: Research and Development Division, Helpage India.

Sen, T., (1991): "Senescence in Different Ecological Settings", I.J. Prakash (ed.), *Quality Aging: Collected Papers*, Varanasi (India): Association of Gerontology.

—, (1996): "A Health and Socio-Economic Profile of the Aged Bangali Women", Vinod Kumar (ed.), *Ageing: Indian Perspective and Global Scenario*, New Delhi: Vinod Kumar, AIIMS.

SGR, (1996): The Plight of Elderly Females in India, Unpublished Report of the National Seminar on the Need for Focusing Attention on the Plight of Elderly Females, Dec. 22–24, New Delhi: Organized by The Society for Gerontological Research, New Delhi.

Shah, A.M. (ed.) (1973): *Household Dimensions of Family Life in India*. New Delhi: Orient Longman.

Shah, A.M., (2000): "Changing Family and their Impact on the Elderly", *Helpage India Research and Development Journal*, Vol. 6, No. 2, February-March, 32–38.

Shah, Anupama, (1991–92): Ageing Women Belonging to Low Socio-Economic Status, (Unpublished Project Report) Baroda: Department of Home Science, Maharaja Sayajirao University of Baroda.

Shah, S.Y., (1991): *An Encyclopaedia of Adult Education*, India: National Literacy Mission, Directorate of Adult Education, Ministry of Human Resource Development, Department of Education, Government of India.

Shah, Vimal P., (1993): *Study of Elderly in Gujarat*, Ahemdabad: University of Gujarat.

Shanas, Ither, (1968): *Old People in Three Industrial Societies*, London: Routledge and Kegan Paul.

Sharan, A.B. and Sandhwar, A.N., (1990): *Problems of Women Workers in Unorganized Sectors*, New Delhi: Northern Book Centre.

Sharma, G.C., (1981): "Life-Style and Aging", *Asian Journal of Psychological Education*, 7(1), 25–26.

Sharma, M.L. and Dak, T.K., (1987): *Ageing in India: Challenge for the Society*, New Delhi: Ajanta Publications.

Sharma, S.D. and Agarwal, Sanjay, (1996): "Ageing: The Indian Perspectives", Vinod Kumar (ed.), *Ageing: Indian Perspective and Global Scenario,* New Delhi: AIIMS.

Sharma, S.D., (1998): "Psycological Problems of Ageing Women", P.C. Bhatla (ed.), *Aged Women: Coping with Life*, New Delhi: NIPHC, 54–57.

Shaul, Muriel P., (1994): "Rheumatoid Arthritis and Older Women: Economics Tell only Part of the Story", *Health Care for Women International*, 15(5), September–October, 377- 383.

Sheila M, Peace (ed.), (1990): *Researching Social Gerontology*, New Delhi: Sage Publication.

Shiva Kumar, D., (1999): "Integration of Strategies for Care of Elderly", *Social Welfare*, 46(7), Oct., 18–22.

Shubha, Suneja, (1999): The Situation of Older People in Rural and Urban India, *The Ageing and Development Report*, London: Earthscan Publications Ltd., 127–130.

Shukla, Manjula and Mishra, Ranjan (2001): "Kanya Bhrun ki Hatya, Jeene ke Adhikar ka Hanan", *Samaj Kalyan* (Hindi), Nov., 17–18.

Siegel, Jacob S. and Taeuber, Cynthia M., (1986): "Demographic Perspective on Long Lived Society", United States: *Daedalus*, 115(1), Winter, 77–197.

Simmons, L., (1945): *The Role of the Aged in Primitive Society*, New Haven, Connecticut: Yale University Press.

Singh, A.K.P.J., Dak, T.M. and Sharma, M.L., (1987): "Work and Leisure Among the Aged Males", M.L. Sharma and T.M. Dak (eds.), *Ageing in India*, New Delhi: Ajanta Publications, 82–93.

Singh, D.P., (1999): "Make Health Care Elder Friendly", *Social Welfare,* 46(1), April, 29–30.

Singh, G., (1997): "On the Status of Ageing Population in India", *Ageing and Society*, 7 (1and 2), 43–52.

Singh, Kanta, R. Singh and M.L. Sharma, (1987): "Problems of Aged Women in Haryana", M.L. Sharma and T.M. Dak (eds.), *Ageing in India: Challenge for the Society*, Delhi: Ajanta Publications, 134–144.

Singh, R.R., (1970): "Welfare of the Aged", *The Indian Journal of Social Work*, 30(4), 327–333.

—, (1995): "Challenge Before the Elderly". In S. Vijay Kumar (ed.): *Challenges Before the Elderly: An Indian Scenario*, New Delhi: M.D. Publications, 53–76.

—, (1996): "Family Change, Elder Care Needs and Social Policy", Vinod Kumar (ed.), *Indian Perspective and Global Scenario,* New Delhi: AIIMS, 171–77

Sinha, J.N.P., (1989): *Problems of Ageing*, New Delhi: Classical Publishing Co.,

Sood, Rita, (1991): *Changing Status and Adjustment of Women*, Delhi: Manak Publications Pvt. Ltd.

Soodan, K.S., (1975): *Ageing in India*, Calcutta: Minerva Associates Pvt. Ltd.

Srivastava, Radhika D., (2000): "Girls are Second Class Citizens Everywhere", *The Times of India* (National Daily Newspaper), January, 17.

Stavenuiter, Monique, (1992): "Research Note: Elderly Women within the Household in Amsterdam in the Period 1851–1891", *Journal of Social History,* 26(2), Winter, 359–366.

Stieglitz, E.J., (1954): *Geriatric Medicine* (3rd ed.), Philadelphia: Lippincott, 3–26.

Strehler, B.L., (1962): *Time, Cells and Ageing,* New York: Academy Press.

Strehler, B.L., (1977): *Time, Cells, and Aging,* Edition 2, Illustrated, Published by Academic Press, Original from the University of Michigan.

Streib, G.F., (1956): "Social Stratification and Ageing", R. Binstork and E. Shanas (eds.), op. cit.

—, (1965): "Are the Aged a Miniority Group"?, A.W. Gouldner and S.M. Miller (eds.), *Applied Sociology*, New York: The Free Press.

Subba Rao, K. and Prabhakar, V. (eds.), (1987): *Ageing: A Multifactorial Discussion*, Varanasi (India): Association of Gerontology.

Subhash, M.N., (1987): "Biochemical Profiles in Subjects Aged 60 Years and Above with Congenital Defects", K. Subba Rao and V. Prabhakar (eds.), ibid., 81–84.

Sudhir, M.A., (2000): *Ageing in Rural India: Perspectives and Prospects*, Delhi: Indian Publishers Distributors.

Sujaya, C.P., (1999): "Some Comments on National Policy on Older Persons", *Economic and Political Weekly,* 34(44) October-November, WS 72–WS 74.

Sundari, S. and Geetha, N., (1999): "The Aged in India: A Demographic Profile", *IASSI Quarterly*, Vol. 18, No. 1, 25–39.

Sureendar, S., M. Vaithilingam, and A.G. Khan, (1996): "Distress of the Aged Widows in Rural Tamil Nadu", *Helpage India Research and Development Journal*, Vol. 2, No. 2, 41–46.

Synge, Jone, (1994): Patterns of Companionship and Sociability among Older Canadian Women: The Weekly Social Round, Department

Sociology Mc Master U, Hamilton Ontario, International Sociological Association.

Tandon, Reena, (1990): Old People in Homes for the Aged (Unpublished M.Phil. Dissertation), Delhi: Department of Social Work, University of Delhi.

Tandon, Sneh Lata, (1998): Unpublished Project Report, New Delhi: Department of Social Work, University of Delhi.

Tester, S., (1996): *Community Care for Older People*: A *Comparative Perspective,* Houndsmills, Basingstoke: Macmillan.

Thakur, A., (1999): "A Post-modernist Enquiry into Women's Workforce Participation", *The Indian Journal of Labour Economics*, Vol. 42(4), Oct.-Dec., 557–66.

The Times of India, (2000): "Formulate Strategies for Tackling Old Age Problems", Jan. 19.

—, (2000): "Life Span Gets Longer But Healthier", January 28.

—, (2000): "Robot Nurses for Sick Elderly", January 14.

—, (A Staff Reporter), (2000): "Discrimination Begins Even Before a Girl is Born", Monday, January 17.

Thomae, H., (1993): "Psychological Aspects of Longevity and Healthy Ageing", J.L.C. Dalf et al. (eds.), *Perspectives in Ageing: The 1992 Sandoz Lectures in Gerontology*, Sandiego: Academic Press, 3–22.

Thurmond, G. and Belcher, J., (1980–81): "Dimensions of Disengagement among Black and White Rural Elderly", *International Journal of Ageing and Human Development*, 12, 245–265.

Tibbitts, C. (ed.) (1960): *Handbook of Social Gerontology: Societal Aspects of Ageing,* Chicago: University of Chicago Press.

Tibbetts, C. and Donahue W., (1960): Ageing in Today's Society. Prentice Hall Inc. N.J.

TISS, (1999): *Elderly in India: Healthy? Happy? Helpless? Reputed? Rewarded? Rejected? An Annotated Bibliography in Search of Answers in the Year of the Older Persons*, Vol. 1, Mumbai: Centre for Health Studies, Tata Institute of Social Sciences.

—, (2001): *Elderly in India: Healthy? Happy? Helpless? Respected? Rewarded? Rejected? An Annotated Bibliography in Search of Answers*, Vol. 2, Mumbai: Centre for Health Studies, Tata Institute of Social Sciences.

—, February. 3, 2006: Researcher's Compilation on the basis of "List of Social Work Institutions", Social Work Education and Practice Cell, Mumbai.

Tout, Ken, (1992): "Does 3rd Age + 3rd World= 3rd Class?", *Community Development Journal*, Vol. 27, No. 2.

Tripathi, Raj Mani, (1999): "Ageing Population and Old Age Pension in India", *Yojana* 43 (11), November, 31–34.

Tripathi, S.N. and Das, Soudamini, (1991): *Informal Women Labour in India*, New Delhi: Discovery Publishing House.

Troll, Lillian E., (1994): "Family Embedded Vs Family Deprived Oldest—Old: A Study of Contrasts", *International Journal of Ageing and Human Development*, 38(1), 51–63.

Tyagi, D., (1993): "Gerontological Research: An Urgency", *Ageing and Society*, 3(3), 26–30.

—, (1996): "Who are Aged? A View Point", Vinod Kumar (ed.), *Ageing Indian Perspectives and Global Scenario*, New Delhi: Vinod Kumar AIIMS, 20–22.

UGC, (2001): *UGC Model Curriculum: Social Work Education*, New Delhi: Prem Verma on behalf of the Secretary, UGC.

UN, (1991): *The Women Ageing Situation*, New York: Centre for Social Development and Humanitarian Affairs, United Nations.

—, (1992): 47th Session Global Targets on Ageing for the Year 2001, www.org/documents/ga/res/47/a47ro86,htm-8k.

—, (1986): Report of the International Seminar to Promote the Implementation of the International Plan of Action on Ageing (Kiev, Ukrainian Soviet Socialist Republic 9–20 September 1985) organized by the UN in cooperation with the Government of the Union of Soviet Socialist Republics with the Institute of Gerontology of the Academy of Medical Sciences of the USSR, New York.

—, (1996): *Global Estimates and Projections by Sex and Age: The 1994 Assessment*, New York: Department of International Economics and Social Affairs.

—, (1999): The Family and Older Persons in Bangladesh, Pakistan and Sri Lanka, Economic and Social Commission for Asia and the Pacific Asia Population Series No. 151, New York.

—, (2002): *World Population Ageing, 1950–2020.*

UNIC, (1999): Towards a Society for All Ages, Proceedings of a Seminar Organized by the United Nations Information Centre, New Delhi to mark the International Year of Older Persons, 1999 on 18 March, New Delhi: UNIC.

Van Mering O and O'Rand, A.M., (1981): "Illness and the Organisation of Health Care: A Sociological Perspective". In C.L. Fry (ed.), *Dimensions, Ageing, Culture and Health*, Prager Publisher, 255–270.

Varghese, N.V., (1993): "Women and Work: An Examination of the "Female Marginalization Thesis" in the Indian Context", A.N. Sharma and Seema

Singh (eds.), *Women and Work: Changing Scenario in India*, Delhi: Indian Society of Labour Economics and B.R. Publishing Corporation.

Vatuk, Sylvia, (1980): "Withdrawal and Disengagement as a Cultural Response to Aging in India", C.L. Fry (ed.), *Aging in Culture*, New York: A.J.F. Bergin.

Victor, C.R., (1984): A Survey of the Elderly After Discharge from Hospital in Wales, Unpublished Ph.D. Thesis, Welsh National School of Medicine.

Victor, C.R., (1987): *Old Age in Modern Society: A Textbook in Social Gerontology*, USA (New York): Croom Helm in Association with Methuen, Inc.

Vijayakumar, S., (1991): "Health of Family of the Aged", Indira Jai Prakash (ed.), *Quality Ageing*, Bangalore: Bangalore University.

Vincent (John A), (1995): *Inequality and Old Age*, London: UCL Press.

Voges, Wolfgang and Hannelore Pongratz, (1988): "Retirement and Lifestyle of Older Women", *Ageing and Society*, 8(1), March, 63–83.

Walker, A., (1981): "Towards a Political Economy of Old Age", *Ageing and Society*, 1(1), 73–94.

Warren, Lorna and Maltby, Tony, (1998): Older Women in the United Kingdom: Lifestyles and Health, Deptt. of Sociological Studies U Sheffield, England: International Sociological Association.

Wasson, S., (1993): Aged Women in Urban Setting, Ph.D. Thesis, Department of Sociology, UP (India): Meerut University.

Weber, Max, (1946): *Essays in Sociology*, H.H. Girth and C.W. Mills (eds.), New York: Oxford University Press.

Weeks, D.J., (1994): "A Review of Loneliness Concepts with Particular References to Old Age", *International Journal of Geriatric Psychiatry*, Vol. 9(5), 345–55.

Wessen, A.F., (1969): "Some Remarks on the Role of Social Medicine in the Practice of Clinical Gerontology", *Interdisciplinary Topics in Gerontology*, Vol. 5, Karger: Basel, 79–82.

Whittaker, T., (1995): "Gender and Elder Abuse", S. Arber and J. Ginn (eds.), *Connecting Gender and Ageing*, Buckingham: Open University Press, 144–57.

WHO, (1990): Technical Report Series No. 797, Geneva, WHO, 34–84.

Whole, John R., (1993): *Coming Health Crisis: Who Will Pay for Care for the Aged in the Twenty First Century?*, Chicago: The University of Chicago Press.

Williams, J.B., Evans, L. and Powell, L.A., (1982): *Politics of Ageing*, Springfield: I.L. Charles, C. Thomas.

Willigen, John Van, Chadha, N.K. and Kedia, Satish, (1996): "Personal Networks of Older People in a Delhi Neighbourhood", *The Indian Journal of Social Work*, 57(3), July, 414–428.

Willium, John Van and Chadha, N.K., (1990): "Techniques for Collecting Social Network Data for Studies of Social Ageing", *Indian Journal of Social Work*, Vol. L1, No. 4, October, 615–621.

Wilson, G., (1993): "Abuse of Elderly Men and Women Among Clients of a Community Psychogeritatric Service", *British Journal of Social Work*, 42, 681–700.

—, (2000): *Understanding Old Age: Critical and Global Perspectives*, London: Sage Publications.

Yadav, K.N.S., Yadav, S.S. and Robert S., Ron E., (1996): "Ageing and Health Hazards in Rural Northern India", *Health and Populations: Perspectives and Issues*, 19(1), 1–18.

Yadav, Satyendra Singh, (1999): Disability and Handicap among Elderly Female Singaporeans, Women's Health and the Nation's Gain: An International Conference with a Special Focus on Women in Asia, Singapore: TSAO Foundation.

Zachariah, K.C. and Rajan, S. Irudaya (2001): "Gender Dimensions of Migration in Kerala: Macro and Micro Evidences", *Asia Pacific Population Journal*, Vol. 16(3), 47–70.

Zusman, J., (1966): "Some Explanations of the Changing Appearance of Psychotic Patients: An Antecedents of the Social Breakdown Syndrome", *Millbank Memorial Fund Quarterly*, 64, 1.

Index